UNITED STATES TRADE POLICY

A Work in Progress

UNITED STATES TRADE POLICY

A Work in Progress

CHARLES PEARSON
The Johns Hopkins University

WILEY

Acquisitions Editor *Leslie Kraham*
Marketing Manager *Charity Robey*
Senior Production Editor *Norine M. Pigliucci*
Design Director *Maddy Lesure*
Production Management Services *Charlotte Hyland*
Editorial Assistant *Jessica Barlett*
Cover Image *©PhotoDisk, Inc.*

This book was set in New Caledonia by Binghamton Valley Composition and printed and bound by Courier Westford. The cover was printed by Lehigh Press.

This book is printed on acid-free paper.♾

Library of Congress Cataloging in Publication Data

ISBN 0-471-26732-5 (pbk)

Printed in the United States of America

10 9 8 7 6 5 4 3 2 1

To Isaiah Frank
Teacher, Colleague, Friend

Unfaithful but not disloyal

Gabriel Garcia Marquez
Love in the Time of Cholera

CONTENTS

DETAILED CONTENTS

PREFACE

The first purpose of this short book is to complement textbook expositions of trade theory with an account of United States trade policy over the past four decades. The twists and turns, lurches and reversals of our trade policy are the raw material for a good story, one that can enliven the spare elegance of trade theory.

International economics textbooks concentrate on developing analytical tools and presenting the principal theories of trade. But textbook expositions, often honed over many editions, have a dry and abstract flavor for many students. The modern approach of inserting "boxes" to illustrate examples from the real world at best gives fragmented snapshots of one trade conflict or another, and at worst it is simply a distraction from the main flow of theory. Moreover, space constraints inevitably mean that students gain little appreciation of how trade policy is actually practiced.

The textbook case for any trade policy other than *laissez faire* is very limited. The principal economic exceptions are the long-standing infant industry argument, the exercise of international market power to affect trade prices (a beggar-thy-neighbor policy), and possibly some configurations of scale economies, externalities, and imperfect competition explored in the strategic trade literature. The strong presumption favoring free trade helps explain its enduring intellectual force. But in the real world, trade policy is a complex, dynamic, rich brew. In the United States and elsewhere, trade policy strays far from the recognized exceptions to free trade. Students need an understanding of the actual practice of trade policy to be measured against the benchmark of theory. If this book is successful, students will gain a deeper insight into the currents and crosscurrents that mark recent U.S. trade policy. With this understanding, and with the analytical tools of trade theory, they will be better equipped to assess and manage the trade issues of the new millennium.

The second purpose of the book is to reach and inform a wider audience—professionals engaged in trade or trade policy, academics whose principal concerns have not been trade, and the chorus of voices praising or damning globalization. Although not formal students of trade, these groups too may gain greater insight into the sometimes quixotic, sometimes pragmatic pursuit of liberal trade in the United States.

Our focus on the evolution of policy in the past four decades is somewhat arbitrary. Virtually all the issues that characterize trade controversies in the past few decades have roots deep in the 19th century. Unfair trade, discrimination, reciprocity, export market access, wage suppression, and national security have been actively debated for two centuries. But a detailed treatment of their historical roots would be excessive and exhausting and would be inappropriate for our purposes. Instead we wish to concentrate on one cycle in U.S. trade policy: the serious deterioration in the liberal trade consensus starting in the 1960s, the patchwork repairs to that consensus by the late 1990s, and the most recent challenge under the antiglobalization banner.

Our task is complicated because U.S. trade policy is neither clearly linear nor clearly cyclical. True, one can mark out periods of high protection—the period following the War of 1812, the long span from the end of the Civil War to 1912, with the Republican Party proudly waving the banner of protection, and the resurrection of that policy in the 1920s, culminating in the notorious Smoot-Hawley tariff of 1930. These were followed by bouts of genuine liberalization, most notably in the immediate post World War II period. But a purely cyclical view of trade policy misses numerous lurches and enthusiasms in quite unrelated dimensions. These include using trade carrots and sticks for noncommercial objectives (e.g., human rights), a taste for regionalism, the ebb and flow in the struggle between Congress and the President for control of trade, the new issue of reconciling trade and environment, and the fair labor standards debate.

We conclude that purely chronological treatment of trade policy in the past 40 years would be tedious and unenlightening. Identifying and tracking a set of issues appear more productive. To get started, however, and to place the issues in context, Chapter 1 presents an overview, or Cook's tour, of the postwar rise, fall, and regrouping of liberal trade forces. The following seven chapters focus on the most prominent issues in U.S. trade policy in this period. Chapters 2 through 4 are closely linked. They analyze a time in which liberal trade was on the defensive and indeed was forced to retreat. Chapter 5 examines questions at the heart of virtually all trade policymaking whatever the era—the impact of trade on jobs and wages. Chapter 6 tells the story of how the United States came to re-embrace preferential trade despite its discriminatory character. Conflicts between trade and environment, dealt with in Chapter 7, first surfaced in the 1970s and became a hot policy issue in the 1990s. Exports have been promoted for commercial purposes and restricted for national security reasons. Chapter 8 analyzes these conflicting policies. Chapter 9 returns to a more chronological format. It examines the events in the 1990s that culminated in a backlash against liberal trade—the Seattle debacle and the aborted attempt to launch a new trade round. Chapter 10 sums up and looks ahead.

It is worth noting at the outset what the book does not attempt. Empirical measurement of trade policy, including advances in using computable general equilibrium (CGE) models, is not covered. Nor does the book present a political economy style analysis of how trade policy is formulated or of the institutions involved in its execution. To do so would require an explicit political economy model, complete with identification of winners and losers and analysis of interest group and bureaucratic politics and lobbying activities. Although important, a proper effort in this direction is beyond the scope of this study.[1] Next, the emphasis is on U.S. trade policy, and attention to the interactions of that policy with international developments is limited. Major international developments that provide a context for U.S. policy include the rise and fall of import substitution in Latin America, the equally ill-fated attempt to create a New International Economic Order in the 1970s, the remarkable expansion of manufactured exports from Asia, the extension and deepening of economic integration in Europe and elsewhere, the trade performance of transition economies, and numerous debt and foreign exchange crises. All of these external developments deserve detailed treatment, but to keep this account manageable they are introduced only as they directly affect U.S. trade policy. Finally, although the focus of this book is on U.S. trade policy, many countries confront similar issues—coping with import surges, striking a balance between preferential and multilateral trade, reconciling environmental and trade objectives, and so forth. We hope that analysis of the U.S. experience will cast light on trade practices in other countries.

[1]For examples of these approaches, see Deardorff and Stern (2000), de Melo and Tarr (1992), Destler (1995), Feenstra et al., (1996), Irwin (1991), Jones and Krueger (1990), and Magee et al. (1989). Research on U.S. trade undertaken by the Institute for International Economics has been extensive and influential and has been valuable in preparing this book.

▶ REFERENCES

Deardorff, Alan, and Robert Stern (eds.). 2000. *Constituent Interests and US Trade Policies.* Ann Arbor: University of Michigan Press.

Destler, I. M. 1995. *American Trade Politics.* Washington, DC: Institute for International Economics.

de Melo, Jaime, and David Tarr. 1992. *A General Equilibrium Analysis of U.S. Foreign Trade Policy.* Cambridge, MA: MIT Press.

Feenstra, Robert, Gene Grossman, Douglas Irwin. 1996. *The Political Economy of Trade Policy.* Cambridge, MA: MIT Press.

Irwin, Douglas (ed.). 1991. *Political Economy and International Economics/Jagdish Bhagwati.* Cambridge, MA: MIT Press.

Jones, Ronald, and Anne Krueger. 1990. *The Political Economy of International Trade.* Oxford: Basil Blackwell.

Magee, Stephen, William Brock, Leslie Young. 1989. *Black Hole Tariffs and Endogenous Policy Theory.* Cambridge, UK: Cambridge University Press.

A NOTE TO READERS

Trade policy is heavily burdened with specialized jargon. Some readers are already expert, but many are not. This book offers a compromise. Excessive use of technical terms has been avoided (although some readers may disagree). When they are used, technical terms are explained in the text, in footnotes, or in the Glossary. The Chronology of Trade Events and the list of Acronyms should also help.

Trade theory poses a more difficult problem. Again, some readers will be well-grounded but others not. Policy cannot be correctly assessed without some theoretical or conceptual framework, but this cannot be the focus of the book. Our compromise here is threefold. First, we give very brief descriptions when theory is referenced. These again are located in the text, in footnotes, or in the Glossary. Examples are the Heckscher-Ohlin trade model and the concept of externalities. Second and more important, we have included nontechnical conceptual or theoretical sections in many chapters. These include a discussion of strategic trade policy (Chapter 3), the conceptual links between trade, jobs, and wages (Chapter 5), the theory of preferential trade (Chapter 6), a review of trade-environment theory (Chapter 7), and others. The intention is to season the policy analysis with a modest dose of theoretical flavoring. Third, we have included bibliographical references to theoretical and empirical literature for those readers who wish to delve more deeply. Finally, for readers interested in trends, the Appendix figures display information on aspects of U.S. trade over the past four decades.[1]

[1]A large number of websites also contain information and analysis of trade policy issues. These include the World Trade Organization (*www.wto.org*), the World Bank (*www.worldbank.org*), United States International Trade Commission (*www.usitc.gov*), United States Trade Representative (*www.ustr.gov*), Bureau of Economic Analysis, U.S. Commerce Department (*www.bea.gov*), Institute for International Economics (*www.iie.com*), the Brookings Institution (*www.brook.edu*), American Enterprise Institute (*www.aei.org*), the Cato Institute (*www.cato.org*), and the Economic Policy Institute (*www.epinet.org*).

Acknowledgments

Washington, D.C., is an ideal vantage point for observing U.S. trade policy. The advantage is not so much the access to documents but the concentration of experts in and out of government, and I have learned much from many. I wish to thank them all. My colleagues at SAIS, Isaiah Frank, to whom this book is dedicated, and Enzo Grilli read the entire manuscript and suggested numerous improvements, and I am grateful. Other colleagues, including Cristino Arroyo, Robert Chase, W. Max Corden, Judith Dean, Jaime Marquez, Michael Plummer, James Riedel, Wendy Takacs, and Frank Weiss, either have commented on individual chapters or shared their insights by osmosis over the years. They too have helped educate me, although none should be held responsible.

The development of this book was aided by colleagues who reviewed drafts of the manuscript. They provided many valuable suggestions and my thanks go to the following individuals: Chad P. Bown, Brandeis University; Gregory J. Buchholz, Missouri Southern State College; Winston W. Chang, State University of New York at Buffalo; Santanu Chatterjee, University of Georgia; David Hummels, Purdue University; and Robert E. B. Lucas, Boston University.

I also wish to thank Cesar Munoz Acebes, Armando Anfosso, John Paul Ferguson, Zeynep Gürgüç, Iva Illieva, and Tisha Loeper-Viti for dedicated research assistance. Additionally, many of my students at SAIS have shown a healthy skepticism for austere trade theory, and their curiosity about policy helped motivate the research and writing. Patricia Calvano, assisted by Rosa Bullock and Jill Freeman, prepared the many drafts, and once again, without their help I would have been helpless. Thank you. Finally, the SAIS libraries in Washington and at the Bologna Center have been professional and exceptionally helpful, and I am grateful.

ACRONYMS

ACP — Africa, Caribbean, and Pacific (countries)
APEC — Asia Pacific Economic Cooperation (organization)
ASEAN — Association of Southeast Asian Nations
BEM — Big Emerging Markets

CAP — Common Agricultural Policy (EU)
CGE — Computable General Equilibrium (trade models)
CITES — Convention in International Trade in Endangered Species
COCOM — Coordinating Committee for Multilateral Export Controls
CU — Customs Union

DISC — Domestic International Sales Corporation

EC — European Communities
ECSC — European Coal and Steel Community
EEC — European Economic Community
EEP — Export Enhancement Program
EFTA — European Free Trade Association
ET — Extraterritorial Income Exclusion (tax law)
EU — European Union

FDI — Foreign Direct Investment
FCPA — Foreign Corrupt Practices Act
FPE — Factor Price Equalization (theorem)
FTA — Free Trade Agreement
FTAA — Free Trade Agreement for the Americas
FSC — Foreign Sales Corporation

GATS — General Agreement on Trade in Services
GATT — General Agreement on Tariffs and Trade
GMO — Genetically Modified Organisms
GSP — Generalized System of Preferences

H-O — Heckscher-Ohlin (trade model)

IIE	Institute for International Economics
IMF	International Monetary Fund
IS	Import Substitution
ISIC	International Standard Industrial Classification
ITC	International Trade Commission
ITO	International Trade Organization
MAI	Multilateral Agreement on Investment
MEA	Multilateral Environmental Agreement
MFA	Multifiber Arrangement
MFN	Most Favored Nation (nondiscriminatory tariff)
MITI	Ministry of Trade and Industry (Japan)
MNCs	Multinational Corporations
MOSS	Market-Oriented Sector-Specific (trade talks)
NAAEC	North American Agreement on Environmental Cooperation
NAALC	North American Agreement on Labor Cooperation
NAFTA	North American Free Trade Agreement
NGOs	Nongovernmental Organizations
NICs	Newly Industrializing Countries
NTBs	Nontariff Trade Barriers
OECD	Organization for Economic Cooperation and Development
OMA	Orderly Marketing Agreement
PNTR	Permanent Normal Trade Relations (for China)
PPP	Polluter Pays Principle
PTA	Preferential Trade Agreement
QR	Quantitative Restriction (quota)
RTA	Reciprocal Trade Agreements Act (1934)
S-S	Stopler-Samuelson (theorem)
SSI	Structural Impediments Initiative (trade talks)
TAA	Trade Adjustment Assistance
TPA	Trade Promotion Authority
TPM	Trigger Price Mechanism
TRIMs	Trade Related Investment Measures
TRIPs	Trade Related Intellectual Property Agreement

UNCTAD	United Nations Conference on Trade and Development
USTR	United States Trade Representative
VER	Voluntary Export Restraint
VIE	Voluntary Import Expansion
WTO	World Trade Organization

CHRONOLOGY OF TRADE EVENTS

GATT/WTO trade rounds

Year	*Name*	*Main Subject*
1947	Geneva*	Tariffs
1949	Annecy*	Tariffs
1951	Torquay*	Tariffs
1956	Geneva*	Tariffs
1960–61	Dillon Round	Tariffs
1964–67	Kennedy Round	Tariffs, Agriculture, Dumping
1973–79	Tokyo Round	Tariffs, Nontariff Trade Barriers (NTBs)
1986–94	Uruguay Round	Multiple, including agriculture, MFA, services, intellectual property, investment, VERs
1999	Millennium Round	(Aborted)
2001	Doha* (Development Round)	See Chapter 10

**Location, not name.*

Other trade events

Year	*Event*
1930	Smoot-Hawley Tariff Act
1934	Reciprocal Trade Agreements Act (RTA)
1948	Havana Charter signed, creating the subsequently aborted International Trade Organization (ITO)
1948	General Agreement on Tariffs and Trade (GATT) established
1948	"Peril Point" requirements adopted
1950	ITO withdrawn from Congress and scrapped
1951	Escape Clause formalized in U.S. trade law
1955	Japan enters GATT; MFN treatment withheld by several members
1955	Voluntary Export Restraint (VER) with Japan on cotton textiles
1957	European Economic Community (EEC) established by Rome Treaty
1960	Kennedy pledges support for textile industry

1960	GATT elaborates concept of "market disruption"
1961	Short-Term Agreement on cotton textile imports
1962	Long-Term Agreement (LTA) on cotton textile imports
1962	Common Agriculture Policy (CAP) established by EEC
1962	Trade Expansion Act establishes Office of the Special Trade Representatives (later USTR) and the Trade Adjustment Assistance Program (TAA)
1963	"Chicken War" with the EEC
1965	U.S.–Canada Automotive Products Agreement
1969	Voluntary Exports Restraints on Steel (Europe and Japan)
1971	First U.S. trade deficit
1971	Nixon shocks: Ends convertibility of dollars to gold, forces dollar devaluation; imposes temporary import surcharge, imposes temporary wage and price controls. Bretton Woods monetary system collapses by 1973.
1971	Burke-Hartke quota bill introduced (ultimately rejected)
1971	Textile VER with Japan extended to wool and synthetic fibers
1972	First oil price shock
1973	Multi-Fiber Agreement (MFA) for textiles succeeds LTA
1974	Trade Act introduced fast track; creates Section 301, authorizes Generalized System of Preference (GSP)
1974	Jackson-Vanick Amendment denying MFN treatment for the Soviet Union on the basis of its emigration policies
1976	United States introduces GSP scheme
1978	Trigger Price Mechanism (TPM) for steel introduced
1981	Voluntary Export Restraint on automobiles from Japan
1982	U.S. proposal for new GATT round fails
1982/83	First Semiconductor Agreements with Japan
1984	Caribbean Basin Initiative offering preferential market access to the United States
1985	Dollar peaks, Plaza Accord to bring down value of dollar
1985	Reagan creates Trade Policy Strike Force
1985	Market-Oriented Sector-Specific talks (with Japan)
1985	U.S.–Israel Free Trade Agreement
1986	Gephardt Amendment (protectionist; fails)
1986	Voluntary Import Expansion (VIE) on semiconductors with Japan
1987	U.S. trade deficit peaks
1988	Omnibus Trade Bill introduces Super and Special 301; requires annual Foreign Trade Barrier Reports

1988	Canada–U.S. Free Trade Agreement
1989	Structural Impediments Initiative (SSI) talks with Japan
1990	Enterprise for the Americas Initiative to explore Western Hemisphere FTA
1992	Agreement reached with Japan to open its auto and auto parts market
1993	North America Free Trade Agreement (NAFTA) ratified
1993	Big Emerging Markets initiatives
1994	Uruguay Round concluded, World Trade Organization (WTO) established
1994	COCOM disbanded
1994	Chile invited to negotiate agreement to join NAFTA
1994	Summit of the Americas agrees to negotiate a Free Trade Agreement of the Americas (FTAA)
1995	Clinton administration threatens Japan with 100 percent tariffs on imported autos in effort to open the Japanese auto market
1997	WTO agreements on information technology, financial services, basic telecommunications services
1998	Multilateral Agreement on Investment (MAI) talks collapse
1999	United States imposes sanctions in beef and banana disputes with EU
1999	WTO effort to launch Millennium Round (Seattle) collapses
2001	Banana dispute with EU settled
2001	Bush initiates Escape Clause (section 201) case on steel; positive finding of injury at International Trade Commission (ITC)
2001	Fast track authority (trade promotion authority) passes House (one vote margin)
2001	WTO rejects U.S. Extraterritorial Income Exclusion Act (ET), successor to DISC and FSC
2001	Doha meeting of WTO launches new trade round
2002	Bush imposes tariffs on steel under the Escape Clause
2002	Congress grants Bush fast-track (trade promotion) authority in Trade Act of 2002
2002	U.S. farm legislation dramatically increases domestic agricultural subsidies
2002	United States proposes sweeping liberalization of agricultural trade at the WTO
2002	WTO again rejects FSC (U.S. tax break for exports) and authorizes EU to impose tariff sanctions of up to $4 billion annually
2002	U.S. trade deficit hits record level

LIST OF FIGURES

Text

Appendix

CHAPTER

1

AN OVERVIEW

This chapter sketches the highlights of United States trade policy from its decisive turn toward liberalization in 1934, through its retreat in the 1970s and 1980s, to a new, modified liberal stance in the 1990s.[1] This progression is the backdrop against which critics of open trade and globalization raised new protests at the end of that decade. Our purpose here is to understand the historical roots of the challenges faced by the United States at the start of the new millennium and to provide a context for the subsequent issue-oriented chapters.

A TURNING POINT: THE RTA

The year 1934 was the low point in the decade-long economic disaster known as the Great Depression. From its peak in 1929, U.S. economic output had declined 24 percent, and the unemployment rate had soared to 22 percent. A severe deflation had brought farm prices down 38 percent and farm income down 44 percent from 1929 (United States Bureau of the Census, 1975). The stock market had lost 62 percent of its (bubble) value and U.S. trade fell to the level of 1912. From the farm to the mill to the temples of finance, economic depression ruled.

However unpromising the economic climate, 1934 did mark the sharpest and most significant turning point in U.S. trade policy in the 20th century. The Reciprocal Trade Agreements Act (RTA) signed into law by

[1]*Laissez faire* is freedom of enterprise and implies the absence of government intervention in exporting and importing. A liberal trade system accepts a modest role for government. The principal tenets of a liberal trade regime are nondiscrimination among trade partners, a commitment to reduce trade barriers through reciprocal concessions, minimal subsidies or restraints on exports, and a sparing use of trade measures to accomplish noncommercial foreign policy objectives.

President Roosevelt that year set trade policy on a new course, the general direction of which it still tracks despite periods of serious backsliding. The legislation itself did not lower tariffs from the highly protectionist levels set by Congress in the 1930 Smoot-Hawley Tariff.[2] Instead, it granted President Roosevelt three-year authority to enter bilateral negotiations for reciprocal reductions in tariff rates of up to 50 percent. The reductions could be implemented by proclamation, without implementing legislation by Congress. The genius of this arrangement, for which then Secretary of State Cordell Hull receives much deserved credit, is threefold.

First, in reciprocal reductions, the United States advances its own export interests, creating an offset to protectionist objections from our import competing firms. The United States had experimented with reciprocity several times in the period 1880–1933, but the efforts were severely limited in duration and scope and strongly colored by the overarching protectionist doctrine during much of that time (Rhodes, 1993). Broad authority for reciprocal tariff reductions in the hands of a committed free trader such as Hull was another matter.

Second, the effects of reciprocal tariff reductions were magnified because the United States had abandoned the practice of conditional Most Favored Nation (MFN) for unconditional MFN a decade earlier, in 1923. The importance of this switch should not be underestimated. Under conditional MFN, a negotiated reduction in the U.S. tariff on, say, iron from Sweden would mean that other iron exporters would face discrimination in the U.S. market unless they offered similar concessions. (In trade jargon, reducing a trade barrier is termed a concession, even when it benefits the importing country. This is a hangover from the mercantilist view that exports are good and imports are bad.) The discrimination is an invitation for conflict and retaliation.[3] Remember, all preferences are inherently dis-

[2]Eckes (1995, p. 107) calculates the average *ad valorem* equivalent rate on dutiable imports at 59 percent in 1932. Average tariff rates must be treated cautiously. Very high tariffs may preclude imports of some items, and these high tariffs would be given a low or zero weight in a trade-weighted averaging scheme. Also, at that time the United States often used specific, not *ad valorem*, duties. The general decline in prices from 1930 to 1934 increased the protective effect of specific tariffs. Finally, 59 percent is the estimated nominal rate and does not measure the effective rate of protection. With lower tariff rates on raw materials and intermediate inputs, effective rates of protection on final goods exceed nominal rates of protection.

[3]The great trade economist F. W. Taussig argued as early as 1918 that preferential market access causes resentment and international friction (Taussig, 1920, p. 115).

criminatory. With the United States and other major trading nations embracing unconditional MFN, the tariff reduction for Sweden automatically applies to other MFN countries, reducing rancor and further expanding trade.[4] But unconditional MFN also has a downside, much in evidence in the middle post–World War II period. Some countries may act as "free riders," taking advantage of better export market access granted through MFN, without yielding on their own import barriers.

The third positive feature of the 1934 legislation was that it got the Congress out of the business of setting tariffs on individual line items. Under the Constitution the Congress has the authority to regulate foreign commerce and establish tariffs. The President can negotiate with foreign countries but has no authority to change duty rates up or down unless Congress delegates that authority. It was painfully apparent that Congress, in legislating the 1930 Smoot-Hawley Tariff, had little taste or ability to resist imposing protectionist tariffs (Schattschneider, 1935). Virtually all members were subject to intense pressures from local interests and specific industries, and logrolling coalitions among Senators resulted in extraordinarily high tariff rates.[5] By delegation of limited line item tariff authority to the President, the attention shifts from the local to the national interest, thus moderating protectionist pressures. The delegation of trade authority was circumscribed, however, and a tug of war between the executive and the Congress has been a hallmark of postwar trade policy up to and including the recent debate on fast-track reauthorization.[6]

In retrospect, it is clear that the RTA of 1934 set U.S. trade policy on a new course. But the ultimate destination was anything but clear at the time. The case for *some* change in direction was strong. The excesses of the Smoot-Hawley Tariff, with its blatant logrolling and futile search for a "scientific" tariff, were fresh in congressional memory. At the time, the ostensible guiding principle was to establish tariffs just equal to the difference

[4]The reasons for the U.S. switch to unconditional MFN were closely tied to its emergence as a significant exporter of manufactures. Most recently, MFN has been rechristened as "Permanent Normal Trade Relations" in an effort to avoid misunderstanding and improve its image with the public.

[5]Logrolling means vote trading on specific tariff lines.

[6]Fast-track legislation authorizes the President to negotiate a trade agreement with the condition that Congress will vote it up or down, without amendment. It is considered necessary if trade partners are to take the negotiations seriously. Fast track is now known as Trade Promotion Authority (TPA). See Chapter 9.

between U.S. and foreign production costs, to ensure "fair" trade.[7] A moment's reflection reveals that such tariffs, if they could be accurately calculated, would eliminate the basis for and the gains from trade. Additionally, the popular perception in the interwar and early postwar periods was that the Smoot-Hawley Tariff triggered widespread retaliatory tariffs, eroding U.S. exports and deepening the distress. The extent of retaliation, however, subsequently has been questioned, and the effect of that tariff on the Great Depression is unsettled.

At the same time, Congress was not ready for a blanket rejection of protectionism and was leery about giving away its constitutional authority over trade. Roosevelt pledged that trade would be promoted "without injury to American producers" and that "no sound and important American interest will be injuriously disturbed," a pledge subsequently repeated by Presidents Truman and Eisenhower (Eckes, 1995, p. 142, 232–233). The RTA also included penalties for dumping and other unfair trade practices. There was some obvious hypocrisy here. It would have been impossible to sharply reduce tariffs—then averaging 59 percent—without injuring the protected status of import-sensitive industries. In any event, armed with the RTA, the United States made modest progress toward trade liberalization in the years leading up to World War II. As described in the next section, the dominant economic position of the United States in the immediate post-war era consolidated the liberalization trend.

▶ BUILDING A LIBERAL TRADE REGIME

The quarter century following World War II was the high point in American commitment to creating a liberal international economic order. With U.S. guidance and support, new international economic institutions were established, massive assistance was provided for political stabilization and economic recovery in Europe, and multilateralism displaced bilateral and preferential approaches to trade and monetary relations. Protectionism

[7]The level playing field notion is nicely captured in the Republican platform of 1908: "In all protective legislation the true principle of protection is best maintained by the imposition of such duties as will equal the difference between the cost of production at home and abroad, together with a reasonable profit to American industries." Cited by F. W. Taussig (1931), p. 363. This came to be known as the "scientific" tariff. This, almost 100 years after Ricardo (1817) showed that the gains from trade arose from differences in comparative, not absolute, costs!

was officially repudiated, and U.S. tariff rates were reduced from their 1932 peak of 59 percent to 10 percent by 1970.[8] In retrospect, however, we can see that U.S. commitment to liberal trade was guarded and greatly influenced by unique circumstances in the immediate post-war period.

Toward the end of World War II, plans were laid for a triumvirate of international economic institutions. They were designed to remedy the effects of economic nationalism that had contributed to the depression of the 1930s and arguably to World War II and to assist in postwar recovery. Two institutions emerged more or less as planned, but the third received a "second class funeral,"[9] although its presumed temporary predecessor survived for nearly five decades.

The live births were the International Monetary Fund (IMF) and the World Bank. The IMF was given responsibility for oversight of the international monetary system—to phase out wartime foreign exchange controls and establish convertible currencies, to secure a system of fixed but adjustable exchange rates, and to prevent beggar-thy-neighbor competitive devaluations.[10] The second institution, the International Bank for Reconstruction and Development, now known as the World Bank, was given a mandate to provide official funds for reconstruction of war-damaged economies and to lend funds for development projects in poor countries.[11] At the time there was little expectation that *private* capital flows would resume quickly and in volume, and no specific institution to regulate foreign investment was contemplated.[12]

The third leg of this triumvirate was to have been the International Trade Organization (ITO), bringing rules, discipline, and liberal principles

[8]Eckes (1995, Table 4.1). Fifty-nine percent and 10 percent are the ratios of duties collected to dutiable imports. For problems with this measure, see Note 3. In an interesting study, Douglas Irwin (1998) has shown that most of the tariff reduction was accomplished through higher import prices, which reduce the effective rate of the then-prevalent specific tariffs, and not through negotiated reductions in rates. Eckes uses the fall in import prices in the early 1930s to argue that the Smoot-Hawley Tariff only *appeared* high because of widespread specific duties.

[9]Diebold (1952), quoting Italians.

[10]To accomplish this, the IMF controlled funds for financing temporary (not fundamental) balance of payments disequilibria.

[11]Reconstruction lending was minimal and largely superseded by Marshall Plan funding.

[12]The ITO did contain some investment provisions. A belated attempt, the Multilateral Agreement on Investment, collapsed more than 50 years later, in 1998.

to the chaotic trade situation that had prevailed in the interwar period. The concept of the ITO was first broached in 1945, elaborated in 1946, negotiated in several conferences, and completed and signed at the Havana Conference in 1948. It was submitted for ratification in 1949 and effectively killed in 1950, when President Truman quietly withdrew the ITO Charter from Congress. Three factors contributed to the failure. One was the opposition of the "perfectionists"[13] in the business community who saw too many exceptions and escape clauses in the complex provisions and too much government regulation, management, and planning. These opponents argued that the numerous exceptions, for example, trade restraints for balance of payments protection or for maintaining full employment, would vitiate efforts to open foreign markets. The ITO Charter also appeared to them to sanction private and government cartels and commodity agreements. The second source of opposition was the traditional array of protectionist interests, including some but not all elements of organized labor. Recall that the doctrine of protectionism, dominant in the United States at the close of the 19th century, had never been fully and formally repudiated. The third factor contributing to failure was that by 1950 the times had changed since the ITO concept was first introduced in 1945. The spirit of wartime cooperation had worn thin. The Cold War was in full swing, but unlike the Marshall Plan, it was difficult to sell the ITO as stabilizing politics in Western Europe. And in 1948 the Republican party, traditionally the protectionist party, won Congress.

With the demise of the ITO, the General Agreement on Tariffs and Trade (GATT) became the default institution involved with international trade. GATT, which had been negotiated as a trade agreement among mainly industrial countries in 1947, was initially viewed as an interim measure until the ITO would come into force.[14] In fact, GATT, which while narrower contained some of the same provisions as the ITO, proved remarkably durable, surviving and in many respects thriving for almost five decades, until it was folded into the World Trade Organization (WTO) in 1995. Although initially perceived as temporary, GATT was a close reflection of the United States' views on a liberal trade system in the immediate postwar period. For that reason and because it has played a

[13]The term is from Diebold (1952).

[14]As an Executive Agreement, GATT did not need Congressional ratification.

major role in facilitating the explosion of trade in the past half century, it deserves attention.[15]

GATT is not a totally self-evident document. Its language has a pronounced merchantilist flavor: reductions in trade barriers are "concessions," and "compensation" is paid to countries for loss of exports, not loss of imports. Despite the language, the purpose and thrust of GATT have been in the direction of trade liberalization. Also, contrary to popular belief, GATT does not directly regulate trade. Rather, it regulates (imposes "disciplines" on) national governments' export and import policies. Nor does GATT always champion free trade. It permits many types of trade interventions, from escape clause (safeguard) import restrictions to antidumping and countervailing duties in response to "unfair" trade. It also allows trade restraints for national security purposes and explicitly allows countries to ban the import of products made by prison labor.[16] The disciplines themselves are not straitjackets. A member can violate GATT rules any time it wishes, although others whose rights have been nullified or impaired can then withdraw concessions previously granted to the violator.

The GATT has three functions: it is a set of rules for trade policy based on underlying principles, it provides a forum for trade negotiations, and it sets out procedures for settling trade disputes. Fundamental principles on which GATT rules are based are nondiscrimination, expressed in unconditional most-favored nation treatment (MFN); national treatment, meaning that a product once entered into a customs area must be treated in all respects (such as internal taxes and conditions of sale) the same as an equivalent domestic product; and a preference for the use of tariffs rather than quantitative restrictions (QRs, or quotas) when imports are restricted. Some exceptions to MFN are allowed, most notably for formal economic integration arrangements such as free trade areas and customs unions. Quantitative restraints are permitted in agriculture and for balance of payments purposes. Also, as a general rule, GATT permits import restrictions based on product characteristics if they are damaging to health or the environment, but it does not permit import restrictions based on the *manner* in which products are produced or harvested.[17] With regard to trade negotia-

[15]See Chronology for dates of various GATT trade negotiation rounds.

[16]To avoid unfair competition, not for humanitarian reasons.

[17]See Chapter 8 for elaboration. As noted, prison labor products are an exception.

tions, the fundamental principle is reciprocity: a country offering trade concessions should expect concessions from others in return.[18]

In summary, the GATT provides an architecture for international trade relations, much as the IMF provides an architecture for international monetary relations. The basic principles and especially nondiscrimination and reciprocity in trade negotiations were devised in response to the chaotic and harmful trade measures that marred economic relations in the interwar period. At the same time, GATT exemplifies a cautious liberalization. Within limits, members could protect against import surges and could maintain long-standing rights to apply countervailing and antidumping duties. Agriculture received special protection. And the long job of dismantling tariff walls left over from the depression years would be tackled in small steps, while presumably observing reciprocity in concessions.[19]

The U.S. government's commitment to liberal trade in this period was deeply influenced by the economic distress and economic nationalism of the 1930s. But actual tariff reductions were greatly facilitated by its dominant economic position in the immediate postwar years. Europe and Japan desperately needed U.S. exports for survival and to rebuild industrial capacity. Their ability to earn dollars by their own exports was severely limited. In this era of "dollar shortage" and exchange controls, foreign markets were uncontested and serious import competition in the United States was virtually nonexistent.[20]

Moreover, the United States had overriding foreign policy interests in securing political stabilization and economic recovery in Western Europe as a bulwark against communism and in tying Japan to the Western democratic orbit. In these unique and temporary circumstances the United

[18]Bagwell and Staiger (2001) view the GATT as a forum for negotiating market access to expand exports. Reciprocity in market access commitments tends to neutralize adverse terms of trade effects that would follow from unilateral liberalization.

[19]The efficiency gains from multilateral adherence to the principles of reciprocity and nondiscrimination have been demonstrated in a formal general equilibrium model by Bagwell and Staiger (1999).

[20]The U.K. undertook an abortive effort to make its currency convertible for trade transactions in 1947, but the attempt failed (Eichengreen, 1993). In this context convertibility means the ability to buy foreign currencies for trade purposes at market exchange rates. General currency convertibility for trade returned to Europe in 1958. In the meantime, from 1950 to 1958 the European Payments Union attempted to promote intra-European trade and conserve dollar receipts to finance trans-Atlantic imports.

States did not insist that others match it, step for step, in it own pursuit of liberal trade.[21] Indeed, the United States actively encouraged Japanese exports to the United States without reciprocity, supported the creation of the European Coal and Steel Community (ECSC) in 1952,[22] and viewed with favor the creation of the (potentially discriminatory) European Economic Community (EEC) in 1958.[23] Although hugely successful in foreign policy terms, this tolerance for overt discrimination and unbalanced market access, plus the role of the State Department in placing foreign policy objectives over commercial interests, cast a shadow over further trade liberalization in the 1960s.

Finally, we note that in this period the United States itself was hardly a dedicated free trader. Presidents Roosevelt, Truman, and Eisenhower all pledged to avoid tariff reductions that would harm U.S. industries. This was backed up by the "peril point" provisions of trade legislation, in which the quasi-independent Tariff Commission advised negotiators on the minimum tariff rates necessary to protect against damaging import competition. U.S. agriculture sought and won its own protection in drafting GATT language. An escape clause permitting the withdrawal of tariff concessions in the event of serious injury was inserted in U.S. trade legislation in 1947 and also found its way into the GATT.[24] In summary, the United States had a grand vision of a liberal trade order. That system would rest on the principles of nondiscrimination and multilateralism, would be subject to international rules, and would advance toward freer trade through reciprocal

[21]In the first three GATT rounds (Geneva, 1947; Annecy, 1949; Torquay, 1950) the results were modest, with the United States making a disproportionate share of tariff concessions.

[22]The ECSC was clearly preferential for members, and because it fell short of a free trade agreement or customs union, requested and received a waiver from GATT (Patterson, 1966). The original plan for the ECSC proposed by Jean Monet sought to create "competitive virtues" out of traditional "cartel vices" (Gillingham, 1995, p. 154). In the end, however, producer associations and cartel-like behavior came to dominate. The political rationale for the ECSC was not efficiency but integration of French and German heavy industry to a degree that made future war infeasible.

[23]In the interesting parallel to the debate over China's accession to the WTO almost a half century later, the United States promoted Japan's membership in GATT on foreign policy grounds. The EEC later became the European Communities (EC) and, in 1993, the European Union (EU).

[24]The Tariff Commission was designated the investigating agency, as the State Department was perceived as lax in implementing earlier versions of the escape clause.

tariff concessions. But for foreign policy reasons and because of postwar dislocations, the United States tolerated major departures from that vision abroad and indulged in selective protectionism itself.

▶ THE MOMENTUM FALTERS

The American vision of an open global trade system faded in the 1960s and 1970s. There are many reasons, and it is not possible to assign specific weights to each. Events in the world economy contributed. Europe and Japan recovered from the war, and trade competition for the United States market stiffened. The EEC initiated its Common Agricultural Policy (CAP) in 1962, and the CAP's combination of target prices and variable levies was correctly seen as protectionist. Japan had initiated its export drive with labor-intensive manufactures, and the United States responded with new, quantitative restrictions on cotton textile imports.[25] Manufactured imports from the Asian NICs (the Newly Industrializing Countries such as South Korea and Taiwan) began to accelerate.

Domestically, the macroeconomic climate for liberal trade deteriorated. Inflation, which totaled 23 percent for the entire decade of the 1950s, was 31 percent for the 1960s and a remarkable 112 percent for the 1970s. Productivity, measured by output per person in the business sector, which had increased by 32 percent in the decades of the 1950s and the 1960s, fell to 15 percent in the 1970s. The U.S. merchandise trade surplus, which had reached $6.8 billion in 1964, fell to $0.6 billion in 1969 and recorded a $6.4 billion *deficit* in 1972.[26] In August 1971, President Nixon had suspended the dollar's convertibility into gold and reinforced pressure for a devaluation of the dollar (more correctly, a revaluation of foreign currencies), with a temporary surcharge on imports.

The business, labor, and agricultural communities in the United States all found reason for complaint. The conditions for obtaining import relief under the escape clause, which was supposed to protect firms and workers from injurious surges of imports, had been revised and made more restrictive in 1962. From then until December 1969, the U.S. Tariff Commission

[25]The United States had negotiated "voluntary export restraints" in textiles with Japan as early as the 1930s.

[26]All data from Council of Economic Advisors, *Economic Reports of the President.*

rejected 13 successive petitions for relief from imports.[27] No serious progress was made in opening up world agricultural markets to U.S. farmers in either the Kennedy Round (1964–1967) or the Tokyo Round (1973–1979) of trade negotiations. Indeed, Japan maintained almost impenetrable barriers against U.S. exports of rice, citrus, and beef. In Europe, the groundwork for agricultural protection was laid in the early 1960s when the EEC unbound national-level agricultural concessions and created community-wide variable levies on imports from nonmembers to protect its farmers. Of course, U.S. hands were not clean either: the United States had sought and obtained a waiver from GATT obligations in agriculture as early as 1955.

The results of increasingly tepid support for liberal trade principles are easy to identify. Quantitative import restraints imposed in the 1961 Short-Term Cotton Textile Arrangement became the 1962 Long Term Arrangement, and in 1973 they were greatly enlarged in the first Multifiber Arrangement (MFA). Although contrary to the fundamental principles of nondiscrimination and preference for tariffs over quotas, these arrangements received GATT blessings. By 1993 the United States had MFA agreements with 41 countries, covering 70 percent of its apparel imports. Urged by the United States, the GATT itself toyed with the idea of sanctioning new trade arrangements to prevent "market disruption" in 1959 and 1960. The United States introduced "voluntary" trade restraints in steel in 1969, setting the stage for more than three decades of intermittent protection for that industry. In a radical departure from earlier insistence on the MFN principle, the United States concluded a discriminatory trade arrangement in autos and auto parts with Canada in 1965, ostensibly to

[27]Under the revised law the Tariff Commission had to find that import increases resulted "in major part" from earlier tariff concessions and that the increased imports were "the major factor" in causing serious injury to the U.S. industry. Many of the escape clause cases in the even earlier Eisenhower era (1953–1961) appear quaint today. Eisenhower gave tariff relief for items such as watches, safety pins, clinical thermometers, and typewriter ribbon cloth. Among others, he denied relief for brier pipes, wooden clothespins, woodscrews, straight pins, and umbrella frames. The escape clause was only one route to protection for minor industries. In the mid 1930s the Treasury received a dumping complaint on flypaper from Japan and imposed antidumping duties in 1939 (Eckes, 1995, p. 265).

avoid a nasty subsidy–countervailing duty dispute.[28] This was followed up by introducing a Generalized System of Preferences (GSP) scheme in 1976. Although the GSP was authorized by GATT and improved developing country market access in the United States, it was clearly a major departure from MFN. Finally, in 1974 the United States created its principal instrument for pursuing "aggressive reciprocity," Section 301 of the Trade Act (see Chapter 3).

None of this is to say that the earlier liberal trade vision was totally abandoned or that trade anarchy reigned again. The United States pressed ahead with tariff reductions in the Kennedy Round. In an effort to dilute the influence of the State Department in trade policy and its presumed overarching concern for foreign policy, Congress created the Office of the Special Trade Representative in 1962 as the focal point for U.S. trade policy.[29] The 1962 trade legislation also included a novel alternative to erecting trade barriers in response to import surges, the Trade Adjustment Assistance (TAA) program. TAA was designed to give financial assistance to workers injured by import competition and to assist firms to modernize or shift to new product lines. Finally, the Trade Act of 1974 set the stage for addressing the growing significance of nontariff trade barriers (NTBs) in the subsequent Tokyo Round. That effort led to a series of multilateral codes covering such trade-distorting practices as discriminatory government procurement, technical barriers to trade (i.e., product regulations), subsidies and the use of countervailing duties, and dumping and antidumping actions. Although the codes have met with mixed success, the fact that they resulted from *multilateral* negotiations within the GATT framework is significant.

▶ CROSS-CURRENTS

United States trade policy in the 1980s presents a confused picture. Despite President Reagan's *laissez faire* ideology and rhetoric, there was no

[28]Starting in 1963, Canada operated a "duty remission" scheme in which U.S. auto exports would enter duty-free to the extent that U.S. auto manufacturers operating in Canada increase the value of exports over a base period. A United States–based parts manufacturer filed a countervailing duty suit in 1964 asserting that the Canadian scheme amounted to an export subsidy. See also Chapter 6.

[29]This was a compromise. Many in Congress had wanted trade authority to be transferred to the protection-oriented Commerce Department. Now known as the Office of the United States Trade Representative (USTR), it reports directly to the president.

discernable shift toward free trade. Even by the less-demanding criteria of liberal trade, the record falls short.[30] However, despite the backsliding, the Uruguay Round of trade negotiations was launched in 1986. When agreement was finally reached in 1994 it was a major milestone in reviving liberal trade through its inclusion of agriculture, by extending GATT obligations to the new areas of trade in services, protection of intellectual property, and limiting trade-related investment restrictions and by establishing a stronger dispute-settlement mechanism. Moreover, for better or worse, the focus of U.S. policy shifted in the 1980s from its emphasis on import protection to opening export markets, an emphasis that grew even stronger in the Clinton era.

The 1980s was a decade of trade slogans. The buzzwords of *level playing field, fair trade, aggressive reciprocity, managed trade, strategic trade policy,* and *industrial policy* all found advocates in government, business, and (to a more limited extent) academic circles. All imply some departure from liberal trade precepts. All of these notions except perhaps strategic trade policy have roots that go back for decades and often to the 19th century. But they came to full flower in the Reagan years. Why?

We can identify three main reasons. The first flows from the macroeconomic situation. Starting in 1979, the Federal Reserve, under Chairman Paul Volker, tightened interest rates to arrest and reverse an accelerating inflation. The results were swift and brutal but successful. The nominal interest rate (3-month Treasury Bills) rose from 7.2 percent in 1978 to 14.0 percent in 1981. Unemployment rose from 5.8 percent in 1979 to 9.7 percent in 1982. Inflation, however, which was 13.3 percent in 1979, fell sharply to 3.8 percent in 1982.[31] Thus manufacturing and industrial employment started the decade from a weak position. This was compounded by the policies followed in the first Reagan administration of large tax cuts, large budget deficits, and restrictive monetary policy. The predictable consequence was a significant real appreciation of the dollar and rapidly rising trade deficit. Specifically, the dollar rose 85 percent in nominal terms and 35 percent in real terms between 1980 and 1985.[32] The

[30]The most egregious example was the 1981 Voluntary Export Agreement on autos with Japan. See Chapter 3.

[31]Inflation measured by the Consumer Price Index. All data from Council of Economic Advisors, *Economic Reports of the President.*

[32]Trade-weighted broad index of dollar.

trade deficit, lagging the dollar appreciation, increased from $36 billion in 1982 to $160 billion in 1987. The one-two punch of recession and an upward spike in the dollar created severe competition for U.S. export and import competing firms in the first half of the 1980s.

It is difficult now, after the strong economic performance of the 1990s, to fully appreciate the degree of pessimism about U.S. economic prospects that was prevalent in the 1980s. The terms themselves have a scare quality to them: deindustrialization, a hollowing out of our industrial capacity, relative decline in the world economy. These dark views found their way into print. The political economist David Calleo (1982) called inflation the "American disease" and argued that it was deeply rooted in America's society, politics, and world role (although, as noted previously, inflation had fallen from 13.3 percent in 1979 to 3.8 percent in 1982). Writing a decade later, Michael Bernstein and David Adler edited a volume with the ominous title *Understanding American Economic Decline* (1994). Arguing that manufacturing is the main source of prosperity, the economist Ravi Batra (1993) presented a harsh indictment of U.S. liberal trade policy under the title *The Myth of Free Trade.*[33]

Second, frustration with Japan and its trade and industrial policies reached a peak in the 1980s. Although bilateral trade deficits have little economic significance, they can be a lightning rod for political attention. The first substantive trade action in the Reagan administration was to negotiate a voluntary export restraint (VER) restricting imports of Japanese autos. Later, emphasis in the United States shifted to prying open the Japanese market through a 1986 agreement on semiconductors (a Voluntary Import Expansion, or VIE) and through the Market Opening Sector Specific (MOSS) talks in 1985, which were followed by the Structural Impediments Initiative (SSI) negotiations in 1989 (see Chapter 4). The Japanese case is of special importance because it was widely believed that it had achieved an unfair trade advantage through opaque but effective policies: industrial targeting, restrictive business practices, manipulating product standards, and others. This view supported the U.S. quest for *fair* trade, including the use of aggressive reciprocity, and convinced some that the United States itself needed its own industrial policy.

The third factor contributing to the crisis in trade policy was growing

[33]Not all analysts shared this view. Henry Nau's 1990 book, *The Myth of America's Decline,* was a sophisticated and balanced response.

weaknesses in GATT itself. The United States was prepared to launch a major new trade liberalization in 1982, but its GATT partners were not. It was not until 1986, after the United States had signaled its willingness to enter bilateral free trade agreements with Israel (1985) and later with Canada, that the Uruguay Round was launched. Also, there were major areas of trade where the GATT disciplines were absent or ineffective and that had serious trade implications: agriculture, services, dumping in third country markets, and domestic policies such as intellectual property protection and antitrust policies. Finally, when a trade dispute was brought before the GATT, it had no teeth. Any member of the GATT, including the country alleged to be the violator, could block the creation of a dispute settlement panel or the adoption of the panel's report. Such blocking action did occur and discouraged use of the GATT process.

These three factors—the difficult macroeconomic climate, the ready excuse of problems in penetrating the Japanese market, and GATT shortcomings—are sufficient to explain some backsliding from liberal trade principles. But policy responses such as aggressive reciprocity and managed trade were also given some academic respectability with the "new" strategic trade theory, with its emphasis on imperfect competition, scale economies, and externalities and its enhanced role for government intervention in trade.

The specifics of the crisis in trade policy and the departures from liberal trade are described in subsequent chapters. It is sufficient to note here that despite the stress, the international trade system showed great resiliency, and by completion of the Uruguay Round in 1994 the outlook for liberal trade was much brighter.

▶ LIBERAL TRADE REDUX

Several factors were responsible for salvaging the U.S. commitment to an open, liberal trade system. First, the dollar returned to a more competitive level, and the U.S. trade deficit declined steadily from 1987 to 1991. The deficit remained at moderate levels until the Asian financial crisis hit full force in 1998.[34] Second, the United States was enjoying an unprecedented period of prosperity; low inflation, low unemployment, and rising incomes

[34]While the U.S. experienced a rising merchandise trade deficit after 1991, much of this was offset by steady increases in the surplus for international trade in services.

during much of the 1990s. This also took steam out of traditional protectionist pressure. Perhaps most important, Japan was mired in stagnation or recession for an entire decade, discrediting the earlier infatuation with the Japanese model of industrial and trade policy.

Despite delays and breakdowns, the Uruguay Round ultimately produced a remarkably strong agreement (see Chapter 9). Not only did it start a phase out of the most egregious derogations from liberal trade—VERs and OMAs, the MFA, and the untouchable status of agriculture—but it dealt with the "new issues" closest to the heart of U.S. business: trade in services, protection of intellectual property rights, and trade-related investment requirements. Unexpectedly, but equally important, the GATT was folded into a new permanent structure, the World Trade Organization (WTO), and the dispute settlement was greatly strengthened and given teeth. Finally, subsequent agreements in 1997 under the WTO cut tariffs on information technology, opened markets in basic telecommunications, and liberalized trade in financial services. These accomplishments revitalized business support for the trade system but did little to mollify labor. An attempt to put workers rights on the Uruguay Round agenda had failed. Labor also lost in a subsequent battle over NAFTA. All this primed the labor movement to be active at the Seattle meeting at the end of the decade.

The 1990s also saw the reemergence of U.S. interest in preferential and regional trade agreements, an interest that had languished during the previous half century. Whether America's recently acquired taste for preferential trade arrangements—NAFTA, a Free Trade Agreement for the Americas (FTAA), and bilaterals proposed or agreed to with Jordan, Chile, Korea, Morocco, and Singapore—is a step toward or away from the early vision of liberal trade is debatable. But it does seem fair to say that the NAFTA process helped spur the completion of the Uruguay Round while reducing trade barriers in North America. There is a certain symmetry here. In the early 1960s the challenges posed by the newly created Common Market in Europe helped justify the U.S. Trade Expansion Act of 1962, which led directly to Kennedy Round of trade negotiations.

To summarize, by the early 1990s U.S. trade policy had survived the crisis of the 1980s but emerged with a distinctly new emphasis. Overt import protection was generally out; opening export markets was in. Preferential trade was rehabilitated. These shifts were accompanied by a commercialization of U.S. foreign policy, much touted under the emerging markets slogan, and supported by President Clinton's active involvement in trade matters.

The decline in overt import protection should not be overstated, however. As U.S. tariffs were whittled down in multilateral trade rounds, the use of the so-called unfair trade statutes responding to dumping and foreign government subsidies accelerated. Between 1980 and 1998, over 1200 U.S. antidumping and countervailing duty cases were considered, involving some $39 billion in imports. Of these, 35 percent led to antidumping or countervailing duties, 40 percent led to negative determinations by the ITC, and in 25 percent Commerce terminated or suspended the investigation. Investigations are suspended when the foreign government/firm agrees to stop the offending practice.[35] Although the authority to impose antidumping and countervailing duties has deep roots in U.S. trade policy (1916 and 1897 respectively), their use for import protection in the past two decades has been disturbing and much criticized in the economics profession.

▶ SEATTLE—A BLIP OR BACKLASH?[36]

In the penultimate month of the last year of the last century of the millennium, trade ministers from 134 countries met in Seattle to set the agenda for a new round of trade negotiations: specifically, to wrap up old business left over from the Uruguay Round (agriculture, services) and to take up new issues such as trade in cyberspace and harmonizing competition policy.

In almost a literal sense, U.S. and other delegates were ambushed by an unlikely coalition of environmentalists, labor and human rights advocates, and antiglobalists. There had been warning signs. Many in the environmental community were deeply disappointed with the WTO's ineffec-

[35]United States International Trade Commission (1999). Antidumping laws are attractive to industry seeking protection and offer some cover to government officials. The injury test is weaker than in the escape clause. The mere threat of an antidumping case may be sufficient to force a change in exporters' behavior. The U.S. government can be selective in choosing foreign targets and can tout their action as a defense against foreign unfair trade practices.

[36]See also Chapter 9.

tive Committee on Trade and Environment, created at the end of the Uruguay Round, and with the environmental side agreement to NAFTA in 1993 (see Chapter 7). Organized labor blamed trade for a fall in real wages that started in the early 1970s and had fought vigorously if unsuccessfully against NAFTA (and would fight later against normal trade relations with China). President Clinton had reversed himself and decoupled human rights from MFN for China in 1994, antagonizing another segment of society. Clinton, at the last moment before Seattle, also undercut his administration's position and appeared to support the use of trade sanctions to enforce labor and environmental standards.

The debacle was inside as well as outside the conference hall. Indeed, one can fairly say the delegates ambushed themselves. The meeting was poorly prepared, with little prior agreement on basic issues. The United States and Europe, already at odds in ongoing bruising fights over beef and bananas, disagreed on agricultural subsidies and trade in genetically modified foods. Japan and others wanted to negotiate new dumping rules, and the United States refused. Developing countries adamantly insisted on keeping labor standards off the agenda. And there was no satisfactory procedure in place for negotiations among the 134 national delegations.

It was unclear at that point if the failure at Seattle represented a minor setback or a turning point in international trade policy. But two conclusions were apparent. First, as tariffs were reduced, nontariff trade barriers had emerged, and after as at least some nontariff trade barriers had been addressed, the issues shifted toward harmonizing ostensibly domestic regulations—environment, labor standards, competition policy, taxation, investment incentives, and, for some, human rights. The easy days of tariff cutting had given way to far more complex challenges in the new century. Second, after years of courting, the developing countries had come to Seattle ready to participate in the negotiations, but the WTO was procedurally unprepared to accommodate them. The efforts to launch a new round took a beating at Seattle but were not permanently abandoned. Two years later governments met again in Doha, Qatar, and as described in Chapter 10, were successful in their second launch attempt.

The preceding overview of U.S. trade policy sets the stage for the following issue-oriented chapters. It is worthwhile to keep three or four themes in mind. First, overt import protection has been reined in but not eliminated. GATT and now the WTO rules set useful limits on what countries can do. And despite reservations, the recent emphasis on export market access over import protection is preferable. Second, one can see some (re)privatization of trade policy, although the modalities are very different from the blatant politics of setting tariffs in the Smoot-Hawley years. In the modern era, private influence on trade policy is exerted through unfair trade petitions from firms and workers and the Section 301 process, the commercialization of foreign policy that was most evident in the first Clinton administration, and of course lobbying in all its forms. Third, starting in the 1960s and accelerating in the Tokyo Round, trade negotiations have moved beyond tariffs to embrace a wide spectrum of domestic economic and social policies. But there is no consensus on which domestic policies are fair game for international scrutiny in the pursuit of trade. That line has yet to be drawn. Finally, as examined in Chapters 7 through 10, the trade system is enmeshed in seeking many noncommercial objectives: national security through strategic export controls, environmental and labor protections, human rights, and others. Again, there is no consensus on whether trade is the appropriate tool for this job.

▶ REFERENCES

Bagwell, Kyle, and Robert Staiger. 1999. An Economic Theory of GATT. *American Economic Review* 89(1):214–248.

Bagwell, Kyle, and Robert Staiger. 2001. The WTO as a Mechanism for Securing Market Access Property Rights: Implications for Global Labor and Environmental Issues. *Journal of Economic Perspectives* 15(3):69–89.

Batra, Ravi. 1993. *The Myth of Free Trade.* New York: Charles Scribner's Sons.

Bernstein, Michael, and David Adler. 1994. *Understanding American Economic Decline.* Cambridge, UK: Cambridge University Press.

Calleo, David. 1982. *The Imperious Economy.* Cambridge, MA: Harvard University Press.

Diebold, William. 1952. *The End of ITO.* Princeton Essays in International Finance (No. 16). Princeton, NJ: Princeton University Press.

Eckes, Alfred. 1995. *Opening America's Market.* Chapel Hill: University of North Carolina Press.

Eckes, Alfred. 1999. U.S. Trade History. In: William Lovett, Alfred Eckes, Richard Brinkman (eds.). *U.S. Foreign Trade Policy Since 1776.* Chapel Hill: University of North Carolina Press.

Eichengreen, Barry. 1993. *Reconstructing Europe's Trade and Payments: The European Payments Union.* Ann Arbor: University of Michigan Press.

Gillingham, John. 1955. The European Coal and Steel Community: An Object Lesson? In: Barry Eichengreen (ed.). *Europe's Post War Recovery.* Cambridge, UK: Cambridge University Press.

Irwin, Douglas. 1998. Changes in U.S. Tariffs: The Role of Import Prices and Commercial Policies. *American Economic Review* 88(4):1015–1026.

Nau, Henry. 1990. *The Myth of America's Decline.* New York: Oxford University Press.

Patterson, Gardner. 1966. *Discrimination in International Trade: The Policy Issues 1945–1965.* Princeton, NJ: Princeton University Press.

Rhodes, Carolyn. 1993. *Reciprocity, U.S. Trade Policy and the GATT Regime.* Ithaca, NY: Cornell University Press.

Ricardo, David. 1817. *On the Principles of Political Economy and Taxation.* Reprinted in 1971. Harmondsworth, UK: Pelican Books.

Schattschneider, E. E. 1935. *Politics, Pressures and the Tariff.* New York: Prentice-Hall.

Taussig, F. W. 1920. *Free Trade, The Tariff, and Reciprocity.* New York: MacMillan.

Taussig, F. W. 1931. *The Tariff History of the United States.* New York: G. P. Putnam's Sons.

United States Bureau of the Census. 1975. *Historical Statistics of the United States.* Washington, DC: U.S. Bureau of the Census.

United States International Trade Commission (USITC). 1999. *Antidumping and Countervailing Duty Handbook*, pub. 3257 (Robert Carpenter). Washington, DC: USITC.

CHAPTER

2

AGGRESSIVE RECIPROCITY

This chapter and the following two chapters describing U.S. flirtations with managed trade and our turbulent economic relations with Japan are closely interwoven. Aggressive reciprocity, sometimes known as aggressive unilateralism, is only one step away from managed trade, which itself is only half a step away from a "results-oriented" trade policy and its close cousin, industrial policy. The long period of sour trade relations with Japan was the catalyst for many of these initiatives. Also, keep in mind the background context to these three chapters—the purported twilight of U.S. postwar economic dominance in the 1970s and 1980s, the rise of a structural trade deficit, and the shrill emphasis on "unfair" trade.

CONCEPTS OF RECIPROCITY

We start with three distinct concepts of reciprocity in trade relations. The first may be called *protectionist reciprocity*, the second called *liberal* (or *first-difference*) *reciprocity*, as enshrined in the GATT, and the third, *aggressive reciprocity*, as practiced by the United States, especially in the 1980s.[1]

Protectionist reciprocity dates to the last decades of the 19th century. In that period the doctrine of protectionism dominated U.S. trade policy and, indeed, was the key pillar in U.S. industrial policy for much of the 19th and early 20th century. Protectionism was embraced most warmly by

[1]Bhagwati (1988) uses the term "first difference reciprocity" to distinguish the traditional (GATT) concept from both protectionist and aggressive reciprocity. It implies negotiating roughly equal changes in the levels of protection.

the Republican Party, which held the Presidency for 32 of 40 years from 1869 to 1909. The dilemma the protectionists faced was how to expand U.S. exports, especially agricultural exports whose prices were periodically weak, without yielding the U.S. market to competitive imports of manufactures. Two approaches were employed. The first was to negotiate bilateral "reciprocity" agreements. A total of 13 reciprocity treaties were negotiated with other countries in the latter part of the 19th century. The intent was to offer concessions on items that did not directly compete with U.S. production (often raw materials), while seeking improved access for U.S. exports of agriculture and manufactures. Achieving this fine distinction proved difficult, and the great majority of these negotiated treaties failed to find Senate ratification. One exception was a treaty with the then-independent Hawaiian Islands in 1876, offering free imports of sugar. But this was a very special situation. Most of the capital invested in sugar in Hawaii was American, and moreover, Hawaiian sugar was refined by a Pacific coast U.S. monopoly.[2]

Another approach to protectionist reciprocity was coercive—using sticks, not carrots—and this approach resonates with aggressive reciprocity a century later. The McKinley Tariff Act of 1890 gave authority to the President to *reimpose* tariffs on items normally imported freely (e.g., tea, coffee, molasses, hides) if an exporting country failed to provide satisfactory access for U.S. exports of agriculture and manufactures. Indeed, if the president found access "reciprocally unequal and unreasonable," it was his duty to impose new tariffs (Taussig, 1920, p. 121). Protectionist reciprocity attempted to extort market access and expand exports without yielding the protected U.S. market. It was primarily directed at South and Central America and was designed to displace European with American exports in those markets.[3] The unilateral character of this coercive approach and the

[2]Taussig (1920, p. 123). The reciprocity treaty led to the annexation of Hawaii in 1898. The United States also had a reciprocity treaty in 1854 allowing duty-free trade with Canada in agricultural products. This lasted about 11 years but was abrogated by the United States, ostensibly because of unbalanced trade. Times change. In 1910 the Taft administration concluded a second reciprocity treaty with Canada covering agricultural products and raw materials. It passed the House and Senate but was defeated in Canada when the Conservative party was ousted by the Liberals.

[3]The use of retaliatory tariff rates was extended in the Payne–Aldrich Act (1909), which set a two-tiered tariff schedule, the higher rates to be applied to countries that discriminated against U.S. exports. President Taft was loathe to impose the penalty rates and declared there was no undue discrimination against the United States by any country.

willingness to threaten retaliation have strong parallels with the more recent aggressive unilateralism. But there are subtle differences. Although both are cloaked in the garb of "fair trade," fairness is defined quite differently. In 1892, the protectionist Secretary of State, James Blaine, was very clever in seeking concessions in Latin America: "It was the application of the golden rule of commerce—the doctrine of fair trade—to insist that countries whose products had so long been admitted free to our parts should admit our products free to theirs."[4] He neglected to say that free U.S. imports from Latin America were mainly noncompeting food and raw material products and that Latin America was not discriminating between Europe and the United States in its imports. Still, the point is that in this early period, fairness was almost exclusively a question of U.S. *vs.* foreign tariff rates. In the 1980s the basis for unfair trade allegations was much broader, ranging from bilateral U.S. trade deficits to nontariff trade barriers and anticompetitive practices.

Also, the earlier demands for reciprocity were conflated with the maintenance of U.S. protectionism, a feature that had pretty well disappeared by the 1980s. One hundred years earlier, Blaine stated, "The enactment of reciprocity . . . is the safeguard of protection. The defeat of reciprocity is the opportunity of free trade."[5] Indeed, in this somewhat perverse logic, even tariff reductions were viewed as a preemptive device for maintaining the protection system. Writing after the Tariff Act of 1883, John Hayes, the President of the Tariff Commission, stated, "Reduction [in tariffs] in itself was by no means desirable to us; it was a concession to public sentiment, a bending of the top and branches to the wind of public opinion to save the trunk of the protective system. In a word, the object was *protection through reduction*."[6] U.S. aggressive reciprocity as practiced a century later, in the 1980s, was in the service of exports, not protected import sectors.

Protectionist reciprocity contrasts sharply with liberal reciprocity as envisioned in the 1934 RTA legislation and embodied in the GATT. In this second meaning, reciprocity refers to roughly equivalent balance when tar-

[4]Quoted by Williams (1967, p. 257).

[5]Terrill (1973, p. 168), as cited by Rhodes (1993).

[6]Cited by Taussig (1931, p. 249), italics added. There is another important difference between U.S. trade policy in the late 19th and late 20th centuries. Throughout the 19th century, the tariff was the principal source of revenue for the federal government. It is a trivial source today.

iff concessions are negotiated (bilaterally between 1934 and 1947, multilaterally after GATT). If a country cuts tariffs by, say, 20 percent on $1 billion of imports, it seeks and could expect similar-size tariff cuts on $1 billion in its export markets. It is important to remember that in liberal reciprocity, market access is negotiated without the threat of retaliatory tariffs and is generally done on a multilateral basis. And in GATT negotiations the balance of reciprocity could be achieved across sectors, countries, and different forms of trade restrictions, including tariffs but also nontariff trade barriers (NTBs).

The advantages of multilateral balanced reductions in trade barriers are obvious. First, the economic benefit of replacing high-cost domestic production with lower-cost imports is doubled, as resources simultaneously are shifted to expanding, efficient export industries. In its direct effect, unilateral tariff reduction captures only the first benefit. Second, reciprocal tariff reductions moderate adverse terms of trade and trade balance effects. Import expansion is more or less matched by export expansion. Third, the creation of new export opportunities helps offset political opposition from import competing industries, greasing the political process. Finally, first-difference, or liberal, reciprocity has a patina of fairness, wherein countries share the "burden" of opening markets.

There are shortcomings to the practice of liberal reciprocity, however. If countries start from greatly unequal tariff levels, identical reciprocal tariff cuts still leave one group of countries more protected than another.[7] Moreover, as is well known from basic trade theory, both the price and the trade effects of a tariff cut depend on import and export price elasticities. Thus, cutting the tariff from 20 percent to 10 percent on, say, fabricated steel may have very different trade effects than a similar cut on petrochemicals or wool. Balanced tariff concessions may not lead to balanced trade effects. Third, once negotiations move beyond tariffs to NTBs such as technical barriers to trade (i.e., product regulations) or government procurement, the measurement and hence the operation of liberal reciprocity is open to question and dispute. Fourth and perhaps most important, the practice of unconditional MFN means that some countries in a multilateral negotiation may make few if any concessions and yet enjoy concessions by others, the free rider problem.

[7]In fact, it is more complicated. Two countries with identical average tariffs will not be equally protective if one has relatively uniform tariffs among products and the second has large disparities. This is the tariff dispersion issue.

Despite these drawbacks, the concept of first-difference reciprocity was embedded in the GATT and served the trade system well in the early postwar period. Reciprocity was a multilateral, noncoercive approach to reducing trade barriers and opening markets. It did not impugn trade partners as unfair, and it did not require specific, numerical trade results. And it was well suited to both multilateral and multisectoral negotiations.

Aggressive reciprocity as practiced by the United States, especially in the 1980s, was very different. It was unilateral in the sense that the United States offered no concession in exchange for a change in foreign practices (although in some cases the foreign country was being pressured to simply do what it had previously agreed to). It was coercive in the sense that if the offending foreign practice was not altered, the United States threatened to retaliate by raising trade barriers. The unilateral and coercive features are opposite to the spirit of GATT, which is based on carrots, not sticks. Furthermore, aggressive reciprocity is country-specific in that it makes demands on particular countries, either for reducing a bilateral trade surplus with the United States or, more frequently, to cease a particular trade practice. And although it need not do so, it often is associated with numerical (quantitative) trade targets and with "results-oriented" criteria, neither of which is present in the earlier GATT conception of reciprocity.

In summary, all three concepts of reciprocity have been touted as devices for expanding exports. Only liberal reciprocity implicitly acknowledges the benefits of expanding imports. The issue of fair vs. unfair trade has also been present in all three, but in quite different guises. In protectionist reciprocity, fairness resided in relative tariff levels; in liberal reciprocity, fairness requires that all participants bear some of the "burden" of opening markets; and in aggressive reciprocity, the U.S. perception of widespread foreign unfair trade practices was the driving force.

▶ SECTION 301: REGULAR, SUPER, AND SPECIAL[8]

The principal but not the only tool for U.S. aggressive reciprocity was Section 301 of the Trade Act of 1974 and its subsequent amendments and offspring.[9] As we have seen, the roots of Section 301 can be traced to the late

[8]For earlier detailed analysis, see Bayard and Elliott (1994).

[9]Section 337 of the U.S. Tariff Act of 1930 can also be considered a tool of aggressive reciprocity. It allows the complete ban on imports of a product if it is produced in violation of intellectual property rights owned by Americans under domestic U.S. law.

19th century, in particular the Tariff Act of 1890, in which the president was given the power to impose new tariffs on certain articles if the exporting country was deemed "reciprocally unequal or unreasonable." This power was reaffirmed in the Tariff Act of 1897. Moreover, the Tariff Act of 1909 allowed the president to impose *additional* 25 percent *ad valorem* tariffs on goods from countries that unduly discriminated against the United States. Such discriminatory practices were broadly described, to include "tariff rates or provisions, trade or other regulations, charges, exactions or . . . any other manner" or export subsidies or export taxes.[10]

Section 301 provides that if the President determines a foreign government engages in certain practices, the United States can retaliate by suspending previous trade concessions and imposing new duties and restrictions on the imports from that country. The target practices include unjustifiable or unreasonable tariffs, discriminatory policies that are unjustifiable or unreasonable, subsidies that harm U.S. exports in third country markets, and restrictions on U.S. access to supplies of food and raw materials that are unjustifiable or unreasonable. The legislative history indicates that the scope of foreign trade practices covered by Section 301 was to be very broad, including government procurement, restrictive business taxes, import licensing systems, exchange controls, certain product standards, and others (Low, 1993, p. 56).

The coverage of the original 1974 legislation was expanded and procedures tightened in subsequent trade legislation in 1979, 1984, and 1988. Trade-related services were explicitly included in 1979, and certain foreign investment regulations (for example, export performance requirements) were included in 1984.[11] In 1984 the terms *unreasonable, unjustifiable,* and

[10]Taussig (1931, p. 403). Section 252 of the Trade Expansion Act of 1962, although limited to agriculture, was another precedent. The exercise of Section 252 led to the famous "chicken war" between the United States and the EEC in 1963. In the 1950s the United States pioneered new methods of chicken production, with the price falling by half. Exports to West Germany boomed. In 1962 the EEC initiated a variable levy system, with the duty rising from 15 percent to 70 percent by 1965. U.S. exports plummeted. GATT authorized retaliation and the United States raised tariffs against the EEC on imports of panel trucks, potato starch, dextrine, and brandy (Preeg, 1970).

[11]Export performance requirements specify that a foreign firm operating in a host country must export a certain percent of its output. Minimum domestic content requirements imposed on foreign direct investments, which require purchase of locally produced intermediate inputs, were also common in developing countries at this time.

discriminatory were explicitly defined, and these definitions give a flavor of what was meant by fair *vs.* unfair trade at the time. *Unreasonable practices* might not violate U.S. international legal rights but simply be unilaterally deemed by the United States as unfair or inequitable. Examples are the denial of fair and equitable market opportunities or the opportunity for the United States to establish an enterprise. *Unjustifiable practices* violate U.S. international legal rights under GATT or in bilateral trade agreements. *Discriminatory practices* deny MFN treatment for U.S. goods, services, or investment. In 1988 foreign practices that might be construed as unreasonable were broadened to include foreign government toleration of systematic anticompetitive activities by private firms, export targeting, and denial of labor rights such as the right to bargain collectively and the protection of child labor.

The U.S. strategy was to bring perceived foreign unfair trade practices to heel, with Section 301 as the tool for pursuing aggressive reciprocity. This was very cleverly complemented in 1984 by requiring an annual report by USTR to the President and Congress listing, country by country, foreign barriers to U.S. exports of good and services, U.S. foreign direct investment, and impediments to the protection of U.S. intellectual property.[12] The reports are also required to include (if feasible) the dollar value of lost trade and investment opportunities and the Section 301 actions undertaken (or the reason why no action was undertaken). The 1986 report ran some 300 pages, with Japan and Brazil heading the list with 20 pages each. The 2000 report was 429 pages, and the dominant countries were Japan (60 pages), the EU (34 pages), and China (17 pages).[13] As might have been expected, there was a negative foreign response to this public finger-pointing. Japan and Canada have both published accounts of U.S. trade barriers, and in 2000 the EU published its 16th annual compilation of U.S. barriers.

Despite the expansion of Section 301 authority to pursue aggressive reciprocity, some in Congress pushed vigorously in the last half of the 1980s for harsher measures to pry open foreign markets and rein in perceived foreign unfair trade practices. A prime example was the Gephardt Amendment, offered in 1986, which ultimately morphed into the more in-

[12]The National Trade Estimate Reports on Foreign Trade Barriers.

[13]Counting pages, of course, has little to do with ranking serious and pervasive trade-distorting practices.

nocuous Super 301 in the 1988 Trade Act. The Gephardt Amendment, deliberately crafted to bludgeon Japan, was truly draconian. In essence, it would have required USTR to identify countries with "excessive and unwarranted" trade surpluses with the United States and to specify those countries engaged in a pattern of unjustifiable, unreasonable, or discriminatory practices damaging U.S. commerce. These countries would then have been required to eliminate the unfair practices and meet a trade surplus reduction target of 10 percent per year for three years. Failing this, the countries would be subject to severe U.S. trade retaliation.

The Gephardt Amendment was recognized as dangerous overkill, even by many sympathetic to the unfair trade rhetoric of the time. But the idea of publicly identifying priority countries and practices survived in Super 301, which obliged USTR to identify priority countries by the number and pervasiveness of their unfair practices. However, both the exercise and level of retaliation were subject to great discretion, and the mandatory, quantitative trade surplus reduction targets of the Gephardt Amendment were dropped.

As expected, in 1989 USTR identified Japan as a priority country under Super 301. However, the designation was on the basis of specific practices in Japan (in the supercomputer, satellites, and forest products sectors) and not due to systemic unfair trade practices. Brazil and India, the latter of which scarcely engaged in any trade with the United States, were also caught up by Super 301 and named priority countries. Korea and Taiwan bought their way out of Super 301 designation by concluding last-minute trade deals with the United States. Super 301 lapsed in 1991 but was later resurrected by President Clinton through administrative action in a much milder form. By 2000 the Super 301 report was mainly a review of the administration's trade expansion priorities (e.g., to establish permanent normal trade relations with China and press onward with the Free Trade Area of the Americas negotiations) and a list of outstanding trade disputes (e.g., subsidies in the EU to Airbus, Japanese barriers in the flat-glass sector).

The 1988 Trade Act also created Special 301, designed to protect U.S. intellectual property rights. It required USTR to identify countries that denied effective protection of such rights or that denied fair and equitable market access for U.S. persons relying on intellectual property protection. To comply, USTR created so-called watch lists monitoring foreign protection of intellectual property. As of the 2000 report, 39 countries had been placed on the Watch List and 16 countries placed on a Priority Watch List. The Uruguay Round agreement on trade-related intellectual property rights (TRIPs) has codified rules in this area and is now the principal means through which the United States attempts to enforce its rights.

▶ SECTION 301 CASES

Between 1975 and August 1999, the USTR initiated action on 119 Section 301 cases.[14] In addition, 29 other petitions were filed by U.S. firms and industry associations and were subsequently withdrawn or rejected. For certain purposes, these 29 should also be counted as part of the 301 universe, as sometimes the threat of investigation led to a positive response from the target country or, in some cases, the U.S. pursued alternative courses of action.[15]

At first glance it is difficult to find much of a pattern (see Figure 2.1). The number of cases initiated per year fluctuates between 1 and 10, with spikes in 1981, 1989, and 1996. But on closer inspection and especially when the rejected/withdrawn cases are included, it does appear that the 1980s, and especially the latter 1980s, was an unusually active period.[16] This, of course, coincided with the increase in the U.S. trade deficit (through 1987), the creation by President Reagan in 1985 under Congressional pressure of the Trade Policy Strike Force, and the passage of the 1988 Omnibus Trade Act, creating the Special and Super 301 mechanisms. Of particular interest, under the 1984 legislation, USTR can self initiate a 301 action; of the 72 cases since 1984, 42 have been initiated by the government rather than by petition from the private sector. Indeed, in the most recent 50 cases, nearly two-thirds are government-initiated.[17] The initiating role of the government is partly a consequence of the ploy in the

[14]This includes 301 cases originally identified under Super 301.

[15]USTR twice rejected petitions from the U.S. Rice Millers Association (1986, 1988) trying to crack the Japanese rice market. The justification was that negotiations under way in the Uruguay Round were a more effective avenue. Modest relief did not arrive until almost a decade later (1995), when Japan agreed to import four percent of its consumption.

[16]A number of studies have shown that the "demand" for protection through various channels is systematically related to variables such as unemployment levels and the real exchange rates (Takacs, 1981; Grilli, 1988). Section 301 cases are not about U.S. protection *per se* but about opening foreign markets.

[17]Obviously, private interests were behind much of this activity.

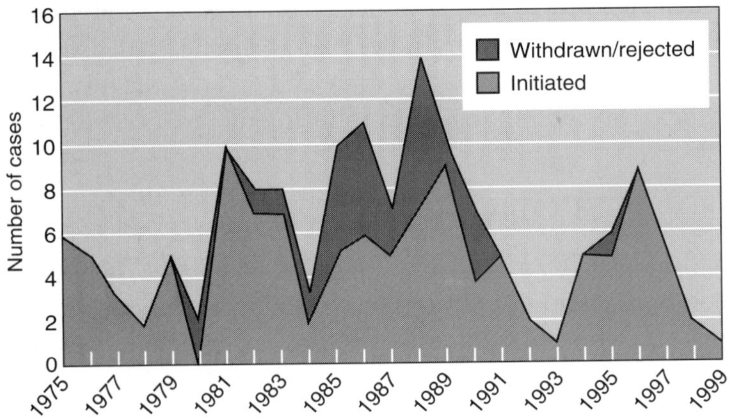

Figure 2.1 Section 301 cases from 1975 to August 9, 1999.*

*Total filed: those initiated and those withdrawn or rejected.

Source: United States Trade Representative.

1984 legislation to require the annual report on foreign barriers and U.S. government responses.

Of special importance was the shift in the Reagan administration's international economic policies in September 1985. Although the dollar had started to depreciate through market forces earlier in the year, it was given an additional shove by the Plaza Accord.[18] At the same time the President ordered the USTR to resolve certain 301 cases or recommend retaliation. USTR itself initiated important new cases in the final months of 1985: Japanese restrictions on tobacco (mainly cigarettes), Brazil's restrictive informatics policies, Korean restrictions on U.S. insurance services, and its allegedly inadequate protection of intellectual property. There was some expectation that with the conclusion of the Uruguay Round in 1994 and the strengthening of the dispute settlement mechanism in the WTO, the United States' use of Section 301 would fade away, but this did not occur. Twenty new 301 actions were initiated in the 1995–1998 period. Nevertheless, Section 301 has lost its sharp unilateral edge since the creation of the WTO. The types of disputes within WTO's purview have been greatly expanded, and the United States must submit these to the WTO's dispute

[18]The Group of Five (U.S., Germany, Japan, France, and the UK) announced their intention to intervene and further weaken what was widely considered an overvalued dollar.

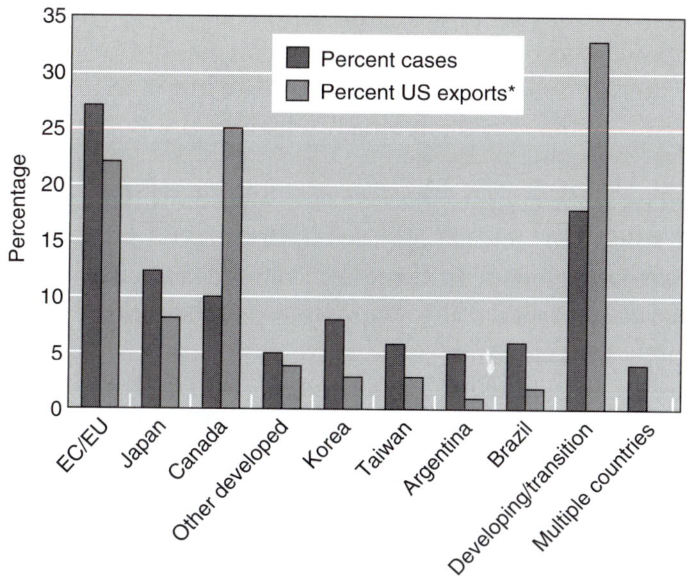

Figure 2.2 Section 301 cases by target country/group.

*U.S. merchandise exports.

Source: United States Trade Representative and Council of Economic Advisors, Economic Report of the President.

settlement process. As Schott (1994) noted, the tradeoff for a more effective multilateral dispute mechanism in the WTO was reduced scope for purely unilateral action under Section 301.

Figure 2.2 presents data on 301 target countries and, for comparison, these countries' share of 1999 U.S. exports. The largest single target has been the EC/EU (27 percent of 301 cases), which exceeds their share of U.S. exports. As one might expect from the intent of 301 legislation, Japan, Korea, and Taiwan were substantial targets, with their share of 301 cases exceeding their share of U.S. exports. Canada was subject to 10 percent of the investigations, although its share of U.S. exports is 25 percent (U.S.–Canadian trade disputes are also pursued through NAFTA's dispute settlement procedures). Argentina, taking 1 percent of U.S. exports, was hit with 5 percent of 301 actions. For those cases identifying a specific sector in which the unfair trade practice occurred, 42 percent were in agricultural products, 39 percent were in manufactures, and 20 percent involved services.

The complaints themselves cover a wide spectrum. For example, Paraguay (1998) was accused of denying protection for intellectual property, Turkey (1996) was accused of discriminatory treatment of U.S. films, and Norway's government procurement practices for highway toll electronic ID systems were challenged (1989). Although some petitions involve multiple accusations, it appears that at least 32 of the 119 cases involved subsidies of some sort, and an additional 15 involved inadequate protection of intellectual property. In three ethically questionable cases, the U.S. government used Section 301 to open up the market for U.S. cigarettes in Japan, Korea, and Thailand.

Evaluating the outcome of the 301 cases is fraught with difficulties, but two earlier studies can be cited. While acknowledging the subjective nature of the exercise, Patrick Low (1993) concludes that 35 percent of 301 cases between 1975 and 1990 led to some liberalization of trade, 55 percent had no identifiable results or uncertain trade results, and 10 percent led to retaliation by the United States. Furthermore, Low finds that the "success" rate against Japan and Korea is relatively high (i.e., 68%), and the "success" rate in cases against the EU is relatively low (15%).[19] Bayard and Elliott (1994) performed a more detailed study of 301 actions. Their analysis of 72 cases between 1975 and 1992 concluded that 35 were "successes" and 37 were "failures," where success is defined as some improvement in market access for U.S. firms.[20] In a somewhat later study, Elliot and Richardson (1997) found that success in resolving 301 disputes was positively associated with the extent to which the target country was dependent on the U.S. market for its exports and with the size of the U.S. trade balance with that country.

▶ ASSESSMENT

What are we to make of this large-scale, persistent effort at attacking perceived unfair trade practices through Section 301? The aggregate direct economic effects are murky but most likely quite small when set against

[19] In an unrelated analysis, Rhodes (1993) found that the EU was relatively more successful than others in resisting U.S. import restraints on steel.

[20] Furthermore, they found that the United States retaliated against the alleged unfair practice in 15 investigations (through 1994), and these led to counter-retaliations in three cases, twice by the EC and once by Canada.

total U.S. exports or, indeed, the U.S. trade deficit. Certainly some additional cigarettes were sold in Asian markets, and it may well be that the U.S. exported somewhat more rice at a somewhat better price to third countries after forcing Taiwan in 1983 to reduce its exports of subsidized rice. Other limited successes could be cited. And it is only fair to acknowledge that the exercise of Section 301 was generally more laser-like than blunderbuss. But there were welfare losses as well. In a complicated and bitter Section 301/countervailing duty case involving softwood lumber with Canada, the final disposition was a 15 percent Canadian export tax, which was estimated to increase new home prices in the United States by \$1000.[21] In a broader sense, unwarranted credibility was given to the view that foreign unfair trade barriers were and remain a major impediment to U.S. exports and are the cause of our persistent trade deficit. Finally, Section 301 gave easy ammunition to foreign critics of U.S. unilateralism.

There are two plausible grounds for a more positive assessment of Section 301. First, at the time it was introduced, GATT coverage of practices affecting trade was limited. There were virtually no international rules covering trade in services or intellectual property or such dubious practices as export performance requirements for foreign direct investment. Moreover, GATT enforcement of existing rules was weak. Dispute panel decisions could be blocked by countries losing decisions at the GATT. It can be argued that foreign resentment toward the unilateral character of Section 301, wielded by a self-righteous United States, has motivated trade partners to develop effective *international* rules and helped lead to a successful Uruguay Round and a stronger WTO. But this is a knife's edge argument—that the discriminating use of a *quasi*-legal unilateral lever strengthens the international rule of law in trade.

The second rationale involves domestic politics. It holds that the early bipartisan consensus for a liberal trade policy had all but collapsed by the 1980s, and the aggressive use of Section 301 was a necessary political defense against a serious, prolonged relapse into protectionism. This is a perception argument—that successive administrations have had to appear forceful in swatting down foreign trade barriers and promoting U.S. commercial interests. There may be a kernel of truth here: it is better to open foreign markets then retreat into import protection. The alternative, of

[21]In 2002, the softwood lumber dispute with Canada entered its third decade, showing that propinquity does not eliminate discord.

course, would have been for the President and trade officials to educate the public: dismiss unfair practices as a rather insignificant source of the trade deficit, demote bilateral trade balances as of little economic significance, and explain that the purpose of trade is efficient allocation of resources and not a vehicle for jobs.

▶ THE FAIR TRADE LAWS

Aggressive reciprocity may be thought of as a unilateral attempt by the U.S. to create a "fair" trade system by forcing changes in foreign trade practices. But our trade partners also have views on *our* trade practices. Before turning to the other strands in this tangle, managed trade and relations with Japan, it is useful to examine how the United States uses it own fair trade laws. The principal ones are the antidumping and countervailing duty statutes.

The antidumping legislation has been most heavily criticized (Finger, 1993; Clarida, 1996). Under current law, imported goods sold at "less than fair value" and that result in material injury, the threat of material injury, or material retardation to a domestic industry producing a like product will be subject to duties set at the level of the dumping margin.[22] Material injury is a less-demanding standard than serious injury found in the escape clause legislation. Whereas economics recognizes a need to protect against predatory pricing, the U.S. dumping law does not require a finding of predation to invoke dumping duties. Moreover, the procedures set forth in the law to determine dumping and the dumping margin are biased against imports and help make the dumping laws the protectionist's instrument of choice.

Bear with us. Commerce has four methods for determining if sales are at less than fair value. The first is to compare the price in the U.S. market with sales price in the home market for similar items at the same stage in the distribution chain (usually an exfactory basis). If the U.S. price is lower, this is deemed dumping. A second method is used when the home market is too small for valid price data. Then Commerce compares U.S. price to the price received by the exporter in some third country market. Again, if the U.S. price is lower, this is dumping. Third, if there is no viable third

[22]The U.S. ITC determines injury and the Department of Commerce determines the margin. The "margin" refers to the difference between the fair value price and the actual selling price of the imports.

country market, Commerce calculates a "constructed value," equal to the firm's total cost of production plus some amount of profit. If the U.S. sales prices are below constructed costs, there is dumping. Finally, for imports from nonmarket economies such as China (and until 2002 Russia), Commerce estimates the physical inputs to production and values these inputs on the basis of prices in some surrogate country that is judged to be at the same level of development as the target country but which operates on a market system. From this, surrogate estimates of constructed costs (including administrative costs and profits) are calculated and then used to compare with selling prices in the United States. Interestingly but unfortunately, this last very questionable practice was reconfirmed for an additional 15 years in the 1999 bilateral United States–China Agreement, paving the way for China's entry into the WTO. While there are real problems with the first (price-to-price) method, the more serious problems are with the last two, constructed cost and surrogate country constructed costs. Dumping is deemed to occur when sales are below average costs, including a "normal" profit. Economics demonstrates that in perfectly competitive markets, firms generally sell at marginal cost or, indeed, below marginal cost if learning-by-doing externalities are present. Marginal costs are often below average costs. Thus, there is a major bias in favor of finding dumping and against imports. Moreover the preferred United States-home market price method is seldom used. Lindsey (2000) finds that in 141 Commerce Department investigations between 1995 and 1998, 20 were based on constructed value, 47 on surrogate country constructed value, and 36 on "facts available," meaning questionable information provided primarily by the petitioner. Only four were based purely on United States–home market price comparisons, and the remainder used mixed criteria.

Ironically, the antidumping virus has now spread beyond the traditional users (United States, Canada, EU, Australia) to developing countries, and U.S. exports have become significant targets (Lindsey and Ikenson, 2001). Brazil, Argentina, and Mexico started intensive use of antidumping laws in the 1980s and have been joined in recent years by South Africa and India. In the 1995–2000 period, worldwide antidumping measures in place increased by 26 percent, and by the end of that period nontraditional users accounted for 45 percent, up from 28 percent in 1995. U.S. exports were the third most popular target in this period. The reason for the accelerated use in developing countries is no mystery. Most have reduced their tariff and quantitative barriers and, taking their cue from the industrial countries, see antidumping measures as the default protectionist instrument of choice. In short, U.S. zeal in using questionable laws in pursuit of "fair" trade has helped spread the protectionist antidumping virus.

In summary, the United States was an active but generally discerning user of aggressive reciprocity to promote its view of fair trade. But its own fair trade laws have been strongly criticized while, at the same time, being copied elsewhere.

▶ REFERENCES

Bayard, Thomas, and Kimberly Elliott. 1994. *Reciprocity and Retaliation in U.S. Trade Policy.* Washington, DC: Institute for International Economics.

Bhagwati, Jagdish. 1988. *Protectionism.* Cambridge, MA: MIT Press.

Clarida, Richard. 1996. Dumping in Theory, in Policy, and in Practice. In: Jagdish Bhagwati and Robert Hudec (eds.). *Fair Trade and Harmonization: Prerequisites for Free Trade.* Cambridge, MA: MIT Press.

Elliott, Kimberly, and J. David Richardson. 1997. Determinants and Effectiveness of Aggressively Unilateral U.S. Trade Actions. In: R. Feenstra (ed.). *The Effects of U.S. Trade Protection and Promotion Policies.* Chicago: University of Chicago Press.

Finger, J Michael. 1993 (ed.). *Antidumping: How It Works and Who Gets Hurt.* Ann Arbor: University of Michigan Press.

Grilli, Enzo. 1988. Macro-Economic Determinants of Trade Protection. *The World Economy* 11(3):313–326.

Lindsey, Brink. 2000. The U.S. Antidumping Law: Rhetoric versus Reality. *Journal of World Trade* 34(1):1–38.

Lindsey, Brink, and Dan Ikenson. 2001. *Coming Home to Roost: Proliferating Antidumping Laws and the Growing Threat to U.S. Exports.* Cato Institute Trade Policy Analysis. Washington, DC: Cato Institute.

Low, Patrick. 1993. *Trading Free: The GATT and U.S. Trade Policy.* New York: Twentieth Century Fund.

Preeg, Ernest. 1970. *Traders and Diplomats.* Washington, DC: The Brookings Institution.

Rhodes, Carolyn. 1993. *Reciprocity, U.S. Trade Policy and the GATT Regime.* Ithaca, NY: Cornell University Press.

Schott, Jeffrey. 1994. *The Uruguay Round: An Assessment.* Washington, DC: Institute for International Economics.

Takacs, Wendy. 1981. Pressure for Protectionism: An Empirical Analysis. *Economic Inquiry* 19: 687–693.

Taussig, F. W. 1931. *The Tariff History of the United States.* New York: G. P. Putnam's Sons.

Terrill, Tom. 1973. *The Tariff, Politics, and American Foreign Policy.* Westport, CT: Greenwood.

Williams, Benjamin. 1967. *Foreign Economic Policy of the United States.* New York: Howard Fertig.

CHAPTER

3

FLIRTING WITH MANAGED TRADE

In a broad sense, all government intervention in trade implies managed trade. From this perspective, all governments, including that of the United States, have been managing trade for centuries. But in the 1980s the term took on a somewhat sharper meaning, with an emphasis on quantitative targets for exports and imports, often specified by country and by sector or product. There was a subtle switch from a focus on trade rules to a focus on trade outcomes, a results-oriented trade policy. This chapter looks at new theoretical justifications and some tools for managed trade *circa* the 1980s.

The active use of Section 301 described in Chapter 2 grew out of a loss of confidence in GATT, an increasingly strident obsession with alleged unfair trade practices, and a surging trade deficit. It was accompanied by two relatively new trade policy instruments: voluntary export restraints (VERs) and voluntary import expansions (VIEs). These new tools reinforced the long-established use of antidumping and countervailing duties and various direct and indirect export subsidies.[1] Underlying much of this activist trade-interventionism was a deep-seated frustration with U.S.–Japan trade relations, considered in detail in the next chapter.

One result of the frustration in obtaining import relief or satisfactory export market access through conventional negotiations was a move to establish numerical targets for trade, by sector and country. VERs and VIEs establish quantitative trade targets, and they became devices for "results-

[1]VERs are identical to Orderly Marketing Agreements (OMAs), except the latter involve formal government-to-government agreements and the former do not. At the time, VERs and OMAs lived in a twilight zone of GATT legality.

oriented" trade agreements and hence tools for managed trade.[2] An activist U.S. trade policy—domestic and export subsidies, tax breaks, import and export targets using VERs and VIEs, industrial policy generally—was given a patina of respectability by a new academic literature on strategic trade policy elaborated in the 1970s and 1980s. As explained below, some of the assumptions of strategic trade policy, especially imperfect competition, foreign government manipulation of trade, and pervasive externalities, appeared to politicians and policy-makers to mesh with actual trade practice. The result was a lengthy U.S. flirtation with managed trade. We start by examining some elements of strategic trade policy, followed by an analysis of VERs and VIEs. We conclude by illustrating the then-new look to U.S. trade policy in three cases: steel, autos, and semiconductors.

▶ STRATEGIC TRADE POLICY

The term strategic trade policy is ill-defined but has come to be associated with government trade actions—defensive or offensive—in the context of imperfectly competitive markets, scale economies, and production externalities. Imperfect competition arises from some degree of market power by firms (monopoly, oligopoly, monopolistic competition). "Strategic" suggests interaction among firms but also strategic interaction among governments and between governments and firms to capture trade benefits.[3]

The underlying assumptions of imperfect competition and externalities, and the related possibility of declining cost curves (economies of scale) provide a rich matrix for constructing models in which it is theoretically possible for governments to intervene in trade and improve national welfare. This contrasts with standard trade theory, where terms-of-trade

[2]The distinction between traditional import quotas, which have been used for many decades, and VERs is not always sharp. It rests on the ostensibly voluntary nature of the arrangement by the exporting country. Quotas can be global or country-specific, but VERs are always country-specific.

[3]The word strategic implies interdependence of actions. It does not necessarily refer to industries that are strategic in a national security sense, nor to industries that have strong backward and forward linkages. There is some question as to how new strategic trade policy really was. Monopoly and economics of scale have long been analyzed. But analysis of strategic interactions between oligopolies and governments in trade was new. For clear analysis, see Pomfret (1992) and Corden (1997). The classic literature includes Helpman and Krugman (1989).

tariffs and infant industry conditions provide the principal economic exceptions to *laissez faire* trade policy. The multiplicity of models in the strategic trade policy literature and the even greater array of policy conclusions (e.g., what might appear to be minor changes in assumptions switch policy recommendations from export subsidies to export taxes) are partly due to uncertainty about oligopolistic conduct and partly the result of living in the murky world of the second best.[4] Imperfect competition and externalities imply gaming behavior and second-best choices, and these are highly sensitive to the specifics of the situation.

The models in this literature fall loosely into four categories: those based on monopolistic competition; rent-snatching models (often presented as duopoly); import restrictions to promote exports; and models in which externalities are central. We start with the first but acknowledge that unlike the latter three, monopolistic competition has seldom been used to justify an active trade policy.

The motivation for melding monopolistic competition and trade is the empirical observation that much international trade involves exchange of similar goods, often among countries with similar income levels and factor endowments. Neither intra-industry trade nor intense trade among similar economies conforms to the standard Heckscher-Ohlin trade theory, which is based on differences in factor endowments. One explanation for intra-industry trade is to postulate variety-specific scale economies in a monopolistic-competition context. In this situation, trade improves welfare by expanding the market, allowing consumers to buy a greater variety of goods at lower cost.[5] It is possible in these models to increase national welfare further through selective tariffs that promote domestic production (lower cost), but this gain must be set against a possible loss of product variety. These product-variety models have been popular in helping explain intra-industry trade, but they have not played a significant role in U.S. trade policy, and we do not pursue them further.

Rent-snatching models come in several flavors. The simplest postu-

[4]See Maggi (1996) regarding uncertainty concerning market behavior in strategic trade models. Second best refers to a situation where economic distortions persist. See Chapter 6.

[5]With long-run adjustment of free entry and exit, the price for each variety equals average cost but exceeds marginal cost. For exposition, see Appleyard and Field (2001), Chapter 10.

lates a foreign monopolist as sole supplier to the home country. If the home country imposes an import tariff, this has the effect of raising the monopolist's marginal cost, reducing its sales to the home country. It is possible although not certain that the tariff revenue gain for the home country (snatched from the foreign monopolist's profits) exceeds the losses to consumers in the home country, and home country welfare improves. The only strategic feature of this model is possible foreign retaliation. It is not very interesting for U.S. trade policy, as most U.S. tariffs are "bound" in the GATT and cannot be arbitrarily changed.

A slightly more elaborate rent-snatching model postulates a duopoly consisting of a home and a foreign firm. It appears to invite a government subsidy so that the domestic firm can capture a larger share of world output and hence duopoly rents (Brander and Spencer, 1985). The model has made its way into trade textbooks and need not be expounded here. The novelty is that under certain circumstances a government subsidy to the domestic firm may add credibility to the firm's output decision and hence cause the foreign firm to reduce its output. Increasing home output at the expense of foreign output increases the share of monopoly profits (and jobs) enjoyed by the home firm and country and may increase national welfare. The interaction of government and the two firms' output decisions is the strategic element and is analyzed with game theory tools. Why one government and not the other seizes this opportunity is not clear.

Although it hardly fits the strict requirements of the Brander-Spencer model, subsidy duels between the U.S. government–Boeing faction and the EU–Airbus faction for the world's commercial aircraft market are often used to illustrate this form of rent-snatching model. In a broader context, it is hard to find examples where this particular trade model casts light on actual practice. Certainly the United States and EU have contested vigorously over agricultural subsidies, but no one suggests that this sector is characterized by oligopolistic rents.[6] Strategic considerations have also played a role in export financing programs and in tax policies. But these actions stray far from the particulars of the duopoly rent-snatching model. It seems unlikely in the extreme that U.S. subsidies attempt the fine calculations needed to maximize domestic welfare that are implicit in this model. Nevertheless, at a general level this strand of the strategic trade policy literature may have provided some intellectual cover for aggressive subsidy and countervailing duty policies.

[6]However, see the novel approach of Bagwell and Staiger discussed in Chapter 8.

The third class of models, in which import restrictions are used to promote exports, has been influential in U.S. trade policy, as the models appear to fit neatly with Japan's so-called industrial policy in recent decades.[7] These models also come in several flavors. A typical example postulates declining costs (economics of scale) in production. If the home market is protected through tariffs, quotas, or more subtle means, the increase in output for the home market lowers average and marginal costs and allows the home firm (or cartelized industry) to expand exports and capture a larger share of world markets. Indeed, in one variation it is possible that the protected home market generates sufficient profit so that an industry that would be fully uncompetitive and would not exist in free trade not only is created but also becomes a successful exporter. The key to these models is declining costs from scale economies, which are obtained through protection of the home market. In short, import protection can nurture exports, a result contrary to traditional trade theory. The perception that Japanese firms in a number of industries have used protected home market profits to penetrate the U.S. market has been influential in setting U.S. trade policy.

Other models of this genre rely on research and development expenditures (R & D) rather than scale economies to demonstrate that import protection can lead to export expansion. In this formulation R & D expenditures reduce production costs (or produce a superior product), and these expenditures are assumed to be a positive function of output levels. It is then easy to demonstrate that reserving the home market for domestic firms through import protection leads to higher levels of R & D, lower costs, and greater export penetration. Neither the scale economies nor the R & D argument are necessarily welfare-damaging for the importing country, but given the *quasi* merchantilist and unfair trade rhetoric of the 1980s, they tended to vindicate an activist U.S. trade policy, especially *vis a vis* Japan.

The final class of models justifying some form of managed trade or industrial policy rely heavily on externality arguments and are generally reserved for high-technology industries. Professor Laura Tyson, who later became Chair of the Council of Economic Advisors in the first Clinton ad-

[7]For example, Edward Lincoln, an expert on U.S.–Japan trade and one-time advisor to Walter Mondale, U.S. ambassador to Japan, asserts the import restriction/excess profit/export promotion argument twice in the introduction to his recent book (Lincoln, 1999, pp. 2, 14).

ministration, was a forceful advocate.[8] In addition to two conventional arguments for managed trade—to reduce the U.S. trade deficit through export expansion and to deflect protectionist pressure—and in addition to the rent-snatching argument discussed above, Tyson asserts that high-tech industries generate substantial spillover benefits to the rest of the economy (positive externalities). Moreover, these industries are characterized by decreasing costs over time, lowering input costs to downstream industries (e.g., the semiconductor–consumer electronics linkage). It does not follow, of course, that such spillover effects, if they occur, are restricted to the home economy or that downstream industries cannot avail themselves of lower cost inputs from abroad.[9] Nevertheless, the view that comparative advantage in high-tech can be *created* through adroit government policies of subsidies, import protection, and negotiated expansion of export markets was attractive to U.S. policy-makers seeking a rationale for managed trade,[10] the more so because of a widely shared view that Japan had mastered the art of managed trade and was thereby profiting at U.S. expense.

In summary, the new strategic trade policy literature had appealing features for those inclined toward managed trade. The emphasis on imperfect competition, economies of scale, and externalities had a more modern aura than Ricardo's wine and cloth vintage theory. And in an era in which foreign unfair trade practices made good political targets, a more robust and active U.S. trade policy found support in business, government, and some academic circles.

VERs, OMAs, AND VIEs

While the tenets of strategic trade policy do not require new trade policy tools, GATT restrictions on the use of traditional tariffs, quotas, and subsidies encouraged the search for new trade intervention measures. Voluntary export restraints and their close cousin, orderly marketing agreements,

[8]See Tyson (1990).

[9]See Irwin and Klenow (1994).

[10]Put a little differently, Tyson (1990) asserts that the rationales for government intervention are (1) social returns from technology exceeding private returns, (2) imperfections in capital markets that limit optimal investment in innovation, and (3) learning-by-doing models suggesting that the value of knowledge increases with the scale of production. The second and third bear some similarity to those for infant industry protection.

were increasingly popular in the 1980s and became a staple of what was known as the new protectionism. The U.S. was not the only eager user. One estimate in 1989, based on an admittedly broad definition, listed 67 for the United States and 127 for the EC and its member states, not including the extensive web of quantitative import restraints under the Multifiber Arrangement.[11]

VERs are usually defined as negotiated, quantitative limits on a country's exports of specific goods to a specific market. The term *voluntary* is a misnomer, as virtually all restrictions are coercive and accepted reluctantly by the exporting country to forestall more onerous trade restrictions. OMAs have the same economic features as VERs. Both are clearly inefficient in economic terms. In addition to the conventional welfare losses from any import restraint (consumer losses, inefficient domestic production), VERs and OMAs, by requiring exporting governments (firms) to restrict sales, encourage and sanction foreign cartel-like behavior. This virtually ensures that the foreign producers capture the difference between production cost and the VER-inflated price in the U.S. market, the so-called quota rent. This contrasts with an import tariff in which the quota rent appears as tariff revenue for the United States. There are additional inefficiencies. Because VERs set quantitative limits on products, there is a strong motive for the foreign firms to ship the most expensive, high-profit models, a response called upgrading (see, for example, the auto VER discussed below). This further distorts the market and tends to penalize low-income consumers. Examples of upgrading and disproportionate burden on low-income consumers were the OMAs on shoes from Taiwan and Korea in the Carter administration and the MFA restrictions on garments. Finally, VERs and OMAs tend to target new suppliers, who are often the most efficient producers, thus shifting import demand to higher-cost, unrestrained suppliers. Indeed, the shift in import demand to unrestrained suppliers under country-specific import quotas and VERs often results in subsequent requests for additional protection, as has been illustrated in color televisions, the MFA, and other schemes.[12]

VERs and OMAs also weaken the international trade system in insidious ways. Because they are country-specific they violate the principle of nondiscrimination. Because they are coercive they undermine the concept

[11]Cited by Low (1993, p. 76).

[12]This trade-diversion effect has also been found in antidumping cases (Prusa, 1997).

of liberal reciprocity as discussed in Chapter 2. Because they are undertaken "voluntarily" they tend to absolve the importing country of an odious protectionist label.[13] This could be termed "immaculate protection." And because the foreign producers are "bribed" through the quota rents, there is an implicit, nontransparent collusion between these producers and the protected domestic industry against the interests of consumers and taxpayers.

These last features, of course, help explain why VERs and OMAs became popular in the trade crisis of the 1980s. They are credible only when initiated by major importers such as the United States or the EU. They can be instituted without the formal analysis and demonstration of injury required in escape clause cases.[14] Moreover, they can be targeted against countries without the economic or political clout to retaliate.[15] And unlike escape clause cases, there was no need to offer compensation to the exporting country in the form of lower tariffs on other goods. In short, VERs and OMAs were clear circumventions of GATT disciplines on protectionism and encouraged bullying in the international trade system. The illiberal and undesirable features of VERs and OMA did not go unnoticed, and to their credit, negotiators in the Uruguay Round agreed to their phase-out. U.S. concern for import surges and ambivalence toward the traditional escape clause did not totally disappear, however. NAFTA contains special safeguards against such surges and very long (15-year) transition periods for sensitive goods. In addition, imports of sensitive agricultural products are controlled through tariff-rate quotas, which set quantitative limits. Neither is in the same class as VERs, but both suggest a desire to manage trade.[16]

[13]President Reagan was almost wistful in his consideration of the 1981 VER on Japanese autos. "I wondered if there might be a way in which we could maintain the integrity of our position in favor of free trade while at the same time doing something to help Detroit and ease the plight of its thousands of laid-off assembly line workers" (quoted by Dryden, 1995, p. 271). He overlooked the more efficient, less expensive alternative of simply giving the auto workers cash payments.

[14]OMAs are also a possible form of relief for Section 201 (escape clause) actions if serious injury is found.

[15]Note that OMAs on shoes (Taiwan, Korea) were not imposed on Italy, a major shoe producer and a member of the EC.

[16]NAFTA has a side agreement on import surges to monitor trade in anticipation of severe import competition. The agreement did not satisfy its chief proponents, the U.S. sugar, citrus, and vegetable sectors (Hufbauer and Schott, 1993). See Chapter 9, Note 16, for the import surge control in trade with China.

Voluntary import expansion agreements were another tool for managed trade developed by the United States in the 1980s. They were used in conjunction with Section 301 actions and presumably responded to alleged unfair trade practices. At first glance VIEs appear more attractive than VERs, as the ostensible purpose is to expand, not restrict trade. On closer inspection, however, the case for VIEs is dubious (Irwin, 1994). As the name implies, the VIE country agrees to a quantitative import target for a specific product, expressed either in absolute terms or as a share of domestic consumption. In this sense the VIEs illustrate the emphasis on results-oriented rather than rules-oriented trade agreements.[17] This new emphasis reflects the view that foreign trade barriers are so subtle and opaque that simply identifying the offending trade practice and negotiating its removal are not feasible. Instead, VIEs bypass these steps and require that the importing country achieve a specified import target.

There are several unattractive features of VIEs, despite their market opening gloss. First, they are unilateral and coercive—exemplars of aggressive reciprocity, not liberal reciprocity as described earlier. Again, they introduce an element of bullying to the trade system.[18] Second, although VIEs need not be discriminatory, in practice they tend to favor the United States. For example, when the United States pressured Korea to open its insurance market, the resulting agreement led to U.S. firms' access to the compulsory fire pool and life insurance markets but no additional licenses for third countries (Pearson, 1989). It appears self-evident that a target country that is under unilateral 301 pressure and is contemplating a VIE with the United States will make efforts to ensure that incremental imports come from the United States. This appears to have been the case in the 1992 auto parts negotiations with Japan.[19] Third, the numerical import penetration target is necessarily arbitrary. Although one could estimate an

[17]This was a hallmark of Clinton's trade policy *vis a vis* Japan and is elaborated in the next chapter. The United States had some experience in negotiating import shares for beef and citrus in the Japanese market in the late 1970s. These were not true VIEs, however, as Japan undertook no obligation to fill an expanded import quota. Still, the monthly quotas on citrus were manipulated to give both California and Florida optimal seasonal access to Japan's market. The beef quota was for "hotel quality," thus giving a bias favoring U.S. grain-fed as compared to Australian grass-fed beef.

[18]Unlike VERs, there is no quota rent to "bribe" the foreign country.

[19]Irwin (1994) cites an early Section 301 case in which Canada doubled its import quota of eggs from the U.S. without changing its overall quota, a clear case of trade diversion.

"appropriate" import level by examining United States market shares for the product in other countries where no unfair trade is alleged, this would hardly be conclusive. Market shares and VIE targets would tend to be politically determined. Finally, under plausible assumptions, VIEs can lead to collusion, not greater competition.[20] This is more likely, as market sharing has explicit sanction from both governments.

In the broadest sense, the case for VIEs must rest on one of two arguments: the first, economic; the second, political. One could make an "infant export industry" argument, in which learning-by-doing and scale economies arising from cumulative production and guaranteed sales in the VIE market result in lower costs and improve international competitive position. But this is implausible for the United States with its large internal market and technological leadership, and in any event, it is arbitrary to single out one export market over another for expansion with a VIE. The political argument is that given the entrenched perception of foreign unfair trade practices, VIEs offered measurable evidence of aggressive U.S. trade policy and maintained core support for liberal trade. But there is an obvious perversion here: to maintain a rules-based system, the United States bent the rules with results-oriented, coercive trade agreements.

The U.S. flirtation with managed trade such as quantitative trade targets, while diminished, has not completely disappeared. In addition to the 2001 proposal for an international steel agreement noted below, the 1999 bilateral agreement preparing for China's entry into the WTO requires China to establish a tariff-rate quota system for the importation of bulk agricultural commodities (e.g., wheat, corn, cotton, rice). Under a tariff-rate quota arrangement, a certain quantity of the product can be imported at a low or zero tariff rate while over-quota imports face higher tariffs. Although technically this is not a VIE, as the importing country does not guarantee a certain quantity of imports from the United States, the rules for allocating the within-quota imports between state trading agencies and private traders, and for reallocating unused quotas, imply minimum quantitative import targets.

[20]Irwin (1994). Greaney (1996), in a game theoretic model, also concludes that a VIE can lead to collusion. The essential reason is that the domestic producer(s) must raise price to make room for the imports and comply with the minimum import target. Note also that VIEs implicitly assume government can direct the behavior of private sector firms.

▶ MANAGED TRADE: A POTPOURRI

Three sectors—steel, autos, and semiconductors—can illustrate the United States' attempts at managed trade.[21] Steel has had almost continuous special protection for over 30 years and might be thought of as the strategic industry of the old (or old-old) economy. The crisis in the U.S. auto industry occurred in the midst of U.S. retreat from the early postwar liberal trade regime and resulted in a comprehensive VER with Japan in the 1980s. Steel and autos represent the protectionist aspect of managed trade. In contrast, the semiconductor industry was the leading edge of the new high-tech economy and the prime example of externality-based strategic trade policy. The trade instrument used was a VIE. All three industries, however, are in the manufacturing sector, and their relevance for trade policy for the new information-based service economy is questionable.

Steel

Steel appears to be a classic declining industry, with sufficient residual political clout to enjoy special protection from the Nixon administration through the second Bush administration in 2002. In interpreting the steel story, it is important to keep in mind certain features of the industry: the cyclical nature of demand and large fixed costs, which suggest frequent periods of overcapacity in the United States and worldwide; large price swings and dumping (selling below average costs); extensive government subsidies, increased competition in this period from new producers, often in developing countries; and new domestic competition from the generally more efficient minimills.

The chronology of U.S. protection in steel has a tedious repetitive quality.[22] It is enlivened, however, by the remarkable diversity of protectionist ploys and the interweaving of protection and politics. The actions include massive filings and threats of filings of antidumping and countervailing duty petitions in the mid-1960s, in 1978, in 1980 (against the EC), in 1982 (over 200!), in 1984, 1989, and 1992, and again in 1998–1999; a Section 201 (escape clause) case on specialty steel in 1974 and again in 1983 and a new

[21]The most durable example of international managed trade is of course textiles and garments under the MFA.

[22]Low (1993) gives a good brief account of earlier activities.

201 investigation initiated by President Bush in 2001; a long series of Section 301 petitions; and direct lobbying of Congress for import quotas in 1966, 1984, and 1999. The results included an extensive patchwork of VERs on a variety of steel products and with a variety of exporting countries (e.g., Europe and Japan, 1969–1971, renewed in 1972; Japan, specialty steel, 1975; EC, 1982; and multiple countries, 1985, many of which were renewed in 1989). In addition, Section 201 quotas on specialty steel were twice imposed. Also in 1978, under President Carter, a novel measure, the trigger price mechanism (TPM), was introduced; it was revised in 1980. The TPM set minimum import prices based on our estimates of steel production costs in the efficient foreign producer, Japan. Imports from any country below the trigger price would automatically start an accelerated dumping investigation. The original TPM ran until 1980 and was strengthened in that year. Thus, the mechanisms for managed trade ran the full gauntlet: quantitative restrictions (quotas) by product, market share targets, and a minimum pricing scheme. Further formal managed trade was proposed in the 1990 Multilateral Steel Agreement talks, but these failed.

The steel trade issue erupted again in 1998–1999 and provided a major test for the Clinton administration's commitment to liberal trade. The proximate cause was the increase in the steel import penetration ratio, which had dipped below 20 percent in the early 1990s but rose to 30 percent in 1998.[23] This was accompanied by a sharp decline in steel prices of about 10 percent in 1998 and a decrease in U.S. capacity utilization from a peak of 95 percent early in 1998 to about 75 percent later in that year. The import surge was triggered by the Asian economic crisis of 1997–1999, which depressed world market demand for steel; currency depreciations in Korea, Brazil, and Japan; and the emergence of Russia as a major steel exporter. The industry again filed numerous petitions under the unfair trade statutes.

Despite very public pressure from the steel industry, the Clinton administration's response was restrained. It opposed a protectionist import quota bill passed by the House and ultimately defeated in the Senate. It did, however, expedite the pending antidumping and countervailing duty cases and availed itself of the "critical circumstances" provision of the trade law, which allows for the imposition of retroactive antidumping duties up to 90 days prior to a preliminary dumping determination. This had a pro-

[23]See United States Department of Commerce (2000).

nounced chilling effect, and imports of hot rolled steel fell 65 percent from November 1998, when the critical-circumstances determination was made, to December 1998. The administration also negotiated a VER with Russia, setting quantitative limits on Russian exports of steel products and pig iron to the U.S. market.[24] Finally, Congress passed a loan guarantee bill to help provide financing for troubled steel companies.

The steel saga did not end. In June 2001 President Bush requested a new escape clause investigation of steel imports by the ITC and sought international negotiations to manage the steel trade through reduced capacity and curtailing government subsidies.[25] The ITC subsequently found injury, and its remedy recommendations range from quotas to tariff rate quotas to straight tariffs of up to 40 percent. Hufbauer and Goodrich (2002) estimated the annual consumer cost per job saved in the U.S. steel industry for the various remedies would range from $304,000 to $584,000. Steel also benefits from the recent Byrd amendment, in which antidumping and countervailing duties are collected by the Treasury and disbursed to U.S. import competing firms. In 2002 President Bush, acting on the ITC recommendations, announced tariffs of up to 30 percent on a wide range of products and countries and again called for an international effort to manage steel production and trade. President Bush's decision to protect steel occurred when Congress was considering whether to grant him new fast-track trade negotiation authority. It is plausible that the steel tariffs were imposed to improve his chances of obtaining that authority from Congress.

This complex history of demand and supply of protection for steel leads to three conclusions. First, the multiplicity of channels available to the industry—Sections 201 and 301 of the trade law, the antidumping and countervailing duty statutes, and direct pressure on Congress for import quotas—tends to be reinforcing. For example, in the 1984 "crisis," the industry had a 15 percent import penetration quota bill pending in Congress, while pursuing an escape clause case and filing a large number of countervailing duty and antidumping duties. The result of these multiple pressures was a new comprehensive round of VERs. More recently, in the

[24]Russia is not a member of the WTO, and thus the phase-out of VERs agreed to in the Uruguay Round did not apply.

[25]The request for an escape clause investigation by the president is unusual. Most are initiated by industry or labor.

1998–1999 steel "crisis," the steel industry deliberately avoided using the escape clause route, as it would have had to show that increased imports were a substantial cause of serious injury. Instead, it pursued the antidumping/countervailing duty route, where the injury test is weaker. But in 2001, following President Bush's signal of support, it successfully followed the escape clause route.

Second, the VER device blurs transparency and allows the administration to profess a commitment to free trade while offering covert protection. Thus, VERs can act as a vehicle for immaculate protection, mentioned earlier. This deception was evident in the 1984 actions under President Reagan. In a split decision, the ITC had found injury and recommended relief in the form of quotas and tariff-rate quotas. The Reagan administration publicly rejected the ITC recommendation as protectionist but at the same time ordered continuation of existing VERs and extension of the VER network to new countries and new products (Low, 1993, p. 104). A numerical market share target for imports was also set. Still, the more transparently protectionist escape clause option is not always better. As implemented by the second Bush administration, the tariffs were selective (NAFTA partners were excluded), and USTR announced that it would entertain requests for exceptions to the tariffs—both of which imply some trade discrimination.

Third, the steel saga illustrates the great difficulty in using administrative trade remedies (mainly Section 201—the escape clause—and the antidumping and countervailing duty statutes) to insulate the President and Congress from political pressures in formulating trade policy. Rules-based administered actions may deflect pressure for minor industries, but given the "easy" out of VERs, they can be bypassed when large industries with political power are involved. The auto industry, discussed next, also illustrates this conclusion. One of the major accomplishments of the Uruguay Round was to circumscribe and eventually eliminate the use of VERs, and this played a useful limiting role in the 1998–1999 steel crisis.

Autos

The auto trade story is less convoluted but still instructive. In the early postwar period of the 1950s and 1960s, the U.S. auto industry had been hugely successful, but it was losing its preeminence by the 1970s. One reason was that it was ill-prepared for the shift in demand to fuel-efficient small cars in the 1970s, a consequence of surging gasoline prices in 1973 and again in 1979. Moreover, production methods and auto technology were becoming outdated, and the industry faced a high cost structure. As a consequence, the Japanese import share of consumption, which had been virtually zero in the early 1960s, rose from 13.6% in 1978 to 22.4% in 1980.

The response of the U.S. auto industry was to go shopping for protection. In 1980 the president of the United Auto Workers union asked Japanese automakers to voluntarily limit exports to the United States but was politely turned down. The UAW and Ford then lobbied Congress for domestic content legislation, but they did not gain the support of the Carter administration.[26] The next stop for Ford and the UAW was the U.S. International Trade Commission and an escape clause petition. In November 1980, the ITC voted three to two against the petition on the grounds that imports were not a substantial cause (a cause greater than any other cause) of serious injury. The ITC determined that recession, high interest rates, and demand shifts were more important. In the meantime, at a campaign stop in Detroit in September 1980, presidential candidate Reagan had promised assistance to the industry. Early in 1981, after Reagan was inaugurated, the pressure of the auto industry resumed, and highly restrictive quota legislation was introduced in Congress. Despite free trade rhetoric and the recent ITC decision against import relief, the Reagan administration caved in and negotiated a VER with Japan that was to last until 1993, although with greatly diminished bite in the latter years.[27]

The economic effects of the auto VER have been extensively studied.[28] Feenstra, for example, estimates the VER increased import prices by 8.4 percent but that about two-thirds of the price increase was due to quality improvements. This is the upgrading effect discussed earlier. Its long-term impact was to help make Japan a formidable competitor in high-priced, high-quality, high-profit models. Dinopoulos and Kreinin (1988) estimate that the VER saved a total of 22,358 U.S. jobs in 1982, at a cost (welfare

[26]A domestic content law would require that some (high) fraction of parts and components be manufactured in the United States.

[27]The VER was set at 1.68 million units the first year, with some increase in subsequent years.

[28]Studies include Feenstra (1984), Tarr and Morkre (1984), and Dinopoulos and Kreinin (1988).

loss) of $181, 000 per job saved! Also, as expected from theory, the diverted demand allowed European exporters to raise their U.S. prices by about one-third.

One question raised by the auto trade case is whether it can be viewed as a strategic trade policy game. On the surface, the answer appears to be yes. U.S. production was controlled by a tight oligopoly. Despite cyclical fluctuations, there tended to be oligopolistic surpluses in the industry. These were taken as either profits or inflated wage levels. Japanese production was less concentrated but still might be classified as oligopolistic. And as expected from the strategic trade policy literature, the U.S. industry appealed to its government for commercial assistance, and the Japanese government became deeply involved in the production/export decisions of its own firms.

However, on closer inspection, the auto case is far removed from the simple strategic models set forth earlier in the chapter. The first and the last models can be easily dismissed. There may be elements of monopolistic competition in the form of product variation, but this is not the auto trade restraint story. No one seriously believes that the U.S. restricted imports to achieve scale economies. Also, no one claims the auto sector represents cutting edge technology, with significant technological spillovers and dynamic scale economies from cumulative production (learning by doing). It is true that autos can embody high-tech features (e.g., navigational systems and computer-controlled fuel mix), and their construction can involve state-of-the-art production and inventory management systems, but auto production is not an originator and incubator of technological externalities.[29]

The second class of models, rent-snatching, does not appear relevant. As presented earlier, it suggests government subsidies to establish the credibility of domestic production and capture a larger share of world markets. The auto story is mainly a defensive action to maintain U.S. producers' share of the U.S. market. Japan responded not to U.S. government subsidies but to credible threats of protection. If there was rent-snatching, it was Japan capturing the quota rents. The auto VER tale is better told as an old, well-worn protection story.

The third class of models, import protection to expand exports, is a bit more persuasive. There are numerous allegations and some evidence that

[29]This is not to dismiss the importance of the auto industry in the macro-economy.

Japan protected its domestic auto market through its initial growth period.[30] This may well have been old-fashioned infant industry protection. But there is very little evidence that the second requisite of this model—the use of home country profits in a cartel-like arrangement to fund subsidized auto exports or R & D expenditures—took place. Despite the limited number of firms, the Japanese auto industry was highly competitive in its home market and resisted direction by MITI. It initially entered the U.S. market in a niche position of small, well-engineered, fuel-efficient cars. And it was from this market position that it could respond to the demand shift of the 1970s. The Japanese auto success is more a matter of luck, timing, and the OPEC oil price increase than of finely calculated strategic trade policy.

There is, however, a strategic policy story here that is better told as a trade/foreign direct investment tale. One of the older explanations for FDI is "tariff jumping," establishing production within a tariff-protected economy, partly to maintain access to the market and partly to forestall further protection. Following the VER there was an influx of investment in the United States by Japanese auto makers. Honda increased its U.S. capacity and Nissan, Toyota, Mazda, and Mitsubishi all established new U.S. plants. At least in this case, a strategic trade policy model without an FDI component is incomplete. In a broader study, Blonigen and Feenstra (1997), using escape clause and antidumping data, have shown that the *threat* of protection had a substantial effect on Japanese FDI in the 1980s.

Semiconductors[31]

The semiconductor case comes closer to true managed trade than either steel or autos. It also is the poster child for models of strategic trade policy based on externalities and dynamic economies of scale. The essential facts are as follows. Until the mid-1970s, the U.S. semiconductor industry led the world in innovations, technological capacity, and production. By 1980, however, Japanese production and incursions in the U.S. market were being felt. The perception and allegation was that Japan's success was the result of home market protection, selective government subsidies, and dumping in foreign markets, including the United States. U.S. producers

[30]The U.S. industry claims that nontariff barriers prevented its sales in Japan.

[31]For a detailed account, see Tyson (1992).

wished to see a halt to alleged Japanese dumping here and in third country markets and improved access for U.S. firms in Japan. Two informal agreements for the latter were reached in the early 1980s but proved unsatisfactory. In 1985, when the dollar reached a peak and Congressional dissatisfaction with Reagan's trade policy also spiked, the U.S. Semiconductor Industry Association filed a 301 complaint. This was buttressed by three antidumping petitions, an antitrust suit alleging predatory pricing, and a patent infringement suit (Section 337) against Japanese and Korean firms.

In this inhospitable climate the United States and Japan concluded the first formal semiconductor agreement, covering a five-year period. The public portion of this agreement included a commitment by MITI in Japan to monitor and prevent dumping in the U.S. and third country markets and to work toward increasing U.S. semiconductor sales in Japan. In a secret side letter, subsequently denied by Japan and revealed by the United States, Japan "recognized" the U.S. expectation that the import share of the Japanese market would rise from the then-current 8 percent to 20 percent within five years (Dryden, 1995, p. 320). The original agreement was extended for another five years in 1991, and the 20 percent market share target was made explicit.

The arrangements did not go down smoothly, however. The EC complained to the GATT on a number of grounds, including potential discrimination, and won a favorable ruling *vis a vis* Japan. The United States also complained that the provisions of the original agreement were not being met, and less than a year later it imposed tariff retaliation against Japan on $300 million of imports from that country. Moreover, U.S. downstream industries acting through the American Electronics Association complained about higher semiconductor prices consequent to the agreement and won some changes in procedures for determining "fair market" value.[32]

In retrospect, the semiconductor agreements represent the high (or low) point in U.S. flirtation with managed trade. A VIE was imposed by the United States on Japanese industry at the behest of U.S. producers and

[32]The VIE was part of a broader U.S. industrial policy *vis a vis* semiconductors. Legislation in 1984 had strengthened protection of intellectual property in this industry and gave some antitrust relief to collaborative R & D. In 1987, Sematech, a consortium of 14 U.S. semiconductor firms, was established and was allocated annual government subsidies of up to $100 million. In an empirical analysis, Irwin and Klenow (1996) conclude that Sematech induced members to *cut* their independent R & D expenditures by about $300 million per year.

with the acquiescence and cooperation of MITI. This was backed by a credible threat of trade retaliation. In addition to numerical import market share arrangements, minimum prices in the U.S. and third country markets were contemplated.[33] The selection of this industry for "management" was not arbitrary. Semiconductors were viewed as strategic in three senses: first, as a component in weapons and military communication equipment; second, as essential in downstream computer and consumer electronics industries; and third, as generating positive technology externalities and exhibiting dynamic economies of scale (cumulative production). Empirical studies, however, have challenged the proposition that strategic trade policy was warranted for semiconductors. Irwin and Klenow (1994) found that learning "spillovers," or the external economy argument for government involvement in this sector, occurred as much between firms in different countries as between firms within a given country. Udayagiri and Schuler (1999) found only weak evidence of knowledge spillovers across several semiconductor memory products, also undercutting the appeal of strategic trade policy. Finally, semiconductors appeared to fit the strategic trade policy model in which Japan, by protecting its domestic market, attempted to capture export markets. Whether the aggressive VIE/minimum price strategy was an effective response by the United States is another question. Some analysts have pointed out that the agreement simply raised profits for Japan's firms, allowing them to commit heavy R & D expenditures for the production of the next generation of chips. And in the current era, in which software is the hot product, the 1980s concern for the hardware, chips, has a somewhat dated quality. Whether or not effective, the semiconductor agreements, by establishing numerical targets, were clear evidence of the trend toward managed trade.

Flirting can be a passing fancy or can lead to serious courtship. The U.S. experience with managed trade turned out to be the former. But to

[33]The U.S. Commerce Department determined cost data, firm by firm and product by product, for Japanese suppliers. If they sold below average cost plus an 8 percent profit margin, they were presumed to be dumping. This is very severe. Not only do firms, including U.S. firms, frequently price at marginal cost below average cost, but also the average costs of technology products often fall with increased production ("learning by doing"), and firms thus have an incentive to price below (static) marginal costs. The establishment of minimum prices is similar to the trigger-price mechanism applied to steel imports a decade earlier.

understand its attraction at the time, it is useful to look more deeply into the contentious U.S.–Japan trade relation.

▶ REFERENCES

Appleyard, Dennis, and Alfred Field. 2001. *International Economics,* 4th ed. New York: McGraw Hill.

Blonigen, Bruce, and Robert Feenstra. 1997. Protectionist Threats and Foreign Direct Investment. In: Robert Feenstra (ed.). *The Effects of U.S. Trade Protection and Promotion Policies.* Chicago: University of Chicago Press.

Brander, James, and Barbara Spencer, 1985. Export Subsidies and International Market Share Rivalry. *Journal of International Economics* 18:83–100.

Corden, W. Max. 1997. *Trade Policy and Economic Welfare,* 2nd ed. Oxford, UK: Clarendon Press.

Dinopoulos, Elias, and Mordechai Kreinin. 1988. Effects of the US-Japan Auto VER on European Prices and on U.S. Welfare. *Review of Economics and Statistics* LXX(3):484–491.

Dryden, Steve. 1995. *Trade Warriors.* New York: Oxford University Press.

Feenstra, Robert. 1984. Voluntary Export Restraints in U.S. Autos, 1980–81: Quantity Employment and Welfare Effects. In: R. Baldwin and A. Krueger (eds.). *The Structure and Evolution of Recent U.S. Trade Policy.* Chicago: University of Chicago Press.

Greaney, Theresa. 1996. Import Now: An Analysis of Market-Share Voluntary Import Expansions (VIEs). *Journal of International Economics* 40:149–163.

Helpman, Elhanan, and Paul Krugman. 1989. *Trade Policy and Market Structure.* Cambridge, MA: MIT Press.

Hufbauer, Gary, and Ben Goodrich. 2002. *Time for a Grand Bargain in Steel?* Washington, DC: Institute for International Economics Policy Briefs.

Hufbauer, Gary, and Jeffrey Schott. 1993. *NAFTA: An Assessment.* Revised edition. Washington, DC: Institute for International Economics.

Irwin, Douglas. 1994. *Managed Trade: The Case Against Import Targets.* Washington, DC: American Enterprise Institute.

Irwin, Douglas, and Peter Klenow. 1994. Learning by Doing: Spillovers in the Semiconductor Industry. *Journal of Political Economy* 102(6):1200–1227.

Irwin, Douglas, and Peter Klenow. 1996. High-Tech R & D Subsidies: Estimating the Effects of Sematech. *Journal of International Economics* 40(3/4): 323–344.

Lincoln, Edward. 1999. *Troubled Times: U.S.-Japan Trade Relations in the 1990s.* Washington, DC: Brookings Institution.

Low, Patrick. 1993. *Trading Free: the GATT and U.S. Trade Policy.* New York: Twentieth Century Fund Press.

Maggi, Giovanni. 1996. Strategic Trade Policies with Endogenous Modes of Competition. *American Economic Review* 86(1):237–258.

Pearson, Charles. 1989. *Free Trade, Fair Trade: The Reagan Record.* Washington, DC:

SAIS Johns Hopkins Foreign Policy Institute.

Pomfret, Richard. 1992. *International Trade Policy with Imperfect Competition.* Princeton, NJ: International Finance Section, Princeton University.

Prusa, Thomas. 1997. The Trade Effects of U.S. Antidumping Actions. In: Robert Feenstra (ed.). *The Effects of U.S. Trade Protection and Promotion Policies.* Chicago: University of Chicago Press.

Tarr, David, and Morris Morkre. 1984. *Aggregate Costs to the United States of Tariffs and Quotas on Imports.* Washington, DC: Federal Trade Commission.

Tyson, Laura. 1990. Managed Trade: Making the Best of the Second Best. In: Robert Lawrence and Charles Schultze. *An American Trade Strategy.* Washington, DC: Brookings Institution.

Tyson, Laura. 1992. *Who's Bashing Whom?: Trade Conflict in High Technology Industries.* Washington, DC: Institute for International Economics.

Udayagiri, Naren, and Douglas Schuler. 1999. Cross Product Spillovers in the Semiconductor Industry. *The International Trade Journal* 13(3): 249–271.

United States Department of Commerce. 2000. *Global Steel Trade.* Washington, DC: United States Department of Commerce.

CHAPTER

4

JAPAN AS TRADE TARGET

INTRODUCTION

In 1853 President Millard Fillmore sent Commodore Perry and a fleet of eight warships to open Japan for U.S. trade.[1] Almost a century later, President Franklin Roosevelt, in response to Japan's military incursions in China and Indochina and its alliance with the Axis powers, Germany and Italy, imposed an embargo on exports to Japan (Feis, 1950). Originally an embargo on aviation fuel and then on scrap iron, it was subsequently expanded to all products, including oil. In 1973 President Nixon, in an attempt to control inflation, temporarily restricted exports of soybeans, an essential food import for Japan. And in 1985 President Reagan created his Trade Policy Strike Force, directed largely at Japan. Later, in a relatively rare instance of retaliation, he imposed punitive sanctions against Japan for its failure to fully implement a trade agreement on semiconductors. To put it mildly, United States–Japanese trade relations have not gone smoothly.

This chapter considers United States–Japan trade and rounds out our examination of the crisis period in U.S. trade policy. Postwar trade relations between the two countries fit into a simple, broad framework. In the early period, the United States sponsored and supported Japan's reintegration into world trade. In the second phase, United States policy was characterized by import protection in specific sectors as Japan gained competitive advantage. With a few exceptions, the import-protection phase ran its

[1]The United States acquired California in 1848, and in addition to trade with Japan, it was seeking port facilities to expand its Asian maritime trade (Beasley, 1999, pp. 191–192).

course by the 1980s and was replaced by vigorous and often contentious actions to improve access for U.S. exports in Japan. In the last half of the 1990s, the market access drive lost some of its intensity, but remnants have persisted in a less public fashion.

In many respects the drive to open the Japanese market to U.S. exports (and investment) is of greatest interest. It reflects a widespread view that Japan's economy and trade are fundamentally different than those of other countries and require a special trade response. Japan was perceived to engage in strategic trade policy, a linking of private commercial interests and government policy dubbed Japan Inc. The U.S. response was to use the new tools of Section 301 and VIEs and toy with managed trade itself. In doing so, the Clinton administration made the almost Talmudic distinction between "quantitative targets" and "quantitative indicators" for exports, all within the framework of a new emphasis on results-oriented trade policy.

Economists have been divided on the issue of how unique Japan's economy and trade really are, and in a latter section of the chapter we review some of the arguments and evidence. We also describe some of the highlights of the export market access drive in the late 1980s and the first Clinton administration. In any event, the Japanese economic model became greatly tarnished during the 1990s by poor performance and has lost stature and respect. The economic and commercial threat to the United States that some observers saw a decade and more ago has greatly dissipated. The chapter concludes by raising the question of whether the U.S. export offensive was worth the effort.

▶ THE EARLY AND MIDDLE PHASES

The United States maintained a positive trade balance with Japan from 1945 through the early 1960s.[2] Initially this surplus was made possible by substantial aid flows in the occupation period (1945–1952), by U.S. financing of cotton exports to revive the Japanese textile industry, and by large military procurement expenditures in Japan during the Korean War period. Hunsberger (1964, p. 35) has estimated that Japan's cumulative net global trade deficit for goods and services for 1945–1962 was $7.5 billion,

[2]Except 1959.

and this was financed in its entirety by U.S. economic aid and military expenditures of $7.9 billion.[3]

In this early period the principal challenge was to resurrect Japan's war-damaged economy so that it would not become a permanent ward of the United States. The choice was aid, trade, or starve, and the Cold War climate ensured that for foreign policy and security reasons the last was not a viable option. As Eisenhower stated, "Japan cannot live, and Japan cannot remain in the free world unless something is done to allow her to make a living" (Lovett, Eckes, Brinkman, 1999, p. 79). Accordingly, the United States took the lead in sponsoring Japan's entry into the GATT, as a provisional member in 1953 and full member in 1955. The reception was rather grudging, however, and 14 of the 34 GATT members invoked Article 35 and withheld full MFN treatment.[4] Moreover, even in the early 1960s, Japan was subject to a number of price or quantity export restraints in OECD markets, often but not exclusively on textile items. Some of the U.S. trade restraints were the result of escape clause cases. Between 1951 and 1961 the United States initiated 24 investigations involving Japan, covering such diverse items as umbrellas, baseball gloves, clinical thermometers, plywood, and textile items (Hunsberger, 1964, p. 270). To be fair, there were severe trade restrictions on the Japanese side as well. Until 1963, Japan justified quantitative controls on imports for balance-of-payments reasons. Indeed, after the IMF found the balance-of-payments rationale no longer justified, Japan removed only nine of 174 quotas in the 1964–1969 period (Trezise, 1971, p. 186).

It was cotton textiles that initiated the middle phase of sector-specific import protection in postwar United States–Japanese trade relations.[5] The textile case is instructive for several reasons. First, textiles and garments are classic examples of products exported by low-wage countries in the early stages of industrialization. Indeed, in the 1930s, Japan had become a substantial world exporter of cotton and woolen textiles when the interna-

[3]Net capital movements for the period, estimated at an outflow of $0.5 billion.

[4]Hunsberger (1964, p. 233). Article 35 permits GATT members to withhold tariff concessions from new members as they join. Patterson (1966) gives a detailed account of Japan's uncordial reception in GATT.

[5]This was a revival and extension of U.S. "voluntary" export restraints imposed on Japan in the 1930s. Those agreements included cotton cloth, floor coverings, hosiery, velveteens, and corduroy (Metzger, 1971, p. 171).

tional silk market collapsed. Thus Japan's textile exports in the 1950s reflected its attempt to restart an earlier successful export engine.

Second, U.S. and international response to Japanese exports of textiles illustrates the "slippery slope" quality of departures from liberal trade. The United States pressed a five-year VER on Japan in 1956 for cotton goods. From that action, trade restraints blossomed into a multinational Short-Term Arrangement for cotton textiles in 1961 and were quickly followed in 1962 by a five-year Long-Term Agreement on cotton textiles, designed to prevent so-called market disruption. The restrictions were extended to other fibers, including wool and synthetics (and ramie!), and other exporters were subsequently added and folded into the expanded Multifiber Arrangement (MFA), which persists in modified form to this day.[6] While Japan was an initial target, the burden of the MFA shifted over time to three generations of developing-country exporters, first Korea/Taiwan/Hong Kong, later countries such as Thailand and Malaysia, and most recently the newest manufactures exporters such as Bangladesh and Cambodia. In short, the initial trade restraint had a viruslike quality of reproducing itself in new products, fibers, and countries to the point where it became and remains the single most important barrier to developing-country exports of manufactures.

Third, the cotton textile agreements and subsequent incarnations are the antithesis of liberal trade principles—that is, they are unilateral, quantitative, and discriminatory. The willingness to subvert GATT principles and avoid the disciplined procedures of the escape clause illustrated a rather shallow commitment to freeing up trade in the United States and other industrial countries. It also weakened the authority of GATT and laid the basis for the subsequent surge of OMAs and VERs discussed in Chapter 3.[7]

Textiles ushered in a series of import protection actions against Japan that extended to the mid-1980s. The specific sectors reflect the increasing sophistication of Japanese exports—steel (VERs, 1969), color televisions

[6]Technically, the MFA was superseded by the 1995 WTO Agreement on Textiles and Clothing, which calls for all quotas to be abolished by 2005. High tariffs will remain.

[7]It is worth noting that the U.S. textile industry did not seek escape clause relief in 1955 and 1956, presumably because total imports of cotton manufactures were less than 2 percent of U.S. production and imports from Japan were less than 1 percent. Thus, it would have been difficult to demonstrate the injury from imports (Metzger, 1971, p. 174).

(dumping, 1971),[8] autos (VER, 1981), motorcycles (escape clause, 1983), and machine tools (VER, 1986). The semiconductor affair in the latter half of the 1980s was both import protection and export promotion. The days of umbrella frames, typewriter ribbons, and stainless steel flatware that dominated the escape clause actions of the 1950s were over. It is not necessary to describe these trade disputes in great detail. It is sufficient to note that the vehicles used for protection covered the full spectrum, from the escape clause to the unfair trade statutes to the newly popular OMAs and VERs; that virtually all the sectors seeking and receiving protection were, in an earlier time, preeminent examples of successful U.S. manufacturing; and that in several cases (color televisions, autos, semiconductors) U.S. firms had or were to establish significant foreign production capabilities or joint venture partners. Only in the case of autos, however, did U.S. trade policy result in significant foreign investment by Japan in the United States.

One other feature deserves comment. It has been argued that in at least four of these sectors (steel, televisions, autos, and semiconductors), Japan secured its formidable export competitiveness through a combination of imported technology, government industrial policy, and protection of the home market, the characteristics of strategic trade policy.[9] This view was persuasive in setting the stage for the subsequent phase in U.S.–Japanese trade relations and the attempts to open the Japanese market to U.S. exports, and it remains a popular view. Lincoln (1999, pp. 209–212), for example, supports continuing vigorous efforts to open the Japanese market, and his argument is based in part on the strategic trade concepts of scale and external economies. We now turn to the third (market access) phase of the relationship.

▶ IS JAPAN'S TRADE UNIQUE?

By the time the Tokyo Round tariff cuts were fully implemented (1983 for Japan, 1987 for the United States), Japan had lower average tariffs and a smaller number of quantitative restrictions on industrial products than

[8]The actual imposition of dumping duties was subject to protracted delays. A 1971 escape clause petition was denied.

[9]The tribulations of the steel, television, auto, and semiconductor industries are analyzed in Zysman and Tyson (1983). Both the United States and Japan used discriminatory government procurement to protect and support their supercomputer industries (Bergsten and Noland, 1993, p. 147).

most advanced countries, including the United States.[10] There were, of course, barriers to important agricultural products (citrus, beef, rice), but both the EC and the United States also engaged in substantial agricultural protection. Despite the modest level of barriers at the border, there was a strong feeling in business, in government, and among some academics that the Japanese market remained highly protected with a web of nontariff trade barriers, many of which were sanctioned and encouraged by the Japanese government. Recall also the strategic trade policy view that protection of the domestic market can confer an unfair export advantage.

Lincoln (1990) lists a number of these barriers—manipulation of product standards and testing and certification procedures to exclude imports, inadequate protection of intellectual property, biased government procurement practices that circumvented GATT agreements, industry collusion (including the *keiretsu* system, which allegedly works against imports), and administrative guidance from the Ministry of Trade and Industry (MITI) to industry to discourage imports. In addition, he describes a number of policies and characteristics that he asserts distort the Japanese economy toward an excessively large manufacturing sector, and he attributes Japan's great export competitiveness and low imports of manufactures in part to this distorted structure. These policies and characteristics include excessive working hours (which supposedly limits consumer demand for and production of nontraded services), a close relation between large business and government that tends to exclude consumers and labor from policy-making, and restrictive land use policy, pushing up residential housing costs and thus promoting high savings. Finally, according to Lincoln and a number of other observers, in addition to the informal and often opaque import barriers and social and economic characteristics that lead to excessive investment in manufacturing for the home and foreign markets, the Japanese government has been adept at delay and circumvention of market opening agreements.[11]

To a surprising extent the debate over Japan and its trade performance

[10] Bergsten and Cline (1985, p. 54) show weighted average tariffs of 2.8% for Japan and 4.4% for the United States.

[11] Lincoln (1999) cites as examples the procurement policies of the *quasi*-governmental Nippon Telegraph and Telephone Company as well as bilateral agreements on flat glass (1992, 1995), paper (1992), and insurance (1996). Prestowitz (1988) gives numerous examples. The subtitle to his book carries his message: *How We Allowed Japan to Take the Lead.* Crudely put, the United States emphasizes consumption; Japan stresses production.

thrived on anecdotes, of which there was no shortage. For example, in opening a new international terminal at Narita Airport in 1992, Northwest and United were left in the dingy and cramped old facilities while ANA went to the new terminal (Lincoln, 1999, p. 65). Japanese health and safety testing had a way of discouraging imports; standards for skis were set for Japan's "different" snow, to the disadvantage of imported equipment; fiberglass boats were tested by dropping them; imported tulip bulbs were sliced open to check for insects.[12] The United States and Japan squabbled over whether or not Nippon Telegraph and Telephone was sufficiently privatized to escape WTO rules on government procurement. Although most of the examples were directed against Japan, a minority of observers asserted that U.S. business was simply unwilling to invest for the long term in selling in the Japanese market. The slow pace of U.S. auto makers in introducing right-hand-drive vehicles in Japan was often cited.

The allegations that protection thrived in Japan despite a modest level of tariffs and quotas led to a spirited search for indirect economic evidence of covert barriers to imports. One approach was to compare the import penetration ratio for manufactures (imports of manufactures as share of GDP or as share of domestic consumption of manufactures) with other industrial countries. The hypothesis was that if the ratio is unusually low, this is *prima facie* evidence of import protection.[13] There is little question that import penetration—especially manufactures import penetration—in Japan was and is low when compared to other industrial countries. But theory suggests that these ratios depend on many factors—economic size, level of industrialization, transport costs, raw material endowments—and strong econometric evidence for a clear-cut protectionist explanation of the level and composition of Japan's imports has been difficult to demonstrate.

A second approach seeking indirect evidence of protection—examining the level of intra-industry trade—suffers from the same limitation. The

[12]Japan is not the only country that uses product standards to limit imports. For example, Thailand has complained in the WTO that Australian sanitary regulations on imported durian, a tropical fruit, require that 450 fruit must be cut open and checked for insects and disease for every consignment of 1000 or less fruit, the normal air freight shipment size (World Trade Organization, 2000).

[13]For a sampling, see Lincoln (1990, 1999), Saxenhouse (1986), Lawrence (1987), and Balassa and Noland (1988). The exceptionally low level of foreign direct investment in Japan as compared to that in other industrial countries reinforced the view that Japan engaged in opaque but effective protection.

hypothesis is that absent serious trade barriers, countries' intra-industry trade in manufactures tends to increase the larger the country and the higher the per capita income. The underlying logic is that the combination of product differentiation and economies of scale leads countries to specialize in particular products within a broader product classification, hence intra-industry trade.[14] Again, the data indicate that Japan engages in relatively low levels of intra-industry trade (increasing, however). This "unusual" characteristic has been interpreted as evidence of import protection and, perhaps, export targeting. But once again, theory suggests many reasons why intra-industry trade may differ among countries, even if they all were to engage in free trade. Thus, it has been difficult to find hard empirical evidence, through econometric analysis, that Japan's intra-industry trade is remarkable and reflects an unusual level of covert protection.

A third indirect approach to inferring informal protection in Japan was to examine price differentials for tradeable goods. The idea is simple enough. If, after accounting for transportation costs and residual formal trade barriers (i.e., tariffs and quotas), the prices of tradeable goods is significantly higher in Japan than in other world markets, it suggests the influence of informal barriers and covert protection. Testing the hypothesis, however, is not altogether simple. The results depend in part on the time frame and especially the exchange rate between the dollar and the yen (which has fluctuated widely); the extent and timing of exchange rate "pass-through"; the specific products to be compared (goods, tradeable services), their quality, size, and after-sale service; and the location and style of retailing (e.g., neighborhood stores vs. outlet malls). In particular, the finding of relatively high prices in Japan is often explained on the basis of high-cost inefficient distribution and retailing services and not on covert trade barriers.[15]

The allegation that Japan pursued export targeting and covert protection was a dominant theme throughout the 1980s and persisted well into the 1990s. It was given some popular credibility by the aggregate trade

[14]Empirical evidence of substantial intra-industry trade, especially among OECD countries, has been a serious challenge to factor-endowment-based theories of trade. Models employing imperfect competition and scale economies have attempted to accommodate intra-industry trade.

[15]Bergsten, Ito, and Noland (2001, Chapter 4) review many of the price comparison studies.

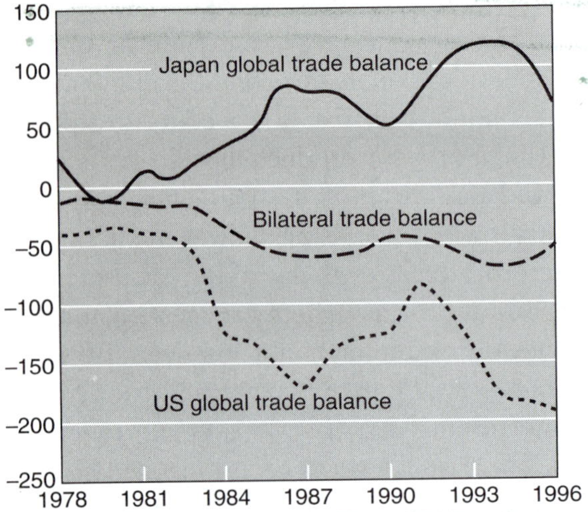

Figure 4.1 Global and bilateral merchandise trade balances, United States and Japan, 1978–1996 (billion U.S.$).
Source: International Monetary Fund, Direction of Trade Yearbooks.

data. Figure 4.1 displays the U.S. and Japanese merchandise trade balances and the bilateral U.S. deficit with Japan over a two-decade period. By and large, the figure appears to tell a simple and compelling story: fluctuating but generally increasing U.S. trade deficits, fluctuating but generally increasing Japanese trade surpluses, and a bilateral U.S. deficit that was an important component of the aggregate balances in both countries. Whereas bilateral trade balances have virtually no economic importance, these numbers provided political grist for targeting Japan and its trade practices. But a moment's reflection suggests that the trade *trends* fail to confirm covert protection in Japan. While protection might help explain the *level* of Japan's trade surplus, there is no evidence and no argument that protection was increasing in this period. Hence, it is difficult to argue that protection in Japan explains the *increases* in its trade surplus. Instead, the data suggest a different story.

▶ MACRO-ACCOUNTING BALANCES

As an alternative to seeking evidence of covert protection to explain trade performance, some analysts sought an explanation in divergent macroeconomic structures in the United States and Japan. This approach is most persuasive in the 1980–1987 period, when the U.S. trade deficit went from $25 billion to $160 billion, the Japanese trade surplus went from $2 billion to $92 billion, and the bilateral deficit increased from $12 billion to $60 billion. The analysis starts with a pair of national accounting identities in which the trade balance is definitionally equal to the difference between national savings and national investment. In notational form, this can be expressed as (X – M) = (S – I) + (T – G). This identity can be interpreted as saying that the trade balance (X – M) must be equal to private sector saving minus private sector domestic investment (S – I) plus the government surplus or deficit, T – G (taxes minus government expenditures). By accounting definitions, a trade surplus (X – M> O) must be accompanied by an excess of private and public savings over domestic investment. Conversely, a trade deficit must be accompanied by a shortfall in private and public savings relative to domestic investment.[16] It is important to remember that this is simply an accounting relation and does not constitute a theoretical relation among the variables. Nevertheless, it does provide some insight into the sharply divergent macroeconomic performance of the United States and Japan in the first half of the 1980s, which set the stage for two decades of trade disputes.

Table 4.1 displays the X – M balance, the S – I balance, and the T – G balance for the United States and Japan for two years, 1980 and 1984, expressed as a percentage of that year's GNP. At the start of the 1980s the United States had a virtually zero current account (X – M) balance, an excess of private savings over private domestic investment of 1.2 percent GNP, and a government deficit of 1.2 percent GNP.[17] In the same year, Japan had a modest current account deficit of 1 percent GNP, an excess of private savings over private domestic investment of 3.5 percent GNP, and a substantial government deficit of 4.5 percent GDP. By 1984 the macrostructures had changed dramatically, in the opposite direction. The U.S. external deficit had risen to 2.8 percent GNP, the savings–investment balance remained positive at 1 percent GNP, but the government deficit

[16] A second interpretation is that an economy in trade deficit must be absorbing more real resources through consumption, investment, and government expenditures than it is producing.

[17] Federal, state, and local, combined. It did run a $10 billion merchandise trade deficit with Japan. The current account balance includes unilaterals, or gifts and grants abroad.

TABLE 4.1 Accounting Balances, Expressed as Percentage of GNP

Year	Country	(X–M)	=	(S–I)	+	(T–G)
1980	U.S.	0.0	=	1.2	+	(–)1.2
	Japan	–1.0	=	3.5	+	(–)4.5
1984	U.S.	–2.8	=	1.0	+	(–)3.4
	Japan	2.6	=	5.2	+	(–)2.6

Source: Bergsten and Cline (1985, Table 2.2).

had grown to 3.4 percent GNP. In contrast, Japan had increased its excess of private savings over private investment to 5.2 percent and had decreased its government deficit (dissaving) to 2.6 percent GNP. The excess of national savings in Japan (private savings less government dissavings) allowed it to run a current account surplus of 2.6 percent GNP, a swing in the external balance of 3.6 percent GNP in four years.

These data were well known at the time and led to two interpretations. One was that U.S. and Japanese trade performance in this period could be explained primarily on the basis of divergent macroperformance, especially fiscal policy moving in opposite directions, without recourse to import protection and export targeting types of arguments. Most analysts concluded that macroeconomic variables, including the exchange rate, and not trade barriers explained the growing bilateral trade deficit with Japan. The second interpretation was that Japan engaged in "excessive" savings, and a long-run solution would require dampening Japanese savings and boosting its consumption. This prescription found its way into the subsequent Structural Impediments Initiative talks discussed in the next section.[18]

[18]There were major changes in the accounting balances by 2000. In the United States the current account deficit reached 4.3 percent of GDP, private savings fell short of private investment by about 5.2 percent of GDP, and the government moved from a deficit to a surplus. (Personal savings as percent GDP fell from 7 percent in 1980 to 0 percent in 2000). The fact that the U.S. current account deficit *increased* while the federal budget swung from a deficit to a surplus undercut the "twin deficit" thesis that had been popular earlier—the view that the current account deficit was simply the mirror of the federal budget deficit. In Japan the 2000 current account surplus still exceeded 2 percent of GDP, the government budget swung to a massive deficit of almost 8 percent of GDP, implying an excess of private savings over private domestic investment of about 10 percent GDP.

▶ THE MARKET ACCESS DRIVE

Efforts to improve market access in Japan accelerated in the 1980s as the import protection phase of the relation wound down. This followed a major successful push in 1977–1978 to increase Japan's import quotas on beef and citrus. Although as noted previously bilateral trade balances have little economic significance and overall trade balances are primarily the consequence of macroeconomic forces, it was politically attractive to focus on market-opening initiatives. The increasingly shrill allegations of foreign unfair trade practices, the ready availability of Section 301 in the trade policy tool box, and the emerging literature on strategic trade policy all argued for a concerted effort to penetrate the difficult Japanese market. By and large the shift in U.S. policy from import protection to export expansion was a welcome change, as the latter has the potential for opening, not closing, markets. Nevertheless, aggressive unilateral demands for market access carry risks and can degenerate into unproductive hectoring.

Congressional concern for U.S. trade and especially trade with Japan reached a peak (or nadir) in the mid-1980s. In response, and in addition to the activation of Section 301, the Reagan administration initiated the bilateral Market-Oriented, Sector-Specific (MOSS) talks with Japan in 1985. Previous market access talks had resulted in some progress in citrus and beef, and the lesson drawn was that Japan required sustained targeted pressure. The MOSS talks concentrated on specific sectors in which the United States felt it had a comparative and competitive advantage that was not fully realized in the marketplace. The priorities were telecommunications, pharmaceuticals, medical equipment, microelectronics, and various wood products. Supercomputers were added to the MOSS talks in 1987 and illustrate the limited success of the negotiations. Under pressure, Japan agreed to buy two U.S. supercomputers, but the purchase was subsequently considered to be mainly symbolic, and a new agreement had to be negotiated in 1989 (utilizing Super 301 provisions of the 1988 trade legislation). Even under the new and more favorable agreement, USTR felt the need to investigate its implementation in 1993. The review found some positive developments in U.S. supercomputer sales in Japan in the previous three years, with six of 15 purchases from the United States. Nevertheless, there was grumbling from U.S. business; five of the six sales were "massively parallel processing" machines made by five different U.S. firms, leading to speculation that Japan's motive was to learn and possibly leapfrog U.S. technology (Bayard and Elliott, 1994).

Frustrated with the so-called retail approach to market access negotiations, in 1989 the Bush administration launched the Structural Impediments Initiative (SII) talks, directed at generic problems underlying trade disputes. In a sense this initiative was a refreshing departure from the almost endless series of product-specific disputes. The premise was that both the United States and Japan would identify structural causes for trade problems in each other's economy and commit to remedy those identified by the other. The SII talks were in fact a rather sophisticated recognition that after overt trade barriers at the border (i.e., tariffs) are removed and after the most egregious nontariff trade barriers (NTBs) are brought to light (e.g., discriminatory customs valuation classification), there remain a host of other government policies that influence international trade, even if their ostensible purpose is domestic in nature.

This point is worth stressing. At present, trade barriers at the border for industrial countries are minimal (excepting textiles, steel, agriculture, and certain services). Most overt NTBs are more or less subject to international rules as set out in the GATT and the WTO. The next step in trade negotiations, which is neither essential nor necessarily desirable, will be to try to harmonize domestic policies (labor, environment, competition, health, retirement, savings) that give rise to differences in production costs and hence international competitiveness. In this sense the SII talks can be thought of as an early encounter with many of the unresolved post–Uruguay Round trade issues. The U.S. shopping list in the SII talks covered much ground, ranging from "excessive" Japanese savings thought to depreciate the yen and protect Japanese industry, to land use restrictions allegedly increasing housing costs and discouraging Japanese consumption of imports. In the end, there was limited progress on the more-specific demands.[19]

The Clinton administration, in keeping with its emphasis on the priority of economic and commercial relations, promised an aggressive stance *vis a vis* Japan. Two buzzwords were a "results-oriented" policy, first introduced by the Bush administration, and "quantitative indicators," the latter presumably influenced by the quantitative target established earlier in the

[19]The Large Scale Retail Store Law allowed Toys R Us to enter the market, most likely selling merchandise made elsewhere in Asia.

Semiconductor Agreement. United States objectives *vis a vis* Japan were formalized in the so-called Framework Agreement of 1993 and among other matters dealt with the then all too familiar list of market access issues: government procurement, financial services, competition policy, intellectual property, etc. The novelty was to have been in monitoring trade results "based on objective criteria, either qualitative or quantitative or both as appropriate" (Lincoln, 1999, p. 127). Thus, improvements in market access were to be measured even if specific numerical targets were not fixed and agreed to.

The results of Clinton's Framework Agreement and other trade initiatives *vis a vis* Japan were modest.[20] In two high-profile cases, the United States managed a draw on the first and lost the second. Access to Japan's auto and auto parts market had been a longstanding sore point, not resolved despite a 1992 agreement reached by the Bush administration. The Clinton administration initiated a market access Section 301 case in 1994 and followed up in 1995 with the announcement of punitive 100 percent tariffs against luxury auto imports from Japan, and it also initiated a WTO case. The actual collection of the duties was delayed, and in the meantime Japan filed a counter-case at the WTO, claiming the unilateral U.S. tariffs violated its WTO rights. At the last minute, Japan agreed to modest regulatory changes, both sides issued separate (and conflicting) analyses of the agreement, the United States withdrew its threat of tariffs, and Japan withdrew its WTO case. Hardly a triumph.

The color film case involved two dominant oligopolists, Kodak and Fuji, which controlled some 75 percent of the world photo film market. Following a 1993 dumping action initiated by Kodak against Fuji and a second Japanese firm, Konica, and its circumvention by Fuji, which shifted production to the U.S., Kodak filed a Section 301 complaint against Japan in 1995.[21] The positive 301 finding led the United States to file a WTO case rather than take unilateral action. The WTO panel accepted certain theoretical points advanced by the United States but on the substantive issues ruled against the United States and, indirectly, against Kodak.

During the second Clinton administration, the aggressive trade approach toward Japan faded. One critical reason was that the new dispute

[20]Limited agreements were reached on intellectual property, certain government procurements, and financial services.

[21]Bergsten, Ito, Noland (2001, pp. 22–26).

settlement procedures of the WTO trumped unilateral action under Section 301, as illustrated by both the auto and photo film cases. A second reason was that the Japanese bubble economy had burst, exposing deep faults in its economic structure and development model. Japan remained a serious competitor, but its credibility as an alternative to the U.S. model suffered. The Asian financial crisis starting in 1997–1998 and the rise of China as a trade power created further distractions.

▶ LESSONS

There are few easy lessons to be drawn from the long period of troubled trade relations with Japan. The least controversial is that the United States acted correctly and with good judgment in leading the support for Japan's reentry into the world trade system in the early postwar period. But even here our policy has been criticized for being soft on Japan's failure to liberalize in a timely fashion (Eckes, 1999). The middle phase in our trade relations was characterized by repeated challenges to industries in which the United States felt it had a permanent comparative advantage. In fact, it was the rapidity with which Japan altered *its* comparative advantage, from labor-intensive to capital-intensive and then technology-intensive manufacturing, that caught the United States by surprise and contributed to our scramble for protectionist response.[22] Although many conditions are different, the rapid rise of China in international trade may pose a similar challenge to established U.S. industries in the next decades.

But it is the sustained drive for market access in Japan, starting almost 30 years ago in the Carter Administration and continuing in subdued form today, that is most difficult to judge. Was it necessary and desirable to invest so heavily in a trade policy directed toward a single country?[23] On the one hand, it is reasonable to suppose that the Japanese market would be less open today had it not been for these efforts, although surely Japan it-

[22]In a sense, this was a novel experience for the United States. The rise of the UK's industrial prowess predated that of the United States. The trade effects of Germany's formidable economic rise in the early part of the 20th century was blunted by lingering protection in the United States.

[23]The United States, of course, had intense trade relations with Europe throughout the postwar period. The essential difference was that most key issues were addressed through the multilateral GATT negotiations, especially the Kennedy, Tokyo, and Uruguay Rounds. For the flavor of these negotiations, see Eckes (2000).

self would have seen some virtue in at least limited liberalization. But the tactics used—unilateral pressure, VIEs, Section 301, quantitative indicators and targets—came with a cost in both foreign policy terms and erosion of liberal trade principles. Although these derogations from liberal principles have become moderated in recent years, it was the collapse of Japan Inc. as an economic model and the resurgence of the U.S. economy, not trade pressures, that eased the tension.

REFERENCES

Balassa, Bela, and Marcus Noland. 1988. *Japan in the World Economy.* Washington, DC: Institute for International Economics.

Bayard, Thomas, and Kimberly Elliott. 1994. *Reciprocity and Retaliation in U.S. Trade Policy.* Washington, DC: Institute for International Economics.

Beasley, W. G. 1999. *The Japanese Experience: A Short History of Japan.* Berkeley: University of California Press.

Bergsten, Fred, and Marcus Noland. 1993. *Reconcilable Differences?: United States–Japan Economic Conflict.* Washington, DC: Institute for International Economics.

Bergsten, Fred, Takatoshi Ito, and Marcus Noland. 2001. *The United States–Japan Economic Relation.* Washington, DC: Institute for International Economics.

Bergsten, Fred, and William Cline. 1985. *The United States–Japan Economic Problem.* Washington, DC: Institute for International Economics.

Eckes, Alfred. 2000. *Revisiting U.S. Trade Policy.* Athens, Ohio: Ohio University Press.

Feis, Herbert. 1950. *The Road to Pearl Harbor.* Princeton, NJ: Princeton University Press.

Hunsberger, Warren. 1964. *Japan and the United States in World Trade.* New York: Harper & Row for Council on Foreign Relations.

Lawrence, Robert. 1987. *Imports in Japan: Closed Markets or Minds? Brookings Papers on Economic Activity.* No. 2. Washington, DC: Brookings Institution.

Lincoln, Edward. 1990. *Japan's Unequal Trade.* Washington, DC: Brookings Institution.

Lincoln, Edward. 1999. *Troubled Times: U.S.–Japan Trade Relations in the 1990s.* Washington, DC: Brookings Institution.

Lovett, William, Alfred Eckes, Richard Brinkman. 1999. *U.S. Trade Policy: History, Theory and the WTO.* Armonk, NY: M. E. Sharpe.

Metzger, Stanley. 1971. Injury and Market Disruption from Imports. In: Commission on International Trade and Investment Policy. *United States International Economic Policy in an Interdependent World.* Papers, vol. 1. Washington, DC: GPO.

Patterson, Gardner. 1966. *Discrimination in International Trade: The Policy Issues 1945–1965.* Princeton, NJ: Princeton University Press.

Prestowitz, Clyde. 1988. *Trading Places: How We Allowed Japan to Take the Land.* New York: Basic Books.

Saxenhouse, Gary. 1986. What's Wrong With Japanese Trade Structure. *Pacific Economic Papers.*

Trezise, Philip. 1971. U.S.–Japan Economic Relations. In: Commission on International Trade and Investment Policy. *United States International Economic Policy in an Interdependent World.* Papers II. Washington, DC: GPO.

World Trade Organization. 2000. *Focus.* No. 49. Geneva: WTO.

Zysman, John, and Laura D'Andrea Tyson. 1983. *American Industry in International Competition.* Ithaca, NY: Cornell University Press.

CHAPTER 5

TRADE, JOBS, AND WAGES

No aspect of trade is more influential in policy than the issue of jobs. Economists have argued for hundreds of years that the purpose of trade is efficiency in the allocation of resources, not providing employment. By and large, this has fallen on deaf ears, and each new trade measure, whether it be the auto VER with Japan, the creation of NAFTA, or granting China permanent normal trade relations, is debated and assessed on the basis of the number of jobs gained and lost. As explained in this chapter, the connection between trade, jobs, and wages is important, but not in the sense that it is often discussed. Trade and trade liberalization seldom have a marked effect on the overall level of employment in the United States. Indeed, toward the end of the 1990s, the United States was enjoying one of its lowest unemployment rates in 30 years, while also experiencing its highest ever ratio of imports to GDP and a record trade deficit.

Nevertheless, while the overall level of employment is not primarily determined by trade, there are two important links that deserve attention. Trade affects the sectoral composition of employment and, when sufficiently rapid, changes in trade can cause involuntary unemployment in export- and import-competing industries. This is the labor adjustment or labor displacement issue and is a valid and serious concern. Moreover, trade affects relative and absolute wage levels and has been implicated in wage suppression and increasing income inequality in the United States. These two channels are not unconnected. If real wages are flexible downward, this will tend to reduce labor displacement.

We start with a brief review of how U.S. labor's position on trade has shifted in the postwar era. We continue with some conceptual and methodological issues in relating trade and employment. The next sections consider job displacement, labor adjustment costs, and the checkered history of the Trade Adjustment Assistance program. Following that we examine the (inconclusive) debate on the role of trade in wage suppression and income inequality. A final trade–labor issue—linking trade policy to fair labor standards abroad—is deferred to Chapter 10.

▶ LABOR'S U-TURN

U.S. labor has not always opposed trade liberalization. Cordell Hull had labor support for the 1934 Reciprocal Trade Agreements Act; in the late 1940s it was business interests more than labor that defeated the ITO without even a Congressional vote; and the AFL-CIO supported President Kennedy's Trade Expansion Act of 1962.[1] Some of this early labor support was made easier by the pledges from Roosevelt through Eisenhower, that trade concessions would not be allowed to harm import-sensitive industries. And of course, since the 19th century, the Democrats, the party of the working man, had generally opposed Republican business support for high tariffs.

The turning point came in the 1970s, when large unionized American industries such as steel and autos came under increasingly severe import competition and when the traditional U.S. trade surplus evaporated. Import competition was only part of the story. U.S. foreign investment, much of which was direct investment by multinational corporations, went from $10 billion in 1970 to $73 billion in 1980. The "export" of jobs by multinational corporations (MNCs) was a hot issue. As described below, the effort to woo back labor support for liberal trade (and investment) through Trade Adjustment Assistance (TAA) was unsuccessful. By the 1990s, the historical stance of labor and business had been reversed; with exceptions, business generally abandoned protection and favored liberal trade, and labor abandoned its low tariff support and took up the task of opposing or rolling back trade liberalization.[2]

The peeling off of labor support for further liberalization of trade and

[1]Destler (1998). Katz (1998) notes that the craft unions of the AFL were less supportive of liberal trade than the industrial unions of the CIO.

[2]This should be taken as a generalization. Labor was *not* active in opposing the Uruguay Round legislation, and some business interests opposed NAFTA and permanent normal trade relations (PNTR) with China.

its vehement attitude toward MNCs is nicely captured in labor's minority dissent to the 1971 Williams Commission Report, which laid the groundwork for U.S. participation in the subsequent Tokyo Round. I. W. Abel, head of the United Steelworkers union, and Floyd Smith, president of the International Association of Machinists and Aerospace Workers, asserted that "sharply rising foreign investments of U.S. companies . . . have caused a rapid transfer of American technology, production and employment to foreign operations" and that "the impact of managed national economies in other industrial nations, the internationalization of technology and the emergence of multinational corporations and the international banks have made obsolete old theories of free trade and protection."[3] They recommended controls on the outflow of capital and technology, tax measures to halt "global runaway" MNCs, and a system of import quotas to protect the U.S. economy.

By and large, organized labor's major initiatives for new protection or to halt further liberalization bore little fruit. Labor was, of course, successful (together with business interests) in obtaining protection in steel, autos, and textiles and has helped craft protectionist antidumping and countervailing duty legislation. It may also have gained some jobs from the switch in policy emphasis starting in the mid-1980s to export expansion and knocking down foreign trade barriers. And together with some elements of the environmental community, labor contributed to disrupting the Seattle WTO ministerial meeting and delaying new trade initiatives. But the most egregious derogations from liberal trade—the 1971 Burke-Hartke legislation, which would have mandated import quotas and restricted foreign investment; congressionally set quotas on autos (1982); and the hardcore Gephardt Amendment of 1988, requiring phased reductions in bilateral trade deficits—were all defeated. And labor failed big time to block NAFTA in 1992 and permanent normal trade relations with China in 2000.[4]

There are many explanations for this unimpressive record. Surely the decline in union membership, which fell from 30 percent of the labor force in 1960 to below 15 percent in the 1990s, was one. Moreover, union mem-

[3]Commission on International Trade and Investment Policy (Williams Commission) (1971, pp. 340–341).

[4]The textile lobby may have helped cause Clinton to scrap the first provisional agreement with China.

bership has shifted toward service industries, many of which do not directly compete with imports.[5] The switch toward an export expansion trade strategy has also played a role. In the 1990s the advent of full employment and the stabilization of employment in manufacturing took the edge off organized labor's position on trade and its influence.[6]

▶ THINKING ABOUT TRADE AND EMPLOYMENT

The simplest notion linking trade and employment is that increasing imports adversely affect employment. When aggregate trade is considered, this idea contains a kernel of truth and a large dose of error. A *general* increase in imports can arise through buoyant aggregate demand during an economic upswing. This was the U.S. experience through much of the 1990s. Demand spills over to imports (and often exportables), and the trade balance declines. In this situation increased imports do not displace domestic output and jobs (see Figure 5.1). If imports do not displace domestic production and jobs, there are no adjustment costs to labor from involuntary unemployment. Remember, we are considering trade aggregates, not the trade position of individual industries.

In contrast, if aggregate costs and prices in the United States move out of line with other countries (a loss of competitive position) due to inflation or an unwarranted real appreciation of the currency, after some lag imports will increase and exports will languish. The deterioration in relative international prices *switches* demand from domestic to foreign sources. This appears to have been the case in the early and mid-1980s (see Figure 5.2). In the event of demand switch, increased imports tend to displace domestic production and employment, and workers may suffer involuntary unemployment. The fundamental remedy is then a restoration of international competitive position through the exchange rate and, most likely, restrictive macroeconomic policies to contain associated inflation. But

[5]The fraction of the nonagricultural labor force producing goods fell from 38 percent in 1960 to 20 percent in 2000, while the fraction engaged in services increased from 49 to 66 percent. The weight of consumer interests vs. labor interests in the setting of trade policy may also have shifted. The consumer goods fraction of total imports increased from 41 percent in 1965 to about 47 percent in 2000.

[6]Manufacturing employment peaked in 1979. It hit a 14-year low in 1993 but recovered slightly in the 1994–2000 period. It fell again in the 2001 recession.

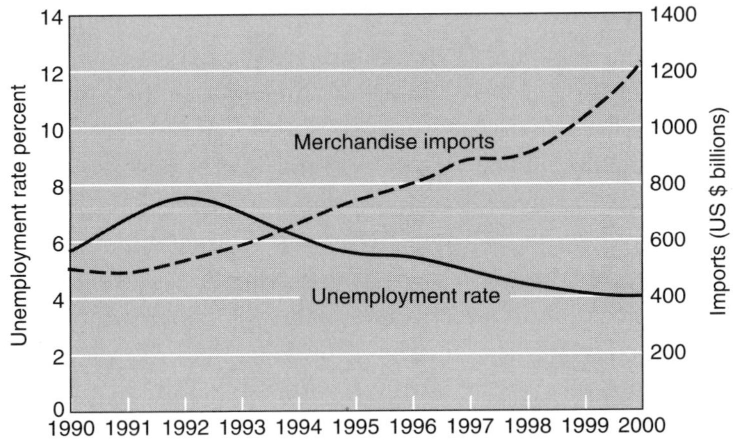

Figure 5.1 U.S. imports and unemployment rate.
Source: Council of Economic Advisors, Economic Report of the President.

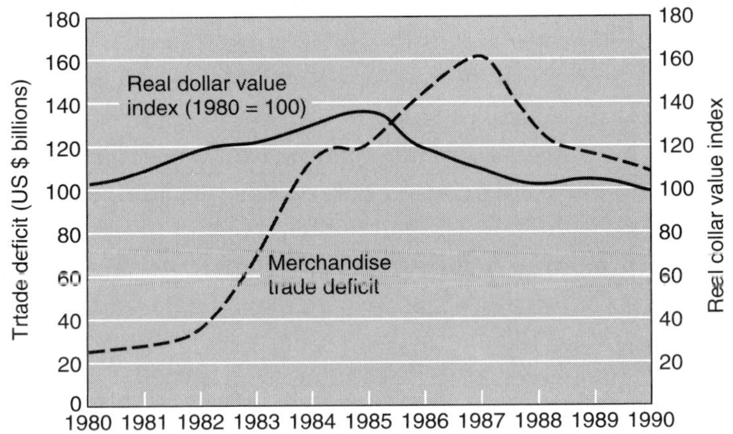

Figure 5.2 U.S. trade deficit and dollar exchange rate.
Source: Council of Economic Advisors, Economic Report of the President.

there may also be an economic case for some form of labor market policy to improve the functioning of the labor market (to reduce the loss of output from unemployed workers) and a social argument for cushioning income loss during unemployment. Import protection in these circumstances is not warranted. It would tend to further worsen the loss of competitiveness through a variety of channels.[7] The efficiency and social arguments for labor market policy are not limited to job displacement due to trade but are relevant for all involuntary unemployment. In summary, trade policy should *not* be used for aggregate employment objectives.

The analysis of trade and jobs is different at the level of specific industries. Imports of a particular good can increase and output and employment in that industry decline for many reasons. These include policy changes affecting individual industries (e.g., tariff reductions, foreign subsidies, new and expensive pollution control regulations), labor or raw material cost increases specific to that industry, improvements in foreign production technology, and changes in tastes favoring the foreign product (implying product differentiation). In these situations, if market growth in the industry is slow and if the rate of decline of domestic output exceeds normal rates of labor attrition (voluntary quits, retirements) then involuntary unemployment (layoffs and downsizing) results.[8]

In these instances the basic policy choices are to (1) do nothing beyond providing normal unemployment benefits, (2) grant temporary protection through the escape clause provisions (or the unfair trade statutes, if appropriate), and (3) provide some form of trade-adjustment assistance to workers to improve efficiency in the labor market (re-employ workers more rapidly) and to cushion income loss for unemployed workers. The choice between the latter two policies depends in part on whether the industry's loss of competitiveness is thought to be temporary and reversible or whether it represents a more permanent shift in comparative advantage. As described below, the United States has vacillated among these three responses. Temporary trade protection given to a permanently uncompetitive industry may draw in new resources—labor and capital—and increase subsequent adjustment costs. Firms inevitably claim that temporary protection will give them time to restructure, increase productivity, and regain competitive position. The one clear example of success was Harley-David-

[7]For example, higher prices for intermediate inputs would worsen the competitive position of export and import competing firms.

[8]This is an oversimplification. Even with increasing domestic output in the industry and a "high" rate of normal labor attrition, involuntary unemployment can result as some firms exit the industry and as firms shift production from one facility to another. Moreover, the quit rate is likely to be endogenous, higher in expanding industries as workers see opportunities for their skills in other firms. See Haveman (1998) and Brechling (1978). Industry may also relocate within the U.S. At one time New England was the center of a thriving textile industry that subsequently moved to the South in search of lower labor costs.

son, which used its period of import relief in the 1980s to introduce a new and popular line of smaller motorcycles. But examples of protection that restore competitive position are rare.

Before turning to analytical approaches linking trade and job displacement, it is useful to make two distinctions. The first is between hypothetical job loss and actual job loss (involuntary unemployment). It is superficially easy to calculate the number of hypothetical jobs that would have been maintained or created if imports were lower than they actually are. All that is needed is the appropriate labor:output coefficient. But the "loss" of these hypothetical jobs is just that: hypothetical. The calculation of these hypothetical jobs does not mean an actual worker is laid off. In contrast, job displacement by imports means an actual layoff or firing and some period of unemployment for a real worker, a loss of output for the economy, and often reemployment of the worker at a lower wage. In contemplations of the labor-adjustment cost of trade, it is actual and not hypothetical job loss that is important.

The second distinction is between social and private adjustment costs. The social adjustment costs of trade-related job displacement primarily consist of the loss of output to the economy during the period the worker is unemployed.[9] The private adjustment costs borne by the displaced worker include his or her earnings loss during unemployment, net of various unemployment benefits, plus job search costs, plus the net present value of any reduction in reemployment wages, which is often substantial.[10] Labor policy is concerned with both types of adjustment costs. But the distinction is important in order to separate analytically efficiency and equity objectives.

▶ ANALYTICAL APPROACHES

Trade-Employment Balance Studies

A popular but questionable approach has been to subtract from the number of jobs associated with exports the (hypothetical) number of jobs that

[9] If wages equal value of marginal product of labor, these costs might be measured by loss of earnings. The more accurate measure is earnings in the next-best-alternative employment. Physical capital (for example, trucks) may also be temporarily "unemployed," and this also is a social cost.

[10] If trade makes a job-specific skill obsolete, this is a human capital loss to the individual but not a social cost.

would exist if imports were replaced by domestic production.[11] If the result is negative, the easy but incorrect conclusion is that trade is "destroying" jobs. Trade-employment balance studies can be *ex ante,* anticipating trade changes from trade liberalization, or *ex post,* looking back at the effects of previous trade changes.[12] They can be done on the basis of existing trade levels or changes in these levels. They can also be done on a country- or industry-specific level: for example, the job content of U.S. trade with Japan or with developing countries and the job content of U.S. trade in manufactures.

These studies are subject to serious misinterpretation and misuse. At the most basic level, it is not the purpose of trade to provide employment, and a negative employment balance for aggregate trade is of no economic concern.[13] Measuring the employment content of trade by region or product sector requires sophisticated effort at modelling substitutions in trade by source and product (e.g., does an increase in imports from China simply displace imports from other Asian countries?). Even if properly done, the result is of little significance; there is no economic reason to expect or desire employment balance in our trade with China or employment balance in trade in, say, chemicals.

However, if done carefully, *ex ante* trade employment balance studies of specific trade policy proposals (for example, the extension of NAFTA southward in the FTAA, as is currently contemplated) can provide some useful information on labor adjustment requirements by industry. But to reach conclusions with regard to real labor adjustment costs (that is, involuntary unemployment), it is necessary to estimate the time profile of imports and adjust for projected demand growth in the industry (exogenous and growth attributable to lower-priced imports). Even with falling demand and domestic output, normal labor attrition may accommodate some increased imports without involuntary unemployment.[14] In any event, if

[11]The calculation requires industry-specific, direct, and indirect labor:output coefficients derived from input–output tables.

[12]Pearson and Salembier (1983) discuss a number of the earlier studies.

[13]Measuring the factor content of trade does have a long and reputable history in testing trade theories, dating to Leontief's work in 1953.

[14]The best studies use a general equilibrium approach, take into account what would have happened in the absence of the trade measure (inherently hypothetical), and incorporate foreign investment responses to the trade measure.

the purpose of the analysis is to estimate labor adjustment costs, it is the gross change in imports, not the net trade change including increased exports, that should be the starting point. A *specific* worker laid off in an import-competing firm is unlikely to be immediately reemployed in expanding export sectors.

Trade-employment balance studies have been remarkably important in U.S. trade policy, in part because of the erroneous but politically popular view that the purpose of trade is jobs and in part because superficial studies can suggest large job losses. Indeed, most of the NAFTA debate was couched in terms of jobs to be lost or gained. A number of studies estimating NAFTA's job impacts were undertaken, using econometric and CGE models but also with less formal approaches. Researchers at the Institute for International Economics (IIE), for example, estimated gross job gain of 316,000 from additional exports attributable to NAFTA and gross job loss from increased imports of 145,000, for a net gain of about 170,000 jobs.[15] These were calculated using the typical trade-employment balance approach of multiplying projected increases in exports and imports by direct and indirect labor coefficients per billion dollars of trade. No effort was made to trace the job losses to specific industries, and thus the actual, as opposed to hypothetical, job loss was not measured.[16] The authors did make the questionable assertion that from the standpoint of the U.S. economy as a whole, what counts is how many net jobs are created by NAFTA.[17] The IIE study was said to be the most frequently cited study of NAFTA and was widely circulated among policy-makers, confirming the political importance of trade-employment balance studies.

Import Surge Studies

If policy-makers are concerned with actual job losses—workers made unemployed because of trade—and not hypothetical jobs that might exist if trade flows were different, the rapidity of increase in specific products imported is important. If concentrated in a short time period, layoffs may re-

[15]See Hufbauer and Schott (1993), Table 2.1.

[16]The authors did, however, examine the occupational structure of the jobs displaced, with the largest impact on precision, production, craft, and repair workers, followed by sales workers.

[17]See Hufbauer and Schott, p. 14.

sult. If spread over several years, domestic output and employment can contract without layoffs. Motivated by the popular but undocumented view that Japan and the developing countries were flooding the U.S. market and displacing labor, Pearson (1984) examined the role of import surges from these countries in the United States and 10 other industrial country importers. He found that for the United States, the increase in the share of imports from all countries in domestic consumption of manufactures for the entire decade of 1970–1980 was only 3.1 percentage points, with additional imports from Japan accounting for 0.8 percentage points and the Asian NICs accounting for 0.7 percentage points.[18] Put somewhat differently, over the 11-year period, imports supplied only 10 percent of the *increase* in U.S. consumption of manufactures, and domestic producers in the United States supplied 90 percent.

The study then went on to look at detailed sectors at the ISIC four- and five-digit levels to identify and classify import surges. Defining an import surge as an increase in the ratio of imports to domestic production plus imports of at least 5 percentage points over three years, and a "serious" import surge with labor adjustment implications to occur when domestic output was falling, the study identified a total of 1662 surges for the 11 countries over the 11-year period, of which 549 were "serious." Contrary to the then-popular view, the United States was not the main target for import surges, accounting for only 27 of the 549. Of these, only a fraction could be attributed to Japan and the Asian NICs. The study concluded that the popular view of the United States as a target for a flood of imports was greatly exaggerated and that true labor-adjustment costs to imports from Japan and Asian NICs were very modest.

Decomposition and Other Studies

It is useful for policy purposes to compare job losses due to trade with job losses arising from other causes. If trade-related job loss is small, the case for trade liberalization is strengthened. Decomposition studies shed light on this question, although the results should be interpreted cautiously. The method is simple, perhaps too simple. The growth rate of employment in an industry is by definition equal to the sum of the growth of consumption

[18]The 3.1-percentage-point increase was far less than the simple average for the other 10 industrial country importers, which was 9.8 percentage points.

of that product, the growth of labor productivity (negative if productivity is increasing), and the share of imports in consumption (negative if the import penetration ratio is increasing).[19] Early studies for the United States found that, as expected, domestic demand growth and productivity changes were more important than imports as a source of employment change in most industries (Frank 1977, Krueger 1978).

One cannot dismiss the labor-adjustment cost issue on the basis of decomposition studies, however. One reason is that this is an accounting exercise, not based on a theoretical foundation. Both productivity and consumption growth are likely to be related to the import penetration ratio, and to calculate trade-related employment change without explicitly incorporating these relations is unsound. Also, like the trade-employment balance studies, this approach measured hypothetical (not actual) job loss due to imports. Moreover, if productivity-related job losses are concentrated in high-growth industries and trade-related job losses are in low-growth industries, actual job loss from productivity growth may be minimal, and job loss from trade in the slow growth sectors may be substantial, but this will be concealed in aggregation. Finally, productivity-related job changes may be spread evenly throughout the industry and accommodated through normal attrition, and trade-related job losses may be concentrated in a few firms that shut down entirely.

A study by Kletzer (1998) bears on the issue of actual, not hypothetical, job loss. In this research the worker-displacement rate for an industry is defined as the ratio of involuntary job terminations during a year to the employment in that industry. The displacement rate is then regressed on the change in the import penetration ratio in that period, and there is some statistical evidence that increases in the import penetration ratio increase the displacement rate. This is further refined by adding domestic demand change as an explanatory variable (to capture cyclical variations in displacement) and by controlling for industry-specific characteristics. The results show that industry-specific characteristics (e.g., differential rates of voluntary quits and accessions) are important in determining displacement rates. In this more complete analysis, the evidence that displacement rates are related to increases in import shares is weak.

Haveman (1998) has also investigated trade-related job displacement

[19]Labor productivity (output per worker) can increase with more capital per worker or through technological improvements or both.

in the United States. The intuition behind his econometric model is that changes in import competition, measured by changes in import and export prices relative to domestic prices, will increase displacements beyond some normal industry level if trade prices are falling and decrease labor displacement if these prices are rising. By comparing actual displacements by industry with estimated displacements had there been no change in the U.S. international competitive position (again measured by trade vs. domestic prices), he estimates trade-related job displacements by industry for the decade of the 1980s. As might be expected because of the strong dollar and falling trade prices in the 1981–1985 period, estimated trade-related job displacements reached a cumulative 75,000, or 2.6 percent of all reported job displacements in all industries. In the 1986–1989 period, as the dollar fell and the United States regained its competitive position, rising trade prices *reduced* the number of displacements by about 76,000 (4.7 percent of total displacements in this period). Overall, the study suggests that trade-related job displacements, the concept that most closely relates to worker hardship, were generally modest but significant in certain industries: for example, mining, primary metals, and (surprisingly) meat products.

Labor-Tracking Studies

Involuntary job loss due to trade (labor displacement) tells part of the story. It is also useful to track what happens to trade-displaced workers to determine the length of their unemployment and their reemployment wage. Early studies (Corson et al., 1979; Neumann, 1978; Jenkins et al., 1978) were handicapped by ad hoc and incomplete data, but the general conclusions were that adjustment costs were higher for older, more skilled, and higher-wage workers and that lower subsequent wages were an important part of private adjustment costs (Pearson and Salembier, 1983). Data started to improve in the 1980s with the Bureau of the Census Survey of Displaced Workers. Kletzer (1998), for example, investigates worker characteristics and finds that workers displaced from high-import-penetration industries have poorer reemployment prospects then workers displaced from low-penetration sectors.[20] This appears to result from the high proportion of females displaced and not their skill levels.

[20]Note that this speaks to the level of the import penetration ratio, not changes in import penetration. See also Kletzer (2001).

Jacobson et al. (1993), using detailed data for Pennsylvania, confirm that lower subsequent reemployment wages were a major private adjustment cost for long-tenured workers who were displaced.[21] The earnings of these workers recovered very slowly, so that five years after separation their losses still amounted to 25 percent of their pre-displacement earnings. Losses tended to be larger for workers in heavily unionized industries and workers displaced from very large firms. The results suggest that serious adjustment costs are concentrated in a subset of displaced workers and are a legitimate concern for social policy.

TRADE ADJUSTMENT ASSISTANCE (TAA)

U.S. policy responded to the trade-related job displacement issue early on. TAA was established in 1962 with the support of labor as part of legislation authorizing the Kennedy Round. The concept can be traced to a proposal made by David McDonald, of the United Steelworkers Union, in 1953. The idea is attractive. Liberal trade brings economic benefits to many, but adjustment costs are concentrated in a few workers. Rather than forgo trade benefits, TAA could compensate injured workers for these costs and, through retraining and job search provisions, could reduce the period of unemployment and contribute to labor market efficiency.[22]

In its early years TAA was a failure (Fooks, 1971; Destler, 1998). The eligibility requirements for assistance were strict, and all worker petitions from 1962 through November 1969 were rejected. Even when some were subsequently approved, the bureaucratic maze and delay sapped the potential of the program.[23] Organized labor was quick to recognize TAA deficiencies and quick to sour on the concept. By the 1970s, labor was denouncing TAA as "burial insurance." A central purpose of TAA, to garner labor support for trade liberalization, failed.

Mindful of the earlier failure, the Trade Act of 1974, which launched

[21]This study is not limited to trade-related job loss. Long-tenured workers have six or more years at their pre-displacement firms.

[22]The 1962 legislation also provided for technical assistance, loans, and loan guarantees to trade-impacted firms. Direct financial assistance was eliminated in 1986, due in part to budget cutbacks and high default rates. Technical assistance continues at a modest level of about $11 million per year.

[23]Interestingly, a somewhat more efficient system for displaced auto workers was established under the 1965 U.S.–Canadian auto agreement.

the Tokyo Round, liberalized criteria for TAA and streamlined procedures. In hindsight the modifications appear too little, too late, and support for the program was lukewarm. It was not possible to regain organized labor's backing for major new trade liberalization efforts at that time. Still, TAA was used for deflecting some protectionist pressure, and annual expenditures surged to $1.6 billion by 1980. But the combination of very large industries that enjoyed large wage premiums (autos, steel) seeking assistance, the accumulating evidence that TAA payments simply delayed reemployment, and realization that the efficiency objectives of retaining and relocation were not being met, all undercut support for the program.[24] Funding and benefits were cut back by the Reagan administration in 1981. The NAFTA debate reinvigorated support for trade-impacted workers and resulted in a special supplemental assistance program (NAFTA-TAA). Two innovations were to extend benefits to workers in firms that relocated to Canada or Mexico, regardless of whether there was a trade impact, and to give assistance to workers in upstream firms that supply the downstream, trade-impacted firms. As of fiscal 2000, TAA cash assistance and training expenditures were $349 million, with 36,000 recipients, and NAFTA-TAA expenditures were $66 million, with 4000 recipients (Storey, 2000).

In retrospect, the premise of TAA appears somewhat naive. Workers are unlikely to welcome lay-offs, even if they are fully compensated for earnings loss during unemployment and given training and assistance with job searches in a timely fashion. Who wishes to lose tenure and a seniority wage premium and face the psychological costs of unemployment if import protection is an available alternative? Moreover, TAA does not compensate for what are often substantial wage and earnings losses after reemployment. In any event, it is difficult to distinguish between job losses occasioned by trade from losses due to demand shifts, corporate mismanagement, technology, and a host of other reasons. And the fundamental question remains as to why trade-related job displacement deserves special attention.

These considerations, together with a desire to neutralize labor's opposition to further trade liberalization efforts, led to new proposals to assist all displaced workers, regardless of cause. For example, Kletzer and Litan (2001) proposed a system of "wage insurance" and subsidized health insurance for qualified workers. The wage insurance would replace some frac-

[24]Destler (1998).

tion of reduced earnings for workers taking lower-wage jobs; the health insurance subsidy would apply (with time limits) during their period of unemployment. All benefits, however, would be available only when new employment was obtained, providing incentive for an early return to work. The Trade Act of 2002 adopted some of these proposals in its reform of TAA. Taking a cue from the NAFTA-TAA scheme, workers in both supplying and downstream industries may be eligible for coverage; older workers may receive up to 50 percent of any loss of wages when they are reemployed; and certain workers may be eligible for income tax credits for their health insurance costs.

▶ TRADE, WAGES, AND INEQUALITY

Even if trade-related actual job losses were minimal, there would still be a legitimate concern for the effects of trade on wages and income inequality. This concern reached a peak in the United States in the early and mid-1990s, partly as a result of the intense public debate surrounding NAFTA. More fundamental was the long period of stagnation and, for many workers, a decline in real wages and sharply increasing inequality in wages and incomes between educated, skilled workers and workers with lower levels of education and skills. In the latter half of the 1990s the economic boom, the attainment of full employment, and some improvement in wages took the edge off of the debate, even as income inequality increased.[25]

Trends in wages and income disparities for the two decades from the mid-1970s to the mid-1990s were quite dramatic. Between 1973 and 1995 the average real earnings per hour of American workers fell by 0.44 percent per year, despite labor productivity growth of 1.02 percent annually. This was in sharp contrast to the 1960–1973 period, in which real earnings rose by 2.04 percent and productivity by 3.01 percent annually.[26] Increases in earnings inequality was even more dramatic. The lowest-paid 25 percent of male workers lost 18.5 percent in real earnings, although female workers gained 2.1 percent, over the 1973–1993 period. The highest-paid 5 percent of workers gained 13.9 percent (30.7 percent for females) over the same

[25]Average real hourly earnings increased a cumulative 7 percent from 1993 to November 2000 (Council of Economic Advisors, 2001).

[26]Collins (1998 [a], Table 1.1). Labor compensation, which includes fringe benefits, fell from 2.67 percent annually in the earlier period to 0.67 percent in 1973–1995.

period.[27] The increasing income disparity was closely correlated with education, with the ratio of earnings for college-educated vs. high school–educated workers rising from a low of about 1.32 in 1979 to a peak of about 1.74 in 1994.[28] This differential came to be known as the skill premium, although education and skills are not identical.

The deterioration in the absolute and relative earnings of U.S. labor coincided with major shifts in the level and pattern of U.S. trade. Between 1970 and 1987 the ratio of merchandise imports to GDP more than doubled, from 3.8 percent to 8.6 percent, and rose further to 10.1 percent in 1995. Moreover, imports from low-wage developing countries accounted for a rising share of booming imports, increasing from 18 percent of manufactures imports in 1973 to 34 percent in 1995. Thus, it was logical to investigate the role of trade in wage suppression and earnings inequality in the United States, quite apart from specific policy issues such as NAFTA or the Uruguay Round Agreements.[29]

And at least on the surface, standard trade theory tends to implicate trade in these wage trends, especially increasing trade in manufactures with low-wage developing countries. The Heckscher-Ohlin trade model has been the workhorse of trade theory for decades. As all trade textbooks demonstrate, the H-O model leads directly to the Factor Price Equalization theorem (FPE) if certain conditions obtain. The logic is that if technology is the same everywhere and if industrial countries are relatively well endowed with skilled labor and developing countries are relatively well endowed with unskilled labor, trade in goods with different skill labor intensities will tend to equalize product prices and hence wages internationally. To obtain perfect equalization, demanding and unrealistic assumptions must obtain, but a *tendency* for U.S. trade with low-wage/low-skilled developing countries to drive down the wage of unskilled labor in the United States sounds plausible to the general public and, indeed, to many econo-

[27]Collins (1998 [a], Table 1.2, after Burtless).

[28]Collins (1998 [a], Fig. 1.1).

[29]The trade-jobs-wages issue has been muted in Europe, in part because redistributional and labor market policies have been generally successful in avoiding rising wage and income inequality. The European problem, however, has been very high levels of unemployment. In principle, trade liberalization could have manifested itself in the United States through rising wage inequality and in Europe through rising unemployment. Both could reflect a relative decline in demand for unskilled labor, consequent to trade changes. See Brenton and Pelkman (1998) for analysis of the issue in Europe.

mists. Note that this proposition is not the long-discredited pauper labor argument, which would assert that high-wage workers in the United States cannot compete with imports from low-wage countries. That erroneous argument neglects the foundations of *comparative* advantage and neglects differences in the productivity of U.S. *vs.* developing-country labor. Instead, FPE is a fundamental proposition of mainstream trade theory, albeit hedged by highly restrictive assumptions.

A relevant and long-established proposition from the same conventional trade theory is the Stopler-Samuelson (S-S) theorem, which asserts that under certain conditions the real wage of the factor used intensively in producing a good will fall if the relative price of that good falls. The connection of S-S to the wage inequality debate is obvious. If trade with developing countries causes the relative price of unskilled labor–intensive goods (e.g., garments, toys, shoes) to fall, the real wages of unskilled labor in the United States will fall in relative and absolute terms. Thus, basic theory tends to put proponents of trade liberalization on the defensive when seeking explanations for the long decline in the wages of unskilled workers in the United States.

The empirical demonstration that trade was responsible for substantial wage changes in the United States has been difficult and controversial. One reason is that trade is conflated with other dimensions of globalization, including increased capital flows (portfolio and direct investment by MNCs), international flows of technology, and especially for the United States, large increases in legal and illegal immigrants, many of whom are low-skilled workers. Moreover, it is possible to build models and adduce empirical support for technological change, rather than trade, as the prime determinant of wage trends in the United States. In these studies technological change is assumed to be biased in favor of skilled workers, disproportionately increasing the demand for and wages of educated workers and reducing the demand for unskilled workers.

We do not need to describe in detail the empirical debate that engaged trade and labor economists for much of the 1990s.[30] It is sufficient to note the two principal approaches. The first is known as the factor content method and bears some similarity to the trade-employment balance studies described earlier. In its simplest form this method measures the

[30]Good sources include Collins (1998b), Cline (1997), Feenstra (2000), and the articles contained in the Spring 1997 issue of *The Journal of Economic Perspectives.*

changes in the *effective* supplies of labor at different skill levels due to trade. This is accomplished by multiplying a matrix of labor skill coefficients in various industries by a vector of net trade changes (i.e., imports minus exports at the sector level). The results for the United States show increases in effective supply of unskilled labor, working through the imports of unskilled labor–intensive products. The supply shift is then translated into a decline in unskilled labor wages (or relative wages) through an elasticity estimate.[31] One difficulty with this approach, which it shares with the trade-employment balance studies, is that it does not account for interconnections and linkages in an economy. Specifically, the trade changes that precipitate the wage changes are considered exogenous, not endogenous, as they would be in a properly specified general equilibrium model. Another point of controversy in the factor content approach is the appropriate sectoral factor coefficients to use. Wood (1994) argued that the use of U.S. coefficients is incorrect and the coefficients should be drawn from developing-country economies where the unskilled labor coefficients in production were much higher. When this is done the unskilled labor content of increased imports is much higher and the calculated effects of trade with developing countries on unskilled wages in industrial countries is much stronger, suggesting that trade has, indeed, played a major role in increasing wage inequality.

The factor content approach is not an explicit test of the H-O model and the S-S theorem, which in its strict form shows that relative factor prices (relative skilled-unskilled wages) are determined by relative prices of skilled vs. unskilled labor–intensive goods. Accordingly, the second approach to empirical testing of the trade-wage inequality puzzle was to look for evidence that the relative prices of unskilled labor–intensive goods had fallen. Despite some problems with the data, the conclusion was that the price of *skilled* labor–intensive goods had fallen. Some researchers took this as evidence that the role of trade in wage inequality was minimal and, by default, technological changes were responsible for declining demand for unskilled labor and hence decline in their wages. Another awkward fact was that the standard H-O theory predicted that all sectors, producing both skilled and unskilled labor–intensive goods and by implication nontradeables, would shift toward more unskilled labor–intensive production

[31]An inelastic unskilled labor supply in the United States indicates a larger wage fall is necessary to clear the unskilled labor market.

methods as a result of trade. This has not happened, and indeed the opposite occurred in the tradeable and nontradeable goods sectors of the U.S. economy. The techniques of production have become more skilled labor–using. This last finding also supports technological change over trade as the explanation for wage trends.

It may be that the H-O model is too narrow and rigid to use as the theoretical basis for empirical explanation of wage trends. A model that incorporates MNCs and the increase in the practice of outsourcing labor intensive processes might be more suitable. If so, technology would play a different but still key role, as improvements in transport and communications have supported the expansion of MNCs and outsourcing.

It is unclear how much influence this substantive academic debate on trade and wages has had on U.S. trade policy. Labor's shift on trade policy predates the full evidence of declining real wages and certainly predates the academic debate of the 1990s. The labor movement did not need empirical tests of the S-S theorem to claim a threat from low-wage imports. The issue of low-wage imports did find a role in the NAFTA debate, but the dominant concern was for job loss and wage suppression through foreign investment and MNCs (Ross Perot's giant sucking sound). Nevertheless, adding the wage suppression argument to the "runaway plant" and job loss arguments added some respectability to labor's opposition to NAFTA and later to its stance at Seattle. It is interesting that the academic debate (not the popular debate) has centered more on trade than on the wages effect of foreign investment. In any event, a frequent response to those concerned with a low-skill wage threat has been to emphasize that expanding exports would increase demand for and wages of high-skilled workers. This hardly satisfies low-skilled workers and their advocates.

By the time the debate over permanent normal trade relations (PNTR) for China reached full pitch in 1999, many factors had changed. As was repeatedly emphasized, PNTR was asymmetrical—no new U.S. trade concessions toward China but substantial concessions on their part. Also, U.S. unemployment was at its lowest level in 30 years. There were pressures on Congress to *increase* immigration, although this was mainly limited to high-tech firms seeking high-skilled workers. Real earnings of all U.S. workers, including unskilled, had started to rise. Starting in 1997, foreign direct investment into the United States exceeded the outflow by a substantial margin, undercutting runaway plant argument. Perhaps most significantly, organized labor chose to concentrate on the internationalization of fair labor practices and the establishment of core labor standards in new international trade agreements at Seattle.

At this point we can conclude that the widespread perception that the purpose of trade is jobs has been influential but incorrect and that the serious issues are labor-adjustment costs and wage suppression. The newest element in the labor-trade debate is the question of fair labor standards in developing countries, and this is considered in Chapter 10.

▶ REFERENCES

Brechling, F. 1978. A Time Series Analysis of Labor Turnover. In: W. G. Dewald (ed.). *The Impact of International Trade on Employment: A Conference with the U.S. Department of Labor.* Washington, DC: GPO.

Brenton, Paul, and Jacques Pelkmans. 1998. *Global Trade and European Workers.* London: MacMillan Press.

Cline, William. 1997. *Trade and Income Distribution.* Washington, DC: Institute for International Economics.

Collins, Susan. 1998 (a). Economic Integration and the American Worker: An Overview. In: Susan Collins (ed.). *Imports, Exports and the American Worker.* Washington, DC: Brookings Institution.

Collins, Susan (ed.). 1998 (b). *Imports, Exports and the American Worker.* Washington, DC: Brookings Institution.

Commission on International Trade and Investment Policy (Williams Commission). 1971. *United States International Economic Policy in an Interdependent World.* Washington, DC: GPO.

Corson, Walter, Walter Nicholson, David Richardson, Andrea Vayda. 1979. *Final Report: Survey of Trade Adjustment Assistance Recipients.* Prepared by Mathematica Policy Research Inc. Washington, DC: Bureau of International Labor Affairs, U.S. Department of Labor.

Council of Economic Advisors. 2001. *Economic Report of the President.* Washington, DC: GPO.

Destler, I. M. 1998. Trade Politics and Labor Issues: 1953–1995. In: Susan Collins (ed.). *Imports, Exports and the American Worker.* Washington, DC: Brookings Institution.

Feenstra, Robert. 2000. *The Impact of International Trade on Wages.* Chicago: University of Chicago Press.

Fooks, Marvin. 1971. Trade Adjustment Assistance. In: Commission on International Trade and Investment Policy. *United States International Economic Policy in an Interdependent World.* Washington, DC: GPO.

Frank, Charles. 1978. *Foreign Trade and Domestic Aid.* Washington, DC: Brookings Institution.

Haveman, Jon. 1998. The Influence of Changing Trade Patterns on Displacement of Labor. *The International Trade Journal* XII(2):259–292.

Hufbauer, Gary, and Jeffrey Schott. 1993. *NAFTA: An Assessment.* Washington, DC: Institute for International Economics.

Jacobson, Louis, Robert LaLonde, Daniel Sullivan. 1993. Earning Losses of Displaced Workers. *American Economic Review* 83:685–709.

Jenkins, Glenn, Graham Glenday, John Evans, Claude Montmarquette. 1978. Trade Adjustment Assistance: The Costs of Adjustment and Policy Proposals. Ottawa: Economic Analysis Branch, Department of Trade and Commerce.

Katz, Jules. 1998. Comment on I. M. Destler Trade Politics and Labor Issues 1953–1995. In: Susan Collins (ed.). *Imports, Exports and the American Worker.* Washington, DC: Brookings Institution.

Kletzer, Lori. 1998. International Trade and Job Displacement in U.S. Manufacturing: 1979–91. In: Susan Collins (ed.). *Imports, Exports and the American Worker.* Washington, DC: Brookings Institution.

Kletzer, Lori. 2001. *Job Loss From Imports: Measuring the Costs.* Washington, DC: Institute for International Economics.

Kletzer, Lori, and Robert Litan. 2001. *A Prescription to Relieve Worker Anxiety: Policy Brief.* Washington, DC: Institute for International Economics.

Krueger, Anne. 1978. Impact of LDC Exports on Employment in American Industry. Presented at International Economic Study Group Annual Conference, Sussex, England, September.

Neumann, George. 1978. The Direct Labor Market Effects of the Trade Adjustment Assistance Program: The Evidence from the TAA Survey. In: William Dewald (ed.). *The Impact of International Trade and Investment on Employment.* Washington, DC: GPO.

Pearson, Charles. 1984. *Import Surges: The Role of Japan and The Developing Countries.* Washington, DC: U.S.–Japan Study Center, SAIS Johns Hopkins.

Pearson, Charles, and Gerry Salembier. 1983. *Trade, Employment and Adjustment.* Montreal: The Institute for Research on Public Policy.

Storey, James. 2000. Trade Adjustment Assistance for Workers. Washington DC: Congressional Research Service, 1B9803.

Wood, Adrian. 1994. *North-South Trade, Employment and Inequality.* Oxford, UK: Clarendon Press.

CHAPTER

6

THE ALLURE OF PREFERENTIAL TRADE

Preferential trade is the polite name for discriminatory trade. Extending trade preferences to one set of countries automatically and inevitably discriminates against other countries.[1] The United States has exhibited an ambivalent, almost schizophrenic approach to preferential trade agreements. In the past century our policy *vis a vis* preferential trade has made two U turns, effectively completing a full circle and apparently returning to its position at the end of the 19th century. American trade policy entered the 20th century very comfortable with preferential trade, as illustrated by its active pursuit of reciprocity treaties with individual countries and its rather lonely insistence on conditional rather than unconditional MFN.[2] Both positions not only tolerate discrimination (preferences) but virtually require it. The United States dropped its insistence on conditional MFN in the 1920s and became an ardent opponent of most preferential trade arrangements in the early post–World War II period.[3] In the 1980s, how-

[1]An alternative term to preferential is regionalism, but not all preferential agreements involve geographical proximity. Preferential trade agreements (PTAs) include customs unions (CUs), free trade agreements (FTAs), and arrangements in which only some sectors exhibit low or zero trade restrictions *vis a vis* members. The U.S.-Canada auto pact was an example of the last.

[2]Viner (1951) states that conditional MFN is "simply a polite way of not practicing most-favored-nation treatment at all."

[3]For political reasons it accepted preferential trade in Europe, starting with the 1952 European Coal and Steel Community.

ever, the allure of preferential trade again beckoned and, with surprisingly little public debate, preferential trade agreements are now welcomed and indeed actively sought. Although the two U turns have returned preferential trade to favor, the world trade and economic systems are much changed over the past century, and these changes should be borne in mind when current attitudes are considered.

This chapter describes the most recent turn in U.S. policy welcoming preferential trade agreements. But before doing so it is useful to first discuss some conceptual and theoretical issues in preferential trade, and then put U.S. policy in a broader international context. The chapter concludes with some comments on what may be the central issue of concern today—whether preferential trade is a building block or stumbling block to further multilateral trade liberalization.[4]

▶ THE ANALYSIS OF PREFERENTIAL TRADE

Although preferential trade agreements have a long history,[5] modern analysis of their effects starts in 1950 with the eminent economist Jacob Viner.[6] His great insight was that removing trade barriers against one set of countries (the partners), while retaining barriers against others, may or may not increase economic efficiency and welfare. To demonstrate this he developed the concepts of trade creation and trade diversion. If preferential removal of trade barriers shifts the source of supply from higher-cost domestic supply to a lower-cost source in a partner country (trade creation), welfare presumably increases. If, however, preferential tariff treatment shifts the source of supply from low-cost third countries to higher-cost partner countries favored by preferential access (trade diversion), welfare presumably declines. Thus, the efficiency and welfare effects of preferential trade are ambiguous and depend very much on the facts of specific cases.[7] This insight is now recognized as a clear example of the

[4]The terms were coined by Jagdish Bhagwati in 1991.

[5]See Machlup (1977), Pomfret (1988). The volume edited by Bhagwati, Krishna, and Panagariya (1999) contains many of the most significant contributions over the past half century.

[6]Viner (1950).

[7]Simply measuring the *amount* of trade created or diverted does not measure the welfare effects of the trade changes, as the cost differentials among suppliers are critical.

broader Theory of the Second Best, which states that efficiency and welfare may or may not be improved if one economic distortion is removed but others are left in place.[8]

Economic theory since Viner has refined the analysis and has shown that the inclusion of consumption effects, terms of trade effects, and specific initial conditions with regard to tariffs and trade patterns can modify Viner's rather sharp distinction between welfare-enhancing trade creation and welfare-reducing trade diversion.[9] Many of the analytical refinements make the welfare effects of preferential trade increasingly ambiguous. To be specific, Viner's original analysis was vague with regard to PTA-induced expansion of demand (lower prices expanding the market), which affects consumer welfare and hence the net calculation. Moreover, if the preferential trade agreement creates a "large" market, the terms of trade of the member countries *vis a vis* others will be affected. The presumption is that within some range, the greater the amount of trade diversion, the greater the gain for the union as a whole from improved terms of trade, but the exact results and their internal distribution within the preferential area depend in part on the level chosen for the postagreement external tariff(s). The incorporation in the analysis of economies of scale, of trade in differentiated products, and of noneconomic objectives in welfare functions also tended to blur the straightforward welfare distinctions between trade creation and trade diversion.

The static Vinerian approach of trade creation and trade diversion has other serious limitations. Most analysts would agree that a durable preferential trade agreement will increase investment from within and outside the region, but this dynamic effect is difficult to model and measure. And the allocation of that investment among the members will be critical to the internal distribution of the benefits and, hence, the incentives to join and the viability of the agreement itself. The internal allocation of investment among the members of preferential agreements has been of utmost importance for policy-makers but has scarcely been analyzed in theoretical work.

In recent years the theory of preferential trade, while not abandoning

[8]We all live in the murky world of the second best. With multiple, pervasive distortions it is difficult to demonstrate in the abstract that *any* policy intervention, from trade liberalization to antitrust policy to environmental protection, necessarily increases welfare. The specifics of the situation matter.

[9]For a good recent survey, see Panagariya (2000).

Viner's contribution, has pursued new approaches. These include insights from the political economy literature, strategic trade/game theoretic contributions, and economic geography. One question is whether geographic propinquity creates "natural" trade blocs due to low transport costs.[10] Another question in the political economy vein is under what conditions a campaign contribution/lobbying model of trade policy supports preferential trade agreements and whether such agreements are biased toward excluding certain sectors from preferential trade. A final issue, pursued below, is how preferential trade interacts with multilateral trade liberalization: does it facilitate or hinder multilateral trade liberalization? In much of this analysis, the trade creation—trade diversion distinction, which was originally intended to illuminate national and global welfare effects—takes on a new role. If a lobbying model of trade policy formation is used, trade creation and trade diversion estimates shed light on the strength of lobbying activities and, hence, the viability and structure of the PTA. From the point of view of the member's export sector, it is a matter of indifference whether increased demand arises from trade creation or trade diversion; both are welcomed.

Trade conditions have also changed since Viner's analysis. Tariff barriers have been radically reduced in most countries so that tariff discrimination no longer packs the same punch that it did decades ago. At the same time, the functional scope of preferential trade agreements has expanded to include investment provisions, environmental and labor clauses, harmonization of technical regulations and of competition policy, dedicated dispute settlement procedures, and many more features. The analytically simple world of preferential tariffs as the hallmark of formal economic integration has disappeared, and "tight" analytical theories of economic integration that incorporate these new features are scarce. Pref Trade Agree

Empirical research on PTAs is extensive. A standard approach for *ex ante* analysis of proposed PTAs is to build a computable general equilibrium model, to "shock" the model by preferential tariff reductions, and to observe the trade, production, and employment results. Although CGE models can offer some insight into prospective agreements, they also have some well-known shortcomings. One weakness is that the analyst can influence outcomes through his/her model structure and parameter choices. *Ex post* analysis of existing PTAs must establish a hypothetical bench-

[10]See Frankel et al. (1997). The U.S. has or has proposed FTAs from Jordan to Singapore!

mark—what trade would have been in the absence of the PTA—against which observed trade is compared. These studies can use gravity models, extrapolation of trends, or market share analysis to set the benchmark, and from that they infer the trade, production, and employment effects of the PTA.[11] There is general agreement in empirical work that trade creation occurred in Europe, but the picture is mixed elsewhere (Srinivasan et al., 1993).

The theoretical refinements since Viner appear to have had little impact on the actual conduct of U.S. preferential trade policy. Public policy discussions in the United States of the two most significant PTAs, the Canada–U.S. FTA and NAFTA, were driven by the traditional (and questionable) issues of export expansion and jobs, not by trade theory. Political objectives were also important in NAFTA (as they have been in Europe since the 1950s). The empirical studies estimating employment effects were much debated and influential, however.

▶ THE INTERNATIONAL CONTEXT

It is important to recognize that GATT, which generally champions nondiscrimination, contains an explicit exemption for free trade areas and customs unions (Article XXIV). The arrangements, however, should conform to three requirements, the first two of which would help minimize trade diversion and maximize trade creation: (1) postagreement tariffs and other trade restrictions should not on average exceed preagreement levels, (2) the parties to the agreement should eliminate trade restrictions on substantially all trade among themselves,[12] and (3) nonmembers are entitled to compensation in the form of equivalent trade concessions if the agreement results in an increase in trade restrictions facing them. This last provision provoked a brief but bitter dispute between the United States and the EC,

[11]Gravity models explain the geographic pattern of trade on the basis of income, population, distance, and contiguity. Adding a dummy variable for preferential trade measures its effect, if any.

[12]This requirement does not apply to preferential agreements among developing countries. Also, preferential agreements predating GATT were grandfathered.

when accession of Spain and Portugal in 1986 resulted in U.S. export losses in corn and soybeans to these two markets.[13]

By and large, these are reasonable requirements and offer some protection against preferential agreements whose *raison d'être* is pure discrimination without any pretense of real trade liberalization. Moreover, they limit but do not eliminate the temptation to exempt import-sensitive sectors from the agreement. Nevertheless, even if the three conditions obtain, some discrimination is inevitable. More problematic, GATT, which was supposed to review them, has a long history of tolerance for preferential arrangements that fall short of these conditions and has shown little appetite for enforcement.[14] As with other agreements, this tolerant attitude facilitated the U.S.–Canadian FTA in 1989.

GATT's *laissez faire* attitude was the backdrop for two waves of preferential trade agreements. The first wave gained force in the 1960s, and except for the EC and its successor, the EU, it basically failed. This wave consisted exclusively of North–North and South–South agreements. The United States stood apart and did not participate. In the North, the EC flourished, and its less-ambitious counterpart, the European Free Trade Association (EFTA), was essentially absorbed into the EC with the accession of the UK in 1973.[15] Although the United States had serious reservations about the inward orientation of the EC, and especially its agricultural policy, it has been generally supportive of economic integration in Europe on political as well as economic grounds.

[13]U.S. exports of corn and soybeans to Spain and Portugal were about $1.3 billion before their entrance into the EC. Under the CAP they were obligated to shift some import supply to the EC. The compensation agreement negotiated between the United States and the EC provided for a quota for corn imports from non-EC suppliers, a waiver from the requirement that Portugal reserve 15 percent of its grains market for EC suppliers and some EC tariff reductions on other products. Haniotis (1990) estimates the EC enlargement cost the United States $147 million in export sales of corn and soybeans but that the compensation agreement reduced this loss to $88 million.

[14]Grilli (1997); Panagariya (2000). The requirements themselves are not foolproof. Many developing countries set actual tariff levels well below levels bound in the GATT. If they join an FTA, they are free to raise external tariffs from actual to the higher bound levels.

[15]The remnant members of EFTA, Sweden, Finland, Austria, Norway, and Iceland, created the European Economic Area in 1994 as an FTA between EFTA and the EU, but almost immediately four of the five formally joined the EU.

The first wave of preferential trade agreements in the South is in many respects a more interesting story, despite its failures. The principal efforts were the Latin American Free Trade Agreement (1960), the Central American Common Market (1961), the Caribbean Free Trade Association (1968), the ANDEAN Pact (1969, revitalized in 1991), and the East African Community (1967). Asian countries were on the sidelines.[16] It must be remembered that South–South preferential trade agreements flourished in the era of import substitution (IS)–led industrialization. IS, of course, was based in part on an incorrect assumption that developing countries could not be competitive in world markets for manufactures. This proved to be a snare and a delusion, as the divergent performances of Latin America and Asian countries subsequently demonstrated. Nevertheless, if one were to accept the basic assumptions undergirding IS—that primary commodity prices were in secular decline; that there were positive growth and development externalities associated with industrialization; and that world markets for manufactures were out of reach—the logic for preferential trade agreements was plausible. Such agreements would broaden the (regional) market for manufactures and permit attainment of greater economies of scale. Exploiting regional comparative advantage is a more efficient strategy than autarky, and IS at a regional level is more efficient than at the national level. Moreover, payments for intraregional trade could be made in "soft" currencies, and export earnings in dollars or other hard currencies could be conserved for essential imports from the North.

In any event, S-S preferential trade agreements collapsed or became moribund before significant benefits could be realized. An underlying cause surely was the erroneous assumptions of the IS strategy. These included the mistaken view that developing countries were uncompetitive in the export of manufactures, noted above, and the incorrect assumption that if a little judicious and targeted infant industry protection was good, widespread protection of the entire industrial sector was even better. In fact, protection simply raised costs and made exporting more difficult. Moreover, the rents enjoyed by privileged, protected national firms and the political influence of these firms under IS also played a role. Even regional competition was to be avoided. At another level, differences in market size, income levels, and industrialization among member countries in

[16]ASEAN, established in 1977, did not establish an FTA until 1991, and it is still incomplete.

S-S preferential schemes led to skewed patterns of investment and benefits that could not be remediated through intra-bloc transfer payments and differential rates of tariff reduction. Intraregional wrangling over investment planning also contributed.

By and large, the industrial countries, including the United States, took a tolerant attitude toward preferential agreements among countries in the South, although it was apparent that they fell short of true FTAs or CUs. There were several reasons. First, their manufacturing sectors were very small by world standards, and the potential for trade diversion was thought to be minimal. Second, with regional payment arrangements in place, any increase in intraregional trade would free up hard currencies for their imports from industrial countries, whose aggregate exports to the members were unlikely to suffer. Third, this was the high-water mark for the import substitution strategy in Latin America. From the perspective of the United States, the alternative to preferential agreements in the South was likely to be greater efforts at national self-sufficiency and hence an even more inefficient development strategy.

The second wave of preferential trade, starting in the 1980s, was fundamentally different. Import substitution was *passé,* North–South agreements were reached, tariff preferences were of far less significance, and the United States became an active and eager participant. It is therefore time to look more directly at our involvement in preferential trade.

▶ REVIVING AN OLD FLAME

After World War II the United States was a strong supporter of nondiscriminatory (MFN) trade and a staunch opponent of most preferential trade arrangements. This reflected in part the view that preferential trade, and especially the UK's imperial trade system, had contributed to the collapse of trade in the 1930s.[17] The principled U.S. position was slightly marred by the Philippine Trade Act of 1946, which provided that the Philippines would continue to enjoy first free trade and then tariff preferences in the U.S. market for up to 28 years following its independence. In

[17]Trade blocs in the 1930s, reinforced by discriminatory quantitative restraints, included preferences within the British Commonwealth, a bloc centered on Germany and including central and southeast Europe, a France-based bloc including its colonies and protectorates, and Japan's trade bloc in East Asia (Korea, Formosa, Manchuria).

return the United States received preferential status for its exports to the Philippines as well as special and preferential rights to make investments in natural resources and public utilities.[18] The defeat of Japan had brought to an end the ill-fated East-Asian preferential trade system with Japan as hub. The major remaining target was European preferential arrangements with its former colonies, mainly in Africa. The United States did not oppose EC preferences granted to African and other ACP countries but did object to reciprocal preferences granted by these countries to the EC.[19]

The Auto Sector

The U.S. re-embrace of preferential trade arrangements started inconspicuously, with small steps and without great public debate. The first move was the United States–Canada Automotive Products Agreement of 1965 (Trezise, 1971). The origin of that agreement was not some abstract vision of trade liberalization, but instead an effort to deflect a rather nasty trade dispute brewing between the two countries. Canada suffered from high-cost, inefficient production of automotive products, as its small market did not permit economies of scale. Despite a tariff of 17.5 percent on new vehicles and up to 25 percent on equipment parts, the Canadian industry lagged the United States, and Canada ran a substantial automotive trade deficit. In 1962 and 1963 Canada attempted to stimulate its domestic industry by offering tariff remissions to its domestic firms (mostly subsidiaries of U.S. firms), provided they increased their automotive exports. Tying import duty remissions to export expansion is tantamount to an export subsidy, illegal under GATT, and the U.S. Treasury received complaints from U.S. parts manufacturers.

Rather than risk a trade war, the United States and Canada concluded the Automotive Products pact, rationalizing auto production through specialization and scale economies in most of North America. This agreement was greatly aided by cross-border ownership of much of the Canadian auto industry, the absence at that time of significant auto competition from ei-

[18]The new Philippine government also gave up the right to impose export taxes, change the dollar value of the peso, or restrict capital movements without U.S. approval (Power and Sicat, 1971).

[19]ACP (African, Caribbean, and Pacific) refers to those countries, mostly former colonies, that enjoyed preferential access to the EC.

ther Europe or Japan, and strong affiliations between the automotive unions in the two countries. Because the auto pact fell short of the "substantially all trade" requirement for an FTA, a GATT waiver was sought and obtained. Moreover, the agreement did not conform to the common sense meaning of free trade, even in the automotive sector. Some automotive products (e.g., tires, replacement parts, used cars) were excluded from duty-free treatment. Canada allowed duty-free imports of vehicles only by manufacturers; individuals in Canada had to pay a 15% duty. Moreover, and most significant, automotive manufacturers were required to meet minimum Canadian value-added and Canadian production to Canadian sales ratios. In fact, the purpose from Canada's perspective was not free trade but maintenance of a high level of domestic production, and the pact might well be dubbed a "sectoral investment agreement."[20] The agreement undoubtedly increased efficiency and trade but had the hallmarks of managed rather than free trade.

GSP

The origins of the Generalized System of Preferences (GSP) date to the early 1960s, when some developing countries were starting to see the benefits of exporting manufactures. The call for tariff preferences to be granted to developing countries was taken up by the newly created United Nations Conference on Trade and Development (UNCTAD) in 1964. The United States led the opposition (Sapir and Lundberg, 1984). In part, this was a principled opposition to weakening MFN, but it also had protectionist overtones. The United States found few allies, however, and eventually changed its stance. In 1971 GATT voted a waiver from MFN obligations for GSP; in the same year the EC introduced its scheme; and rather grudgingly the United States followed suit in 1976. In the end, the U.S. scheme was hemmed in by limitations on country and product coverage (e.g., footwear, textiles and apparel, and steel items were excluded).[21] The U.S. GSP system continues to this day, but its consequences are dampened through multilateral tariff reductions and newer preferential arrangements such as the Caribbean Basin Initiative and NAFTA.

[20]As pointed out by Sperry Lea (1987).

[21]There were also rules of origin and "competitive need" restrictions, as well as requirements that at some point countries "graduate" from preferences.

US–Israel FTA

The United States entered its first formal free trade agreement by signing an FTA with Israel in 1985. The direct economic stakes for both countries were minimal. Before the agreement, U.S. commercial trade (exports plus imports) with Israel was only 0.6 percent of its total trade in goods. By 1995, at the end of a lengthy transition period, it had risen to 0.8 percent. The United States was Israel's largest single trade partner, taking 25 percent of its exports and supplying 20 percent of its nonmilitary imports (Frenkel, 1988). But 93 percent of Israel's exports to the United States already entered duty-free. The principal economic motivation for the United States was to neutralize any commercial advantage that the EC may have obtained in its earlier (1975) FTA with Israel. On the Israeli side, the main economic objective was to make permanent the duty-free access it was then enjoying under the U.S. GSP program.[22]

In a broader view, however, the U.S.–Israel FTA was of some importance. Through the FTA, the United States signaled for the first time a willingness to consider preferential trade liberalization in addition to multilateral negotiations through GATT. Indeed, it was the U.S. failure in 1982 to convince major trading countries to launch a new round of multilateral trade negotiations that prompted the U.S.–Israel initiative. The use of this device, the active pursuit of preferential liberalization when multilateral negotiations were sluggish or stagnant, was subsequently part of U.S. strategy in the Canada–U.S. FTA process and was used again with NAFTA. It can be argued that the APEC initiative in the early 1990s was a subtle prod to the Uruguay Round process, even though APEC has yet to establish any specific trade preferences.[23] Currently, the proposed FTAA can be viewed as a spur to the new WTO round launched in 2001 in Doha.

A second notable feature is what the FTA with Israel did and did not include. There was no agreement to modify the principal protectionist barriers in the U.S. market: the MFA and the use of import quotas in agricul-

[22]Forty-one percent of Israeli exports to the U.S. benefited from GSP. U.S. MFN duty rates on principal imports then ranged from 2.3 to 9.3 percent, affording Israel some margin of preference.

[23]APEC, which includes developed and developing countries, would not be permitted to establish preferences in only a few sectors. The "threat" of an APEC bloc was not especially credible.

ture.[24] Nor was there any modification of U.S. laws and procedures with regard to dumping and the use of countervailing duties or the escape clause. And when tariff concessions were established, the most import sensitive sectors in the United States received the longest periods of protection in the 10-year transition period. On the other hand, the FTA did break new ground in considering matters beyond tariffs. It limited several of Israel's subsidy programs, liberalized government procurement practices, and prohibited certain trade-related investment requirements such as minimum export and domestic purchase requirements. And the FTA did include a "declaration" concerning trade in services. In this regard the FTA anticipated issues for negotiations in the Uruguay Round and provided something of a model for the broader array of issues addressed in NAFTA.

Looking North

The Canada–U.S. Free Trade Agreement, ratified in 1989, was a decisive step in the rehabilitation of preferential agreements as an integral component of U.S. trade policy. Unlike the U.S.–Israel FTA, the economic and commercial effects were expected to be significant. At the time of the agreement, just over 20 percent of U.S. trade in goods was with Canada, services trade was extensive, and almost 25 percent of U.S. foreign direct investment was in Canada. The stakes for Canada were even higher, with 67 percent of its trade conducted with the United States.

Canadian interest in an FTA grew out of several considerations. Natural resource exports, which had sustained Canada in the distant past, were judged inadequate for future prosperity. Manufacturing, coddled by protection and hampered by the small domestic market, was inefficient and high-cost. With British entry into the European Common Market in 1973, Canada had lost its preferential position in that market. After the 1982 effort to launch a new trade round failed, multilateral liberalization within GATT was stalled. And in Canada's principal market, the United States, support for liberal trade appeared to be yielding to resurgent protection. Especially irksome was U.S. use of administered protection and, in partic-

[24]This must be interpreted carefully. At the time there was no bilateral agreement on textiles between Israel and the United States, and the Commerce Department had authority to set line item quotas if it found "market disruption." The entire FTA almost collapsed when Commerce set a quota of 600,000 units for imported flannel sheets from Israel! (Frenkel, 1988, pp. 181–182).

ular, countervailing duty statutes.[25] Thus, Canada was motivated in part by defensive reasons.

The United States had a direct commercial interest in lower Canadian tariffs, which remained substantial even after the Tokyo Round cuts. More important, the United States was concerned about the climate for direct investment in Canada and access to Canadian energy supplies. In 1973 Canada had introduced its Foreign Investment Review Act to screen investments for their beneficial impact on the Canadian economy. Incoming investors were encouraged to commit to minimum export levels and domestic input purchase targets, employment goals, Canadian R & D expenditures, etc. (Schott and Smith, 1988). Although the requirement for domestic sourcing of inputs was later rejected by GATT in a case brought by the United States and less-restrictive investment rules were instituted in 1984, the United States saw an FTA as a vehicle for securing a liberal investment regime as well as liberal trade. Energy trade had also been contentious, with Canada temporarily cutting oil exports at the time of the Arab oil embargo and actively discriminating against U.S. energy investments. The United States in turn manipulated the wellhead price of natural gas to the disadvantage of Canadian producers and denied Canadian refiners access to potentially low-cost Alaskan crude (Verleger, 1988). Thus, ironing out energy trade disputes was an additional incentive.

At another level the United States, like Canada, was frustrated with the stalled multilateral process in GATT. The United States' view was that an FTA with Canada might serve one of two purposes: either to push the multilateral process forward or, if that were not possible, to experiment with an alternative trade system in which liberalizing-minded countries could do so, unshackled by multilateralism and MFN. Thus, the U.S. re-embrace of preferential trade had the usual commercial motives supported by foreign investment and energy security objectives, but it was also seen as a vehicle for reinvigorating the multilateral system or, failing that, as a fall-back posi-

[25]In an early case (1973), the United States imposed countervailing duties on imports of Michelin tires manufactured in Nova Scotia on the grounds that regional development aids to that depressed area were, in effect, export subsidies. The first softwood lumber subsidy case brought by the U.S. against Canada was rejected in 1983 but reversed with a finding of subsidies in 1986. For dispute settlement under the FTA, see the intriguingly titled book by William Davey, *Pine and Swine* (1996).

tion. In that sense, the FTA with Canada was very different than our 19th century experience with preferential trade.

The completed FTA with Canada moved beyond the earlier agreement with Israel. In addition to chapters on nontariff trade barriers (i.e., government procurement, product standards), it broke new ground in its inclusion of services, especially financial services; in establishing rules concerning investment and trade in energy; and by establishing a new, dedicated dispute-settlement procedure. These, of course, are precisely the areas that the Uruguay Round was in the early stages of addressing, and in that sense the FTA was bound to influence the content of the final Uruguay Round Agreements reached seven years later.

Finally, it is worth noting what was not addressed: environmental protection and natural resource conservation. Despite a long history of environmental and resource disputes between the two countries, dating to the Trail Smelter transboundary air pollution dispute of the 1930s and including acid rain, pollution of the Great Lakes, protection of fisheries, and fresh-water diversion projects, and despite the prominent role of energy and natural resource provisions in the agreement, it is silent with respect to environmental protection and conservation issues. While some environmental organizations in Canada opposed the agreement, the United States environmental community had no comment and, presumably, no interest.[26]

Looking South

The FTA with Canada unlocked a flurry of interest in preferential trade agreements. Studies of possible FTAs with the United States were undertaken in ASEAN, Australia, Japan, Jordan, Korea, Mexico, and Taiwan. By 2002 only one, the North American Free Trade Agreement (1992; United States, Canada, and Mexico) had come to fruition, although the United States had signed (not ratified) an FTA with Jordan, was pursuing FTAs with Chile and Singapore, and, in 1998, had initiated negotiations for a hemispheric arrangement, the Free Trade of the Americas Agreement (FTAA).

NAFTA consolidates U.S. enthusiasm for preferential trade, but in important respects it is unique. It was the first significant attempt to form a

[26]For Canadian environmental concerns, see Shrybman (1991–1992).

free trade area (or customs union) between a rich industrial country and a (relatively) poor developing country.[27] Like the U.S.–Canadian FTA, there was a disparity in absolute size. The U.S. economy was 25 times the size of Mexico's. But unlike the link to the North, the proposed economic agreement with Mexico provoked strong opposition from U.S. labor and, for the first time for *any* trade agreement, the active opposition from many environmental organizations. The raucous public debate on NAFTA has been matched only by the China trade debate of 1999–2000. Finally, the agreement was unique in that the United States had overarching foreign policy interests with Mexico, notably illegal immigration and drug trafficking, that colored the trade policy decisions.

U.S. economic interests in the NAFTA were straightforward. It wished to lock in Mexico's unilateral trade liberalization that had started in 1985 and to obtain full, tariff-free access to the Mexican market. It wished better and more secure access for its investment in Mexico. It wished to negotiate better protection of intellectual property, obtain access for financial services and agriculture, and open the telecommunications market. On a broader political level, the United States wished to "reward" Mexico for turning away from protection and hostility toward foreign investment through its market-liberalization efforts. The prevailing view was that an FTA would help Mexican growth, stimulate U.S. exports, and reduce illegal immigration. Finally, the Uruguay Round negotiations were dragging on in the background and, like the two earlier FTAs, NAFTA was viewed by some as both carrot and stick to bring that much delayed process to conclusion.

The abstract question of whether the United States wished to support MFN over preferential trade was not an issue. That die had been cast. Policy-makers judged that preferential trade was compatible with long-term multilateral liberalization. The attention to the potential for trade diversion vs. trade creation was also muted. Mexico was unlikely to suffer much

[27]In 1992 the average hourly wage in manufacturing was $11.46 in the United States and $2 in Mexico (at prevailing exchange rates). The two economies were already closely tied through the maquiladora program. In that arrangement, in effect since 1965, U.S.-owned plants were established along the border in Mexico to process or assemble imported components for subsequent export to the United States. In turn, the United States assessed import duties only on the value added by the assembly work done in Mexico. The duty-free treatment was permitted under sections 806.30 and 807.00 of the U.S. tariff code. By 1992 maquiladora exports accounted for one-third of total Mexican exports to the United States.

trade diversion, as two-thirds of its imports already came from the United States. The United States might expect to divert some trade in labor-intensive manufacturers away from Asian suppliers to Mexico, but few were bothered by this prospect. Trade diversion was mainly of concern to those small Western Hemisphere countries enjoying Caribbean Basin Initiative preferences.

The public debate over NAFTA centered on jobs, wages, and the environment. The old pauper labor argument was trotted out, together with the more modern embellishment of runaway plants and MNCs setting up export platforms in Mexico. The more serious issues of wage suppression and increasing income inequality were also raised, but the answers were muddied by the small size of Mexico relative to the United States and the difficulty in setting a plausible alternative. If NAFTA were not enacted, would low-wage imports simply come from Thailand or China? If MNCs were unsure of the investment climate in Mexico, would they simply go to Malaysia or Brazil or Indonesia?

The politics of legislating NAFTA in the United States led to two results. First, a number of special deals were cut to protect U.S. labor and the more sensitive sectors. For example, the rules of origin with regard to garments basically require that for duty-free treatment, the finished goods must be cut and sewn from fabric spun from North American fibers, protecting upstream U.S. textile manufacturing. Complicated and stringent rules of origin and transitional domestic-content rules were also established to the satisfaction and protection of U.S. auto makers. In the final crush to secure Congressional approval, President Clinton cut additional protectionist deals on a number of products, including citrus, sugar, and winter vegetables.

Second, President Clinton found it politically expedient to distinguish his support for NAFTA from the agreement reached earlier in the Bush administration. He did so by proposing and negotiating two side agreements, one dealing with labor issues and the second with environmental issues (see Chapter 7). The labor agreement addressed worker rights issues and is examined in Chapter 10.

In the end, organized labor remained strongly opposed to NAFTA, and the environmental community was split. And as described in Chapter 9, NAFTA marked the end of presidential fast-track authority for negotiating new trade agreements for almost a decade. At the broadest level, the passage of NAFTA confirmed the new "two-track" trade negotiation strategy of the United States: multilateral efforts through the GATT/WTO structure and active pursuit of preferential agreements on a bilateral or regional basis. The latter rests on the theoretically dubious proposition that some trade liberalization is better than none. But the century old allure of securing preferential access for U.S. exports to Latin America exerted its old charms.

In summary, the revival of U.S interest in preferential trade did not reflect a deliberate and conscious strategy, but was *ad hoc* and opportunistic. The auto pact with Canada averted a nasty subsidies fight and was aided by cross-border industry and labor ties; GSP was reluctantly granted and hedged with protectionist restrictions; and the FTA with Israel was primarily motivated by political considerations. The U.S.–Canada FTA and its successor, NAFTA, not only involved substantial commercial and investment interests, but also reflected frustration with multilateral negotiations in GATT.

▶ WHAT IS THE CURRENT QUESTION?

Jacob Viner's clean world of trade creation/trade diversion continues to attract some analytical attention, despite an impressive accumulation of theoretical caveats. This can be explained in part because the creation/diversion distinction is useful in illuminating labor-adjustment costs and new export opportunities, even if the welfare implications are ambiguous. These effects are central to recent political economy models of PTAs, and in this new role the concept of trade creation/trade diversion lives on. Nevertheless, Viner's distinction is of diminishing relevance in the new era of PTAs. MFN tariffs are at a historically low level, and therefore tariff preferences have less economic significance. Recall that in conventional static analysis, the welfare cost of a 5 percent tariff is only one-fourth the welfare cost of a 10 percent tariff. While restrictive rules of origin can boost margins of preferences, they have been undercut by lower MFN tariffs.[28] Additionally, while low MFN tariffs erode the welfare significance of both trade creation and trade diversion, modern PTAs are increasingly about liberalizing international investment (and in some cases labor flows), reducing NTBs, harmonizing ostensibly domestic policies (e.g., competition,

[28]We do not wish to push this point too far. Developing-country tariffs are lower but not trivial. And tariffs are often set lower than the bound rates so that tariff increases following a PTA are possible. Rules of origin can be written to maintain substantial effective rates of protection against third-country imports.

environment), and establishing dispute settlement procedures. Trade creation/diversion is only marginally useful in analyzing these provisions.

What, then, is the relevant question to ask of PTAs? Anne Krueger (1998, p. 262) provides a sensible suggestion: ". . . in an important sense the extent to which formation of PTAs is conducive to further liberalization is the key question for analysts." This is essentially the question of whether PTAs are building blocs or stumbling blocs to further multilateral trade liberalization. U.S. policy over the past 20 years has assumed that PTAs are building blocs, but the answer is not so clear cut.

The theory of PTAs is inconclusive on this question.[29] One strand investigates what types of PTAs are more likely to be set up: trade creating or trade-diverting. While the welfare implications of both remain ambiguous, there is a presumption that trade-diverting PTAs take the world further away from the goal of multilateral free trade. Using a political economy model in which government policy responds to campaign contributions from lobby groups attempting to maximize their welfare, it can be shown that FTAs are more likely when they are trade diverting. The intuition is that a trade-diverting FTA increases profits in export expanding sectors as they take advantage of high protected prices in partner countries. This encourages them to pledge large political contributions contingent on government approving the FTA. If politicians are more responsive to these contributions than the general, more diffused welfare loss from trade diversion, they will comply and a deal is struck. In contrast, in a trade-creating FTA, the level of protection against partner countries is reduced, and opposition from domestic firms harmed by import competition is greater. Expected profits from the FTA are lower, the political contributions do not materialize, and the incentives to create the FTA are weakened.[30]

On the other hand, there are some theoretical reasons why once an FTA (not a customs union) is formed, each member may have an increased incentive to reduce its tariff against third countries, nudging the world closer to multilateral free trade. One reason is that once established, an

[29]See Panagariya (2000). Grilli (1997) in his comprehensive review of PTA theory and past experience, is guardedly pessimistic concerning the coexistence of multilateral tariff cooperation and regionalism in trade relations and reminds us that trade discrimination on a regional basis is "second best" policy.

[30]Grossman and Helpman (1995) present a more sophisticated analysis, leading to a similar conclusion.

FTA will lead to the contraction of certain import-sensitive industries. In a political economy model this can reduce those industries' willingness and ability to lobby for continued protection against residual imports from third countries. Moreover, if the member in question had simply diverted its imports from efficient third countries, it has an incentive to minimize the trade diversion loss by adjusting downward its tariff toward third countries.[31] The intuition here is that a member can recapture some tariff revenue lost in the FTA from trade diversion by setting a lower external tariff and reversing the trade diversion.[32]

Another strand of the theoretical literature investigates the incentives to expand membership in PTAs. If expansion continues to be attractive, eventually full multilateral free trade could be reached. Again, the theoretical results are inconclusive and depend on the model used. Up to some point, expansion may provide net benefits to new and existing members, but beyond that point the calculus can shift, and expansion becomes less attractive for either prospective or existing PTA members, or for both. More directly, it can be argued that PTAs, once established, tend to reduce the incentive for additional multilateral liberalization. Sectors that have benefited from partner country trade diversion will resist a reduction in their margin of preference through additional MFN reductions in trade barriers; sectors that have contracted through trade creation will see no gain from further liberalization (all assuming a political economy, not a national welfare approach to trade policy).[33] Moreover, fixed investments may well have been made in the PTA regime that would be threatened by MFN liberalization. These comments do not exhaust the subject but do serve to illustrate the complexity of the interaction between PTAs and multilateral trade liberalization. Even here, however, the theory has paid little attention to the newer attributes of PTAs: investment (Ethier, 1998, is an exception), harmonization of technical standards and other policies, and the use of PTAs as carrots and sticks.

We are left with the empirical record, and that too is subject to differ-

[31]Bringing the price of imports below the partner country will restore tariff revenue loss (Richardson, 1993).

[32]A large PTA might be tempted to set a high external tariff to exploit its market power, but the ability to do so is limited by GATT provisions.

[33]Some developing countries resisted Uruguay Round cuts by the North on the grounds of reduced margins of preference established in GSP schemes, but this argument had little influence.

ent interpretations. One could make a positive case that PTAs are building blocs to multilateral liberalization along the following lines. First, the largest and most significant PTA, the EC, managed to accomplish significant external liberalization in the Kennedy, Tokyo, and Uruguay Rounds, while consolidating its formal integration.[34] Fortress Europe never materialized. Moreover, the EU's eastward expansion has tilted prospective members in the direction of freer trade. For example, Poland, Hungary, Slovakia, and the Czech Republic agreed in 1992 to mutual tariff reductions in anticipation of joining the EU. But this positive record should not be pushed too far. The EU's external liberalization occurred within the framework of a multilateral trade system that in its earlier years was supported and championed by the United States.

As for the United States, a positive interpretation is that its regional PTAs held the trade liberalization constituency together and influential during the uncertain years of 1982–1994. Going further, one could claim that the PTA carrot/stick over the Uruguay Round ultimately proved successful, yielding a strong agreement and no collapse of the trade system into protectionist blocs. Moreover, if one wished to be bullish on PTAs, one could claim that they have had a virtuous domino effect. For example the EC–Israel FTA helped beget the U.S.–Israel FTA, which helped pave the way, along with British entry into the EC, for the U.S.–Canada FTA which, in turn, begat NAFTA and may ultimately result in hemispheric free trade. NAFTA itself has not inhibited Mexico from signing free-trade agreements with Venezuela, Colombia, and Costa Rica and negotiating with the EU for an FTA.[35] Similar liberalizations through FTAs and association agreements have sprung from the EC/EU integration initiative. While this process has not yet run its course, an optimist can see it headed for global free trade. Finally, one can make a case that PTAs have served as a useful testing ground for broadening the functional scope of economic integration. PTAs with provisions in such diverse areas as product standards, environmental protection, and competition policy may make multinational negotiations of these issues easier and more productive.

Still, a dedicated multilateralist is left somewhere between nagging

[34]Agriculture was less successful, but this is true for many countries and now may be headed in the right direction.

[35]Indeed, the British move toward free trade with repeal of the Corn Laws in 1846 set the stage for the 1854 reciprocity treaty, freeing up trade between the United States and Canada (Winham, 1988).

doubts and serious reservations.[36] GATT rules may limit increases in external tariffs following a PTA, but aggressive use of countervailing duties and antidumping may circumvent this rule and result in increased protection (although admittedly this could also happen without the PTA). The threat of PTAs may well have pushed forward the Uruguay Round, but a principal obstructionist, the EU, was itself a PTA. Negotiating among (and within) blocs is not necessarily a productive exercise. And in any event, given their proliferation, the threat of new PTAs may have lost its clout in pressuring multilateral negotiations. Also, there is some evidence that countries such as Israel and Mexico raised their external tariffs following the FTAs, moving the trade system away from free trade. There is also some evidence that unilateral trade liberalization was stalled in Latin America for much of the 1990s. Whether this was the result of multiple new PTAs in the region or other factors is not certain. Another concern is that the broadening scope of PTAs and their negotiations between large countries with market power and small countries suggests an asymmetry and possible bullying that GATT rules and strict adherence to MFN would have defended against. Finally, on a more technical level, the proliferation of PTAs with differing and complicated rules of origin and multiple membership by individual countries creates additional trade distortions, all of which could have been avoided by a clear, simple multilateral MFN liberalization process.

In summary, the United States enters the 21st century as it did the 20th century, as a proponent of PTAs. But the motives are very different and the international trade system is very different. Our two U turns have not, in practice, completed a circle. At a broader level, the question of PTAs as building blocs or stumbling blocs has yet to be resolved.

[36]See Grilli (1997), Panageriya (1999).

▶ REFERENCES

Bhagwati, Jagdish, Pravin Krishna, and Arvind Panagariya (eds). 1999. *Trading Blocs: Alternative Approaches to Analyzing Preferential Trade Agreements.* Cambridge, MA: MIT Press.

Davey, William. 1996. *Pine and Swine: Canada-United States Dispute Settlement.* Ottawa: Center for Trade Policy and Law.

Ethier, Wilfred. 1998. Regionalism in a Multilateral World. *Journal of Political Economy* 106(6):1214–1245.

Frenkel, Orit. 1988. *Constraint and Compromises: Trade Policy in a Democracy: The Case of the US-Israel Free Trade Area.* Thesis. Washington, DC: Johns Hopkins University.

Frankel, Jeffrey, Ernesto Stein, Shang-Jin Wei. 1997. *Regional Trading Blocs in the World Economic System.* Washington, DC: Institute for International Economics.

Grilli, Enzo. 1997. Multilateralism and Regionalism: A Still Difficult Coexistence. In: Ricardo Faini and Enzo Grilli (eds.). *Multilateralism and Regionalism after the Uruguay Round.* New York: St. Martin's Press.

Grossman, Gene, and Elhanan Helpman. 1995. The Politics of Free Trade Agreements. *American Economic Review* 85(4):667–690.

Haniotis, Tassus. 1990. European Community Enlargement: Impact on U.S. Corn and Soybean Exports. *American Journal of Agricultural Economics* 72 (2):289–297.

Krueger, Anne. 1998. In: Jeffrey Frankel (ed.). *The Regionalization of the World Economy.* Chicago: University of Chicago Press.

Lea, Sperry. 1987. A Historical Perspective. In: Robert Stern, Philip Trezise, and John Whalley. *Perspectives on a U.S.–Canadian Free Trade Agreement.* Washington, DC: Brookings Institution.

Machlup. 1977. *A History of Thought in Economic Integration.* New York: Columbia University Press.

Panageriya, Arvind. 1999. The Regionalism Debate: An Overview. *The World Economy* 22(4):477–512.

Panagariya, Arvind. 2000. Preferential Trade Liberalization: The Traditional Theory and New Developments. *Journal of Economic Literature* 38(2):287–331.

Patterson, Gardner. 1966. *Discrimination in International Trade.* Princeton, NJ: Princeton University Press.

Pomfret, Richard. 1988. *Unequal Trade.* Oxford, UK: Basil Blackwell.

Power, John, and Gerardo Sicat. 1971. *The Philippines: Industrialization and Trade Policy.* Oxford, UK: Oxford University Press.

Richardson, Martin. 1993. Endogenous Protection and Trade Diversion. *Journal of Political Economy* 34:309–324.

Sapir, Andre, and Lars Lundberg. 1984. The U.S. Generalized System of Preferences. In: Robert Baldwin and Anne Krueger. *The Structure and Evolution of Recent US Trade Policy.* Chicago: University of Chicago Press.

Schott, Jeffrey, and Murray Smith. 1988. Services and Investment. In: Schott and Smith (eds.). *The Canada-United States Free Trade Agreement.* Washington, D.C., and Montreal: Institute for International Economics and Institute for Research in Public Policy.

Shrybman, Steven. 1991–1992. Trading Away the Environment. *World Policy Journal* 9(1):93–110.

Srinivasan, T. N., John Whalley, Ian Wooton. 1993. Measuring the Effects of Regionalism on Trade and Welfare. In: Kym Anderson and Richard Blackhurst (eds.). *Regional Integration and the Global Trading System.* New York: St. Martin's Press.

Trezise, Philip. 1971. U.S. Canadian Economic Relations. In: Commission on International Trade and Investment Policy. *United States International Economic Policy in an Interdependent World.* Vol. II. Washington, DC: GPO.

Verleger. 1988. Implications of the Energy Provisions. In: Jeffrey Schott and Murray Smith,

(eds.). *The Canadian-United States Free Trade Agreement.* Washington, DC, and Montreal: Institute for International Economics and Institute for Research in Public Policy.
Viner, Jacob. 1951. *International Economics.* Glencoe, IL: The Free Press.
Viner, Jacob. 1950. *The Customs Union Issue.* New York: Carnegie Endowment for International Peace.
Winham, Gilbert. 1988. *Trading with Canada: The Canada-U.S. Free Trade Agreement.* New York: Twentieth Century Fund.

CHAPTER

7

TRADE AND ENVIRONMENT

INTRODUCTION

Reconciling liberal trade and environmental protection was a sleeper issue in the late 1970s and 1980s, attracting little public attention. This changed dramatically in the 1990s. Trade and environment became highly contentious, and as shown at the failed WTO ministerial in Seattle in 1999, highly disruptive. The principal fault lines in the controversy are between North and South and between the environmental and trade communities. This is a tangled web and, at the risk of oversimplification, can be summarized as follows: developing countries in the South fear that collusion between environmental and protectionist interests in the North will use the environment as a pretext for imposing unwarranted environmental standards, restricting the South's export market access. Their concern runs up against divergent views in the North. Some in the environmental community are deeply concerned that trade and trade liberalization efforts in the WTO will trump hard-won domestic environmental protection policies and will promote an international regulatory "race to the bottom" in environmental standards. This concern is but a short distance from allegations of "pollution havens," in which it is asserted that countries deliberately neglect the environment to obtain international competitive advantage. Environmentalists in the North therefore wish to see a strict "greening" of the trade system, both to protect their own environmental policies from being eroded and because they often have a worldwide interest in environmental improvement. Joining them in working for a green trade system are other groups, often organized labor, who wish protection from "unfairly" traded goods originating in pollution havens. At the same time, many trade advocates in the North are equally concerned that the liberal trade system respect legitimate differences among countries with regard to environmental standards and not become overburdened by using restrictive trade measures to accomplish international environmental objectives.

Each of these concerns contains a kernel of truth. For example, environmental regulations can affect market access and trade. Mollerus and Sanchez found that about 15 percent of Asian exports to OECD markets, totaling $47 billion, were subject to some form of environmentally related product measures. But they did not estimate the severity of the restrictions (Pearson, 2000). Also, although there is little empirical evidence of either pollution havens or a regulatory race to the bottom, the analogy to tax havens and competition in tax incentives provides some plausibility. Finally, the advocates of an uncluttered liberal trade system see similarities between obtaining environmental objectives through trade and the use of the trade system in pursuit of fair labor standards and human rights improvements, areas where they do not wish to go.

Reconciling trade and environmental objectives has been complicated by a number of other factors: conflicting results from theoretical and empirical analyses of trade and environment; the emotional character of the debate; the differences in *modus operandi* between environmental and trade decision-making (e.g., open and participatory in the environmental community *vs.* more closed and often secret trade policy proceedings); and the asymmetry between the well-established institutional and legal features of the trade system, as embodied in the WTO, and the absence of an equally robust legal/institutional apparatus regulating international environmental affairs. A careful analysis reveals that much of the apparent conflict between trade and environment is the result of either poor trade or poor environmental policies or is simply a failure of communication. Still, some points of conflict and friction are real and need attending to if progress in liberal trade and environmental protection is to be achieved.

The United States has been at the center of many of the trade-environment controversies. Its policies have been the object of several complaints brought to the WTO/GATT (e.g., the required use of turtle-exclusion devices in shrimp harvesting, reformulated clean gasoline), and the United States itself has brought environmentally related disputes (EU's ban on hormone-fed beef, Canada's landing requirements for salmon and herring, Thailand's restriction on imported cigarettes).[1] On one occasion the United States imposed trade sanctions in support of international environmental objectives.[2] Environmental concerns were center stage in the NAFTA debate, played a major role in the subsequent denial to President Clinton of fast-track trade negotiating authority, emerged in full force at the Seattle ministerial, and were the central question in the Cartagena Protocol on Biosafety dealing with trade in genetically modified organisms. Business interests in the United States have also entered the debate on numerous occasions, often arguing against stringent environmental standards on the basis of loss of trade competitiveness.[3]

The trade–environment nexus is only now being introduced to trade textbooks, and it is useful to start this chapter with a brief review of how traditional trade theory has been modified to incorporate environmental variables. We then present a taxonomy of trade–environment policy issues to sort out the often emotional and confusing controversies, followed by an examination of how the debate has evolved. The chapter continues with a discussion of how the disputes have played out in NAFTA and the Biosafety Protocol and concludes with a discussion of unfinished business.

▶ THEORETICAL CONSIDERATIONS[4]

The overarching questions for both theory and policy are the effects of international trade on the environment (positive and negative) and the ef-

[1]In the clean gasoline case, Venezuela objected to the way in which the United States established a baseline against which Venezuela's cleaner gasoline exports to the United States were to be measured. The WTO panel ruled in favor of Venezuela. Earlier the United States objected to a Canadian requirement prohibiting the export of unprocessed herring and salmon caught in its waters. Canada defended the restriction on conservation grounds, but a GATT panel rejected this claim and ruled in favor of the United States. The tuna-dolphin and Thai cigarette cases are discussed below.

[2]In 1994 the United States imposed prohibitions against certain imports from Taiwan, valued at $22 million. This was done under the Pelly Amendment to the Fishermans' Protective Act and in response to Taiwan's failure to stop its imports of rhinoceros and tiger parts, both animals protected under the Convention on International Trade in Endangered Species (CITES).

[3]Environmental opposition also helped sink plans for a Multilateral Agreement on Investment (MAI) in 1998. See Chapter 9.

[4]Dean, 2001; Pearson, 2000; Antweiler et al., 2000.

fects on international trade of measures to protect the environment. Traditional trade theory, including the Ricardian and Heckscher-Ohlin trade models, do of course accommodate natural resources as a factor of production. The novelty of extending these models to explicitly account for the environment is threefold: first, the environment provides valuable services for direct consumption and for waste disposal that do not have market prices; second, the environment often exists as a common property resource, which invites misallocation and misuse; and third, environmental degradation is closely associated with negative externalities such as pollution, again a prime source of economic distortions. In combination, these three features require extending traditional trade theory.

In thinking about theory and policy, it is useful to keep three distinctions in mind. First, environmental degradation can have a negative effect on directly consumed environmental services, such as loss of scenic amenities or dirty air, but also a negative effect on production, for example, soil erosion reducing agricultural output or the loss of commercial fisheries from water pollution. This distinction helps avoid the popular but erroneous conclusion that poor countries necessarily have a comparative advantage in dirty industries. Pollution that degrades productive resources is every bit as damaging in poor as in rich countries, perhaps more so. Hence, at least some environmental standards may need to be equally stringent in the South. Second, pollution or environmental degradation can arise in either production (the classic steel mill example) or consumption (auto exhaust or post-consumer waste disposal). The trade implication of this distinction is that the country of production and export has principal responsibility for controlling production pollution, and the country of import and consumption has principal responsibility for controlling consumption-based pollution. The final distinction is between environmental effects that are purely local, for example ground-level ozone in an urban area, and transboundary or global pollution, in which environmental effects are felt outside the polluting country. The trade importance of this distinction is that because international management of transboundary and global pollution is primitive, trade measures—coercion or incentives—offer a superficially attractive means to manage these international environmental spillovers.

Early theoretical work concentrated on revising positive trade theory, with the environment treated as an additional factor of production. Three strong conclusions emerged (Pearson, 2000). First, because countries differ with respect to assimilative capacity, industrial structure, income, and preferences, internationally uniform environmental standards are no more appropriate than uniform wage rates. Second, trade can lead to environmental degradation, but *if* appropriate environmental protection measures are in place, trade still improves welfare. Third, trade changes the optimal levels of environmental protection, and hence there is a strong case for jointly establishing trade and environmental policies.

More recent theoretical work has focused on the environment in the context of North–South trade. The results depend heavily on the assumptions and structure of the model. It is possible to build models showing that, following optimal environmental policies, increased North–South trade increases world pollution, but also models with the opposite conclusion. For example, Copeland and Tayor (1994) construct a model in which both North and South follow optimal environmental policies (more stringent in North), production technologies are the same, and trade takes place on the basis of relative costs. When the system is opened to trade, dirty (i.e., pollution–intensive) industries migrate from North to South, where pollution abatement regulations are weaker, and net world pollution increases.[5] But they also construct a second model (1995) incorporating global environmental damages in which net world pollution does not rise. Underlying this latter encouraging conclusion is the assumption that the North responds to increasing transboundary pollution by tightening its own abatement standards.

In the absence of optimal policies, many unpleasant things can happen. For example, Chichilnisky (1994) assumes that environmental resources frequently exist as open access common property resources in the South and that the products of these resources are sold for export at prices below social costs. In this (distorted) context, trade can impoverish exporting countries. Although this comes close to a trade-exploitation situation, it is important to keep in mind that while trade may be the proximate cause of environmental degradation, the root cause is a domestic failure to restrict access to common property resources.

A major advance in trade–environment theory and measurement was to decompose the effects of trade into three elements: a scale effect due to the increased level of economic activity; a composition effect as the mix of

[5]This summary does not do justice to the model, which separates a scale, composition, and technique effect of trade on the level of pollution. See the following paragraphs.

dirty and clean industries changes; and a technique effect that captures the effect of trade, working through increased incomes, on the demand for environmental quality (Grossman and Krueger, 1993; Antweiler et al., 2001). The scale effect on the environment is expected to be negative (more output, more pollution), the composition effect depends on a country's comparative advantage in clean/dirty industries, and the technique effect is expected to be positive as trade increases income and the policy response is stronger environmental standards. Using data on SO_2 concentrations, Antweiler and his colleagues find that freer trade may be good for the global environment.

To complete this review, we note that there is increasing interest in the theory of policy; for example, the appropriate coordination of trade and environmental policy, when one policy might substitute for another, and strategic behavior. A key conclusion from traditional trade theory—that trade measures are not optimal responses for domestic distortions—holds up very well, although this is not so clear-cut when transboundary pollution is present. This last situation is often analyzed with strategic and game-theoretic models.

SORTING OUT THE POLICY ISSUES[6]

Virtually all trade–environment policy issues fall into one of four categories. The first three concern the effects of environmental policy on trade and the trade policy system. The fourth turns the question around and investigates the effects of trade on the environment.

1. Competitiveness Questions

Strict environmental protection measures applied to the production of goods and services tend to increase costs and erode an industry's international competitive position. This is relevant for both export and import competing firms.[7] Even if the environmental protection measures are fully

[6]Pearson, 2000; Esty, 1994.

[7]In some cases cost-savings from energy and materials conservation and resource recovery and recycling may actually improve profits. The extent of these win-win situations is disputed. See Porter and van der Linde (1995); Palmer, Oates, and Portney (1995).

justified on social welfare grounds, the trade-competitiveness effect and the associated job loss have long been a cause for policy concern. For example, Section 6 of the 1972 U.S. Federal Water Pollution Control Act was motivated by this concern and required annual studies of the trade impact of the legislation.

The competitiveness issue has led to a number of proposals for "eco-duties" on imports from countries that do not impose environmental standards equivalent to U.S. levels (Vogel, 1995, pp. 208–210). Such duties presumably would equalize environmental protection costs. These proposals appeal to "fair trade" and "level playing field" type arguments, although there is no economic or environmental justification for identical environmental standards worldwide. Some supporters also see eco-duties as an incentive for upgrading environmental protection in foreign counties. The eco-duty approach conflates protectionist and environmental interests, a potential collusion of considerable concern for advocates of liberal trade.

Thus far, no country has established eco-duties to equalize environmental protection costs affecting production. There are several reasons. First, it is well established that environmental standards and hence environmental protection costs legitimately differ in countries with different assimilative capacity, income levels, industrial structure, and preferences. One size does not suit all. Second, GATT and now WTO regulations disallow country-specific eco-duties. While a WTO member may offset an explicit financial export subsidy by a foreign competitor with a countervailing duty, it is not permitted to offset an implicit export subsidy arising from "low" environmental standards. This raises the issue of "pollution havens" in which a country may seek competitive advantage through environmental neglect and has been a point of contention between environmentalists and the WTO. Third, the OECD moved early on in 1972 to establish the Polluter Pays Principle (PPP). Although the PPP does not attempt to equalize pollution abatement (environmental protection) costs internationally, it does discourage trade distortions arising from differences in *financing* such costs. Finally, and subject to significant caveats, the empirical literature suggests that the trade/competitiveness effects of differential environmental standards have been modest to negligible.[8]

[8]For reviews, see Dean (1992), Jaffee et al. (1995), Pearson (2000).

2. Environmentally Related Product Standards

Restricting imports because of their environmental characteristic poses a quite different set of issues. In general, Article XX of the GATT/WTO permits restriction on the import of products if the *consumption* of those products has an adverse effect on the health, safety, or environment of the importing country.[9] Examples would be auto emission standards and pesticide residue standards for imported fruits and vegetables. The main difficulty has been distinguishing between those import restrictions that serve legitimate environmental protection and natural resource conservation objectives and those that are merely or mainly covert protection in the form of nontariff trade barriers (NTBs). It should be acknowledged that environmentally related product standards raise few new conceptual issues that have not been present in the long-standing problem of health and safety standards, which also can be used for covert protection.

The United States has been on both sides of the product standards issue. For example, it argued before GATT/WTO panels that its ban on the import of tuna caught in a fashion that caused large numbers of dolphin kills was justified on the grounds of natural-resource conservation (tuna and dolphins school together). At the same time, it argued against a Thai ban on imported cigarettes on the grounds that Thailand had alternatives to trade restrictions to mitigate the public health effects of smoking. The U.S. position was that the Thai import ban was not "necessary." The tuna dolphin and Thai cigarette cases are examples where the United States was first the defendant and then the plaintiff at the WTO. The issues in the two cases, however, were very different.[10]

The nuances of the trade–environment debate as it concerns environmentally related product standards are too intricate to fully analyze here. It is sufficient to list certain unresolved issues:

[9]Article XX allows, subject to certain conditions, restrictions on imports necessary to protect human, animal, or plant life or health or to conserve exhaustible natural resources.

[10]In the first tuna–dolphin case, the GATT panel ruled against the United States in part on the grounds that the natural resource to be protected—dolphins—were in the open ocean, outside U.S. jurisdiction. This caused a firestorm among U.S. environmentalists and has subsequently been modified. The United States was successful in opening up the Thai market to U.S. cigarettes. The GATT panel ruled that Thailand could have used a less-trade-restrictive measure to disourage smoking.

- Should the WTO allow trade restrictions to protect natural resources outside the jurisdiction of the importing country, and under what conditions?[11]
- Should countries have the right to restrict imports based on the environmental manner in which the products are produced?
- Is the current requirement that environmentally related restrictions on imported products be based on scientific principles workable? How is the science to be evaluated, and by whom?
- Is the current language of Article XX, which includes the ambiguous terms "arbitrary or unjustifiable discrimination," "necessary," and "disguised restriction on international trade," being interpreted too narrowly so that legitimate environmental objectives are compromised?

A closely related issue involves eco-labeling and environmental certification schemes. In principle, these efforts help inform the consumer, improve the efficiency of the market, and reduce the need for government regulation. But the manner in which environmental criteria are selected and certification is granted can result in *de facto* discrimination against imports and hence be considered NTBs. Eco-labeling has been of concern to developing countries, whose exporters may be disadvantaged (Zarrilli et al., 1997; Jha et al., 1997).

3. Trade Measures to Accomplish International Environmental Objectives

It is possible to carve out a third category of issues concerning the appropriate use of trade restrictions to further international environmental interests. The temptation to do so is clear. There is no supranational Environmental Protection Agency with the authority to protect international environmental resources. Voluntary protection agreements among countries are difficult to negotiate because of free rider problems and primitive

[11]An Appellate Body ruling on the shrimp–turtle exclusion device dispute suggests that some trade measures can be used to protect "shared" environmental resources. In this dispute, the United States had imposed a ban on imported shrimp unless the exporting country was certified to be using turtle-exclusion devices when trawling for shrimp. Asian countries objected and took the case to the WTO.

channels for compensating those countries that bear disproportionate protection costs. Thus, the temptation is to use trade sanctions to coerce agreements and as enforcement tools. Moreover, environmentalists, whose concerns are often global in scope, have neither an effective international market to "buy" environmental improvements abroad nor a direct political voice in foreign governments' environmental decisions. Trade sanctions (or inducements) can provide some leverage. However, the downside is the possibility of "eco-imperialism," coercing countries with little market power to adopt environmental standards and policies that are inappropriate to their circumstances. This might be called the "forced rider" problem. Coercive trade measures for noncommercial objectives may weaken support for a liberal trade system.

A number of multilateral environmental agreements (MEAs) contain trade provisions, although their compatibility with GATT and now the WTO is in question and has yet to be contested and formally tested.[12] These MEAs include the Convention on International Trade in Endangered Species (CITES); the Montreal Protocol, concerned with ozone-depleting substances; and the Cartagena Protocol on Biosafety, which governs trade in living genetically modified organisms. The United States also has a number of laws authorizing trade sanctions in pursuit of environmental objectives. Some reinforce international agreements to which the United States is a party, and some are of a more unilateral character. The actual use of such trade measures has been infrequent; the tuna–dolphin case with Mexico and the U.S. requirement that imported shrimp be caught by vessels with turtle-exclusion devices have been the most widely publicized. As noted above, the United States did resort to trade sanctions against Taiwan (not then a member of the WTO) for its failure to control trade in certain endangered species, and in September 2000 it started a process that could have led to economic sanctions against Japan for alleged illegal whaling.[13]

Trade policy can be used as a carrot as well as a stick. There is little question that the lure of preferential access to the U.S. market motivated

[12]A dispute concerning swordfish between the EU and Chile and involving the UN Convention on the Law of the Sea was brought to the WTO in 2000, but a provisional agreement was reached before a dispute panel was established.

[13]The proposed sanction was to deny Japan fishing rights in U.S. waters, not a direct trade measure.

Mexico to improve its environmental performance, especially in the area of enforcing its environmental laws. In similar and perhaps more dramatic fashion, the Eastern European countries aspiring to full membership in the EU have taken on serious environmental protection obligations in anticipation of the trade and other benefits that membership in the union will confer. The use of trade carrots rather than trade sticks to accomplish environmental objectives is inherently less objectionable, as it leads to freer rather than more restricted trade.

4. Effects of Trade on the Environment

This last category of issues inverts the question and focuses on the effects of trade and trade liberalization on environmental quality. This question has generated great heat but less objective analysis. Trade critics argue that liberal trade can increase pollution and environmental stress in export sectors; contribute to unsustainable levels of natural resource exploitation, especially if resources exist as open access common property; strengthen the hand of commercial interests against environmental interests in setting environmental standards; add a pollution burden from international transport of goods; result in monoculture agriculture and the loss of genetic diversity; and have other adverse (and unforeseen) consequences. At the most general level, some argue that the trade system encourages a regulatory "race to the bottom" to gain competitive advantage.

Proponents of liberal trade argue that certain trade restrictions themselves have negative environmental effects (e.g., protected sugar production in the United States causing degradation of the Everglades ecosystem; excessive use of pesticide and fertilizers in high-cost, protected EU agriculture); that removing trade-distorting subsidies can have positive environmental consequences (e.g., subsidized fishing fleets are an invitation to overfishing and depletion of fish stocks); that most of the immediate negative environmental effects listed in this and the previous paragraph reflect poor domestic environmental protection policies and not trade *per se*; and that trade lifts national income and allows countries to spend more on environmental protection.

Neither theory nor empirical evidence is conclusive. Theory suggests that trade does alter the level and composition of production and consumption and may result in environmental degradation. Logging tropical forests for sawnwood and plywood exports and destruction of mangrove forests for prawn and shrimp cultivation and export in Southeast Asia are often cited as examples. But although trade may be the proximate cause, the underlying problem is most often inadequate domestic environmental policy. On the other hand, the assertion that trade lifts incomes and hence the ability to afford environmental protection falls short of demonstrating that such protection is actually carried out.[14]

▶ EVOLUTION OF THE ISSUE

Contrary to popular view, the trade-environment debate did not spring *de novo* in the 1990s or at the Seattle Ministerial in 1999. The first serious analysis was done in the early 1970s following the UN-sponsored Stockholm Conference on the Human Environment. The principal issues at that time were whether differences among countries in environmental standards and costs would affect competitive position and trade (our first category of issues) and whether environmental standards applied to products would be used as covert NTBs (our second category). The use of trade measures in MEAs was not anticipated, and no one gave serious thought to the impact of trade on the environment. The analysis at the time was done by trade economists and trade officials; the environmental community did not participate.

The trade–environment issue virtually disappeared from sight by the early 1980s. Trade theory was beginning to accommodate the environment as another factor of production (along with labor, capital, and technology) in an expanded theory of comparative advantage, and the OECD had enunciated its famous PPP, which minimized trade distortions arising from different financing regimes, and had also established the principle that environmental standards, like other product standards, should not be used as covert NTBs. Finally, preliminary empirical evidence suggested that for most industries, pollution-abatement costs were a small fraction of total production cost and hence had minimal trade effects, at least in the area of

[14]The connection between income levels and environmental protection/pollution levels has generated a growing literature under the heading of "Environmental Kuznet Curves." (The original Kuznets Curve related income inequality and per capita income levels.) Some research shows an inverted U curve, with pollution rising in the low per-capita income range, reaching a maximum, and then declining at high per-capita income levels. If trade is a vehicle for increasing income, it moves countries along the curve with pollution first rising and then declining (Barbier, 1997).

industrial pollution control. The GATT itself provides evidence of the low level of interest at this time. It established a working group on trade and environment as early as 1971, but the group was not given an agenda and did not convene for 20 years, suggesting a minimal level of concern.

The benign neglect of trade and environment evaporated in the 1990s, and U.S. trade policy struggled for a decade for reconciliation. Four factors contributed to the revival of interest. First, formal economic integration (e.g., the EC-92 effort at creating a unified market in Europe) and market-driven globalization of trade, investment, and technology have made ostensibly domestic environmental policies international in their effects. The post–Uruguay Round trade agenda has been dominated by the question of how to harmonize all manner of national economic regulations—labor standards, competition policy, e-commerce—and the harmonization of environmental policy is no exception.

Second, environmental concerns have expanded from simple industrial pollution to the conservation of natural resources and sustainable development. It is no longer possible to deny a close connection between natural resource conservation/exploitation practices and international trade.

Third, concern has shifted from local to global environmental threats, for example, climate change, depletion of ocean fisheries, and loss of genetic diversity. Trade measures offer a superficially attractive method for inducing or coercing participation in MEAs.

Finally, triggered by GATT's tuna–dolphin decision in 1993 and the negotiations for NAFTA, the U.S. environmental community woke up to the connection between trade and environment. More specifically, it recognized not only that trade and trade liberalization have environmental consequences but also that trade measures might be used to pursue international environmental objectives. Although this recognition was too late to have major influence on the Uruguay Round, the environmental community has played an important role in most U.S. trade policy debates since then.[15]

THE U.S. POSITION AND THE NAFTA DEBATE

The U.S. government position on trade and environment displays some evolution but also considerable ambivalence. In the early years, when ana-

[15]The Uruguay Round did create the WTO's Committee on Trade and Environment.

lytical and policy work was concentrated at the OECD, the United States was a strong supporter of traditional liberal trade values. The original interpretation of the PPP was as a "no subsidy" principle, without ethical connotations. The United States correctly saw the PPP as a defense against government subsidies that would distort trade. It also supported the OECD's stricture against using environmentally related product standards as covert NTBs, although it may have underestimated the difficulty in distinguishing the intent of the product standards. At the time, the United States, along with virtually all other participants, private and public, was unconcerned with the environmental effects of trade. This pro-trade stance gradually has been modified, although certainly not abandoned.

The battle over NAFTA in the early 1990s was the seminal event in the evolution of U.S. trade–environment policy. Indeed, the NAFTA process illustrates cleavages that persist to this day. At the procedural level, preparations for NAFTA brought about advances in the formulation of trade and environmental policy. USTR put prominent environmentalists on its advisory committees and included EPA officials on the negotiating team. At the same time, the EPA created an advisory Trade and Environment Committee with environmental NGOs as members. Still, the merging of environmental and trade interests was neither easy nor complete and has been highly political. As background, it should be remembered that prior to NAFTA the United States and Mexico shared severe and worsening environmental degradation along their border, in part due to growing maquiladora trade, and that the prospect for Mexico to become a low-wage pollution haven had a distinct plausibility. In early 1991 President Bush needed fast-track authority from Congress for NAFTA negotiations and was obliged to promise that U.S. environmental and worker safety laws would not be harmed. He did not, however, agree that environmental negotiations would be integral to the trade negotiations, preferring to relegate them to a "parallel track" process (Johnson and Beaulieu, 1996). During the actual trade negotiations (August 1991–August 1992), U.S. environmental NGOs were active in making their position known but were generally disappointed in the results.[16] The Bush administration left office before Congress could act on NAFTA. In January 1993, newly elected President Clinton chose not to reopen NAFTA but rather to negotiate a

[16]The National Wildlife Federation did give support to NAFTA after the three governments agreed in September 1992 to negotiate a parallel environmental agreement.

supplemental agreement, the North American Agreement on Environmental Cooperation (NAAEC), which was completed in August 1993. This side agreement left the U.S. environmental community split, with many NGOs supporting the NAFTA/NAAEC package but others, including the Sierra Club, opposed. The NAFTA package was ultimately passed by Congress in November 1993 and signed by President Clinton three weeks later.

Although it was the intent of the Bush and Clinton administrations to keep the trade and environmental negotiations separate, this was not fully possible, for two reasons. First, the NGOs actively sought to "green" NAFTA, and second, by its nature, the trade and investment provisions of NAFTA held environmental implications. In the end, NAFTA contained green elements but fell short of environmentalists' goals. NAFTA's preamble contains hortatory language calling for sustainable development, environmental protection, and conservation, the first two of which were absent from GATT language. On the competitiveness issue described previously, NAFTA states members *should not* (emphasis added) waive or derogate from health, safety, or environmental measures to encourage investment—a very mild bow to the pollution haven concern. On the issue of environmentally related product standards, NAFTA (like the Uruguay Round) separated sanitary and phytosanitary measures from other technical regulations and allowed each member to set its own appropriate level of protection, without harmonizing the standards.[17] Thus the worst fear of environmentalists, harmonizing standards downward to a lowest common denominator, was avoided. Still, some restraints apply. Members shall avoid arbitrary or unjustifiable differences in standards, the measures must be "necessary" for protection of human, plant, or animal life, and they must be based on scientific principles. For other types of product standards, NAFTA states that imported products cannot be restricted on the basis of how the product is produced.[18] All these provisions are designed to prevent environmental standards from becoming covert NTBs. All display some ambiguity and can to lead to challenges, which can be taken to NAFTA or the WTO at the choice of the party challenged. Finally, the agreement states that obligations undertaken in certain MEAs (endangered species,

[17]Harmonization of standards is declared as an objective.

[18]Unless the production method is related to the characteristics of the product.

ozone depletion, hazardous wastes) take precedence over NAFTA obligations, an unresolved question in MEA–WTO relations.

In an unexpected turn, the investment portion of NAFTA (Chapter 11) subsequently raised concerns in the environmental community. In an effort to protect investors against arbitrary government actions and improve the investment climate, NAFTA allows private investors to initiate direct actions against host governments to enforce investors' rights and to hold governments to their NAFTA obligations. While conceived as a defense of private investment, some observers saw this unprecedented right as an invitation to investors to shield themselves from new laws and policies, including environmental regulations. One consequence may be reluctance of governments to establish new environmental regulations, no matter how well justified on public interest grounds. This is of concern to environmentalists in all three countries, who rely on legal and regulatory measures to improve environmental conditions. As of March 2001, some 10 cases challenging environmental regulations had been filed by investors under Chapter 11 provisions (International Institute for Sustainable Development 2001).

Given the unsettled state of theory and empirical experience and the highly charged atmosphere, one might expect that the United States would have been scrupulous in attempting to anticipate the environmental effects of new trade liberalization initiatives. This has not always been the case. The United States did conduct a "review" of the expected environmental effects of both NAFTA and the Uruguay Round, but both efforts can at best be described as superficial. The most charitable explanation is that standard methodologies for evaluating environmental effects of trade agreements were and remain quite primitive. A less charitable conclusion is that the trade community and certain commercial interests were and are unenthusiastic about adding environmental hurdles to trade agreements.

The conduct of trade policy is of course a learning process. The ongoing pressure from the environmental community in the United States and the conflation of environmental objectives and denial of fast-track authority led President Clinton to issue an executive order in 1999 to develop guidelines for environmental reviews of trade agreements, and these were completed in December 2000. The guidelines are a compromise between those who wish to keep trade agreements relatively clear of environmental concerns and those who wish to meld trade and environmental policy. The guidelines may not satisfy those with environmental interests who are skeptical of new trade initiatives. One reason is that they put primary responsibility for environmental reviews with USTR, which has few environmental credentials.[19] A second reason is that the guidelines declare that domestic impacts in the United States are the main concern, although global and transboundary impacts *may* also be considered. Local impacts in partner countries will not be analyzed. This is a particularly parochial view of the environmental effects of trade liberalization and is unlikely to find favor with environmentalists, who not only have international concerns but view trade policy as a key instrument for extending their foreign influence. A third problem that environmentalists are likely to point out is that the guidelines fall short of limiting new trade agreements, even if the environmental consequences are judged serious.[20] An interesting footnote, reflecting a general desire to keep trade measures clean of environmental encumbrances, is that Permanent Normal Trade Relations (PNTR) with China was consummated in 2000 without any formal environmental review and despite the 1999 executive order. One might correctly argue that the environmental consequences of PNTR will be felt in large part in China and not in the United States. But that is precisely the issue: should the *foreign* environmental consequences of U.S. trade initiatives be on the trade table?[21]

The trade-environment issue remained unsettled in U.S. politics and policy. A good illustration was the 2000 Cartagena Protocol on Biosafety, following up on the earlier Convention on Biological Diversity.[22] The Protocol ostensibly sets out rules for trade in genetically modified products but is in fact a study in obfuscation. Countries can restrict imports of such products if they have a scientific basis for doing so, but the science need not

[19]Environmental reviews will be conducted by USTR through the Trade Policy Staff Committee. The TPSC is interagency and does include environmental agencies.

[20]The guidelines do require analysis of options to mitigate negative impacts, but this falls well short of a formal benefit-cost requirement.

[21]The FTA between the United States and Jordan was subject to a draft environmental review. Based in part on a USITC study that concluded the FTA would have no measurable impacts on U.S. trade, production, or employment, not surprisingly the review found that the FTA would have neither significant environmental effects in the United States nor transboundary or global effects of concern to the United States.

[22]The Protocol was actually signed in Montreal, as the earlier Cartagena meeting could not reach agreement. The United States was an active observer at Montreal but not a formal participant, as it has not ratified the earlier Convention.

be conclusive. This reflects partial acceptance of the so-called precautionary principle, much beloved by the EU but resisted earlier by the United States in the beef hormone dispute. The Protocol also further muddies interpretation of language found in the WTO's Sanitary and Phytosanitary Agreement. Whether the Protocol's rules trump WTO rules or visa versa is completely unclear; at one point the Biodiversity Convention and the Protocol are asserted as co-equal to WTO obligations, and at another point it is asserted that countries' rights under the WTO are left untouched.[23]

Another issue, largely neglected until now, will be the trade consequences of the Kyoto Protocol addressing global warming, should that environmental agreement or something similar be taken seriously. There are at least three major linkages to the international trade system that will have to be addressed. First, how will countries respond to shifts in international competitive position and trade, as some but not all countries increase fossil fuel prices and costs for energy-intensive industries? Second, should trade measures be used to coerce or induce membership in a Kyoto-like agreement? Third, what are the trade and exchange rate consequences of an international carbon-emissions trading program, a centerpiece of earlier U.S. proposals?[24] Although President Bush did not explicitly cite trade concerns when he rejected Kyoto in 2001, his references to a disproportionate economic burden on the United States strongly hinted that trade concerns influence our global warming policies. Once again, the competitiveness effect of environmental regulations, our first category of policy issues, is relevant.

[23]For further analysis, see Phillips and Kerr (2000).

[24]International emissions trading would presumably appreciate the currency of permit-sellers and depreciate the currency of net purchasing countries. If the United States were to become a major buyer of permits, it would tend to depreciate the dollar and improve the U.S. merchandise trade balance. But of course, higher energy costs for U.S. producers would work against the positive trade effect.

▶ REFERENCES

Antweiler, Werner, Brian Copeland, Scott Taylor. 2001. Is Free Trade Good for the Environment? *American Economic Review* 91(4):877–908.

Barbier, Edward. (ed.). 1997. Introduction to the Environmental Kuznets Curve. *Special Issue, Environment and Development Economics* 2(4):369–381.

Chichlinsky, Graciela. 1994. North-South Trade and the Global Environment. *The American Economic Review* 84(4):851–874.

Copeland, Brian, and M. Scott Taylor. 1994. North-South Trade and the Environment. *Quarterly Journal of Economics* 109(3):755–787.

Copeland, Brian, and M. Scott Taylor. 1995. Trade and Transboundary Pollution. *American Economic Review* 85(4):716–737.

Dean, Judith (ed.). 2001. *International Trade and the Environment.* Brookfield: Ashgate.

Dean, Judith. 1992. Trade and the Environment: A Survey of the Literature. Discussion paper 159. In: Patrick Low (ed.). *International Trade and the Environment.* Washington, DC: World Bank.

Esty, Daniel. 1994. *Greening the GATT: Trade, Environment, and the Future.* Washington, DC: Institute for International Economics.

Grossman, Gene, and Alan Krueger. 1993. Environmental Impacts of a North American Free Trade Agreement. In: Peter Garber (ed.). *The Mexico-US Free Trade Agreement.* Cambridge, MA: MIT Press.

International Institute of Sustainable Development. 2001. *Private Rights, Public Problems.* Winnipeg: IISD.

Jaffee, Adam, Steven Peterson, Paul Portney, Robert Stavins. 1995. Environmental Regulations and the Competitiveness of U.S. Manufacturing: What Does the Evidence Tell Us? *Journal of Economic Literature* 33(1):132–163.

Jha, Veena, Amil Markandya, Rene Vassenaar (eds.). 1999. *Reconciling Trade and the Environment: Lessons from Case Studies in Developing Countries.* Cheltenham, UK: Edward Elgar.

Johnson, Pierre-Marc, and Andre Beaulieu. 1996. *The Environment and NAFTA.* Washington, DC: Island Press.

Palmer, Karen, Wallace Oates, Paul Portney. 1995. Tightening Environmental Standards: The Benefit-Cost or No-Cost Paradigm? *Journal of Economic Perspectives* 9(4):119–132.

Pearson, Charles. 2000. *Economics and the Global Environment.* Cambridge, UK: Cambridge University Press.

Phillips, Peter, and William Kerr. 2000. Alternative Paradigms: The WTO Versus the Biosafety Protocol for Trade in Genetically Modified Organisms. *Journal of World Trade* 34(4):63–75

Porter, Michael, and Claas van der Linde. 1995. Toward a New Conception of the Environment–Competitiveness Relationship. *Journal of Economic Perspectives* 9(4):97–118.

Vogel, David. 1995. *Trading Up: Consumer and Environmental Regulation in a Global Economy.* Cambridge, MA: Harvard University Press.

Zarrilli, Simonetta, Veena Jha, Rene Vossenaar (eds.). 1997. *Eco-Labelling and International Trade.* New York: St. Martin's Press.

CHAPTER

8

A CONFLICTED EXPORT POLICY

United States export policy has had a Janus-like quality, facing in two quite different directions. On one side are the many efforts to support and expand exports. The obverse side faces a different direction and involves numerous restrictions on exports. There is no mystery here, but there is a conflict of objectives. Export expansion is supported for commercial purposes. Restrictions on exports are for national security purposes or as part of economic sanctions packages to secure noncommercial foreign policy objectives.[1]

Some of our export expansion activities such as the vigorous efforts to obtain preferential access to the Latin American market in the second half of the 19th century, the use of Section 301 in the 1980s, and the big emerging markets drive of the early 1990s are described elsewhere in the book. This chapter considers additional export support policies. It also examines export-restricting policies, specifically, the tension between commercial objectives and national security interests and the use of export restraints

[1]Unlike import restrictions such as those authorized by Section 301, export restrictions for commercial objectives have been rare. One major exception was the Embargo Act of 1807. At the time, Great Britain was engaged in the Napoleonic Wars with France. In an effort to limit neutral trade with Continental Europe, it issued Orders in Council mandating its navy to seize the cargo of neutral ships. As a major maritime power, U.S. shipping interests were severely affected. The United States attempted a power play, prohibiting its ships from engaging in international trade, the Embargo Act. This resulted in serious economic consequences for both countries, with U.S. imports from Britain declining 58 percent and the price of wheat, a U.S. export, rising by 50 percent in Britain. In the end the U.S. effort was unsuccessful, and the offending Orders in Council were maintained until 1812 (Selden, 1999).

for a widening variety of foreign policy goals, ranging from human rights to the isolation and destabilization of unfriendly foreign governments.

The structure of the chapter is as follows. The next section starts the analysis of export promotion policy with several theoretical points and a review of the arguments that might favor active export support. The following section considers three principal export subsidy policies, the DISC/FSC tax program, the Export Enhancement Program (EEP) for agriculture and especially the EC–U.S. wheat subsidy war, and export financing support through the Ex-Im Bank. The final section turns to the other side of export policy: controls, restrictions, and sanctions.

▶ CONCEPTUAL ISSUES

It is useful to introduce a few theoretical comments before considering U.S. export policies in detail. The first point is that an export subsidy (tax) has different effects than production subsidy (tax). The export measure drives a wedge between domestic and international price equal to the subsidy (tax); a production subsidy (tax) does not.[2] Thus, for a small country without international market power, an export subsidy drives up the domestic price of the exportable product and an export tax drives down the domestic price. Because of the price distortion associated with an export subsidy, the deadweight or efficiency cost of an export subsidy is larger than that of a production subsidy with equivalent output effect. But of course, the taxpayer cost of the export subsidy is smaller, as it applies to fewer units. Recall also that in general the WTO/GATT prohibits export subsidies but permits domestic subsidies unless they harm the interests of another country.[3]

The second point is that export subsidies (taxes) have different effects for small and large countries. If the country is large (i.e., has international market power), an export subsidy drives down world market prices and an export tax drives up world prices; for a small country, world market prices are unaffected. This suggests that the United States, which is large in at least some export products, should be more interested in restricting than subsidizing its exports to obtain better terms of trade. However, this has

[2]This distinction becomes a little complicated when the subsidy is paid "in kind" through the release of government stocks, as was done in the initial years of the EEP.

[3]For details of international rules on subsidies, see Trebilock and Howse (1999).

rarely been the case. Export subsidies have been the rule, and restrictions on exports for economic or commercial objectives have been the exception.[4] It should be remembered that the Constitution prohibits taxes and duties laid on exports from any state (Moyer and Maybry, 1988, p. 129).

The third theoretical point, rarely acknowledged in policy discussions, is known as the Lerner symmetry theorem (Vousden, 1990). This theorem demonstrates that if trade is balanced, a uniform *ad valorem* tax on exports has the same effect as an import tax set at the same rate, and a uniform subsidy to exports has the same effect as a similar subsidy to imports. Thus, a tariff on imports is in effect a tax on exports; a subsidy to exports is a subsidy to imports. If this result were more widely appreciated, one might expect U.S. import competing industries to more actively oppose U.S. export subsidies.[5] The symmetry between export and import intervention measures is helpful to us, as we can use the theory of import policy as a partial guide to analyzing export policy.

▶ AN ECONOMIC CASE FOR EXPORT ASSISTANCE?

As noted, the United States rarely restricts exports for economic or commercial purposes. But it has assisted exports through tax provisions, direct subsidies, export financing, and trade information and facilitation services, although such assistance has been at relatively low levels. Can this assistance be justified on economic grounds? To some extent the arguments fa-

[4]A few of these exceptions come to mind. Exports of unprocessed logs harvested from federal lands have been banned since 1973. The ban reduces the input costs and enhances the competitiveness of U.S. sawmills, an example of the theory of effective protection. The practical effects may be small, however, as export of logs from private lands is permitted. There was also a ban on the export of Alaskan North Slope oil dating to the 1970s, which presumably was designed to moderate oil prices in the United States and to support U.S. maritime interests in cabotage. In the early 1970s President Nixon imposed a temporary embargo on the export of soybeans to moderate U.S. agricultural inflation. Finally, in the early power-war period, there were temporary restrictions on the export of critical industrial goods in short supply. None of these export restrictions were motivated by terms of trade consideration.

[5]Two caveats are needed. First, in the real world, trade is not balanced because of international capital movements. The effects of trade policy working through capital flows and the exchange rate back on the trade balance can be positive, negative, or neutral. Second, differential export subsidy rates among products, like differential tariff rates, affect relative prices and hence the composition of output and trade.

voring export support parallel import protection arguments, although of course their trade impact is opposite.

Infant Export Industry

The durable infant industry argument for import protection can, with some stretching, be recast to support export assistance. The argument would be that the industry is uncompetitive in its infancy, but if given startup subsidies it is expected to achieve lower production costs and become a profitable exporter. To be persuasive, however, one must show some capital market distortion that prevents the private sector from financing production through the unprofitable infant stage of exporting. The best policy would be to remove that capital market distortion. Moreover, if assistance to the exportable industry is justified, production rather than export subsidies would be more efficient.

Terms of Trade

In general, the terms-of-trade effect of export intervention favors the imposition of taxes that would limit exports rather than subsidies. Limiting exports would tend to increase export price, improving terms of trade. There are some exceptions, however. It is possible to construct a situation in which a country that has some unexploited market power in one export product elects to subsidize the export of a second, marginal product that has no international price power. Working either through a reallocation of productive resources toward the subsidized product or through currency appreciation, the exports of the first product are reduced, and a terms-of-trade gain may be secured for the country (Itoh and Kiyono, 1987). This sort of sophisticated policy is not relevant for the U.S. tax or agricultural subsidy policies analyzed in the next paragraph. The tax breaks are not restricted to marginal exports, and U.S. agriculture cannot be considered marginal in world markets. Improving terms of trade through export subsidies is generally a non-starter.

Strategic Subsidies

It is also possible to construct situations in which a large country can gain through strategic export subsidies, but the conditions for success can be demanding. The simplest case is a predatory subsidy successful in driving out foreign competition and establishing monopoly power. This is not legal in GATT/WTO. The rent-snatching model discussed in Chapter 3 is another example but subject to serious limits, including triggering a wasteful subsidies war. Finally, export subsidies may be used in an attempt to force removal of foreign subsidies (see the wheat subsidy war, described next). The conditions for success are best analyzed with repeat game theory models. Such subsidies can be thought of as "bargaining subsidies" and provide the main justification for the three policies analyzed below.

Neutralize Tariff Distortions

The Lerner symmetry theorem suggests that a country can neutralize a uniform import tariff with a uniform export subsidy. The United States does not have a uniform tariff, and this argument can be dismissed.

Capture Positive Externalities

The production externality argument is similar to the infant industry case. The first best policy would be production subsidy. Because externalities are elusive—often claimed, less often demonstrated—the burden of evidence should be strict before export subsidies are employed. In principle, such subsidies should be finely targeted, but this may be difficult to accomplish.

Jobs

In general, the use of export subsidies to support employment is no more valid than the use of tariffs for aggregate employment purposes. While it is true that export jobs generally pay higher than average wages, there is little evidence that subsidized exports would raise the average wage or labor productivity.[6]

To summarize, the abstract economic arguments for export subsidies are about as weak as arguments for import protection. But as we have seen, economic efficiency arguments concerning trade policy do not always carry the day.

[6]Free trade is of course a powerful engine for efficient production and higher real wages. Removing export disincentives is desirable. But subsidized exports would tend to push trade beyond its efficient point.

The preceding discussion assumes the form of assistance to be an export subsidy. Governments also provide assistance through export financing and insurance. The motivation may be to pump up exports but, alternatively, might be to remedy some defect in capital markets. The Ex-Im Bank assists in financing exports from the U.S. Its experience is described below. We now turn to an analysis of three export-assistance policies.

▶ U.S. EXPORT SUPPORT POLICIES

The DISC-FSC Saga

A long-running controversy in U.S. export policy involves tax subsidies. The dispute traces back to the Revenue Act of 1971, which authorized the creation of Domestic International Sales Corporations (DISCs). The motivation was to give firms a tax break for exporting. Recall that at this time the U.S. economy was sluggish (0.2 percent growth in 1970), the trade balance was headed for its first deficit in many decades, and overseas investment by U.S. MNCs was seen by some as a threat to domestic production and jobs. Moreover, the U.S. business community claimed a competitive disadvantage *vis a vis* Europe due to different tax systems. Europe relies mainly on indirect taxes (e.g., value-added taxes), whereas the United States relies primarily on direct taxes (e.g., corporate and personal income taxes). GATT allows countries to adjust indirect taxes at the border, applying the tax to imports and rebating the tax on exports. It does not permit any adjustment at the border for direct taxes.[7]

The DISC device seemed an ideal response at the time.[8] Tax relief for exporters was thought to help neutralize the competitive disadvantage of our direct tax system, would improve our trade balance, and would tend to

[7]The origin of GATT treatment was a belief that indirect taxes are passed forward in product prices and direct taxes are passed back to the factors of production. If this were true, tax neutrality in price competition would support border adjustments for indirect taxes but not for direct taxes. Subsequent research suggests that the pass-forward, pass-backward assumption is flawed, casting doubt on the GATT treatment. In the longer run and in aggregate, however, it makes little difference, as exchange rate adjustments offset any competitive effect of differential tax systems.

[8]Not everyone was enthusiastic. Stanley Surrey (1971), a prominent law professor at Harvard, wrote a stinging critique, noting that the Treasury's proposal was not supported by data, analysis, or economic studies.

shift investment and jobs back to the U.S. The DISC concept itself was quite simple and inexpensive to firms. U.S. corporations engaged in exporting could set up DISCs and channel exports through them (in a bookkeeping sense, not through physical movement of goods). A fraction of export profits could be allocated to the DISC, which was required to distribute only 50 percent of profits to the parent. U.S. taxes on the remaining 50 percent were deferred indefinitely, amounting to an interest-free loan to the corporation and raising the rate of return on exporting.[9] The ultimate effect was to reduce the cost of capital in exporting activities and, with competition in exporting, reduce the price of U.S. exports relative to other goods and relative to foreign prices. The price advantage would lead to greater export sales.[10]

The DISC export subsidy did not escape the attention of the EC, which filed a complaint with GATT as early as 1972. GATT prohibits export subsidies except for primary products, and even those are limited. The United States defended the DISC program and counterattacked by filing a complaint alleging that the tax systems of Belgium, France, and the Netherlands were themselves implicit export subsidies.[11] In 1976 a GATT panel found that DISCs and also certain European tax practices violated GATT export subsidy rules. The GATT Council accepted the panel ruling in 1981 with certain qualifications. The United States grumbled and did not concede the illegality of DISCs. But to avoid further controversy, it

[9]Firms were given some choice in determining the fraction of export profits that could be allocated to the DISC, but these were generally capped at 50 percent. Thus, up to 25 percent (0.5×0.5) of export earnings were essentially tax-free. The rules were tightened and the subsidy reduced in 1976 and 1982. See Mutti and Grubert (1984) and Desai and Hines (2000) for details.

[10]There are a number of caveats to this line of reasoning (Mutti and Grubert, 1984). First, expanded exports may cause an appreciation of the dollar, adversely affecting import competing firms and export firms that do not take advantage of DISC. Second, by reducing the cost of capital in exporting, DISCs will tend to substitute capital for labor in production, moderating the positive employment effects of expanded exports. In a general equilibrium analysis, the increased demand for capital may trigger capital inflows, further appreciating the dollar and causing distress in non-DISC firms. Finally, the initial effect of the tax subsidy is to decrease U.S. export prices, causing terms-of-trade losses. In short, the trade, welfare, and distributional effects of DISCs are not self-evident.

[11]The basis for the U.S. complaint was that the territorial tax systems of these countries (i.e., exempting foreign earned income from taxation) allowed them to shift income to low-tax countries by not using arms-length transactions prices, a form of transfer pricing.

agreed to change its tax law. Thus, in 1984 DISCs were put to rest, and FSCs, Foreign Sales Corporations, were born.

A profitable subsidy is hard to kill. FSCs were deliberately designed to maintain a subsidy to exporters while nudging the tax law slightly closer to GATT compliance. In purpose and in effect, DISCs and FSCs are interchangeable but the technical details differ. FSC legislation requires the establishment of a *foreign* corporation through which exports are routed (again in a bookkeeping sense only). The most popular sites for FSCs were U.S. possessions (U.S. Virgin Islands, Guam—hardly foreign) and Barbados (Desai and Hines, 2000). FSCs must keep books, hold board meetings outside the United States, and maintain a foreign office. As a result, they were somewhat more cumbersome and expensive to establish then DISCs, and they tended to favor larger corporations.[12] The initial EC response to FSCs was restrained. It requested consultation in the GATT, but no formal complaint was made. By the late 1990s the situation changed. The number of FSCs had grown from 3798 in 1987 to 5136 in 1996, the latter supporting $290 billion in exports, about 50 percent of total U.S. exports. Also, the dispute settlement procedures under the WTO were tighter than under the earlier GATT, suggesting that a successful challenge might have tangible results. And the acrimonious disputes between the United States and the EU concerning beef and bananas were in full flower. In 1998 the EU requested a dispute settlement panel, in 1999 the panel found that FSCs were a prohibited export subsidy, and subsequently an appellate body upheld the finding.[13] The United States responded by devising yet another tax scheme in 2000, the Extraterritorial Income Exclusion Act (ET). Again the purpose was to reduce taxes on export earnings. Again the EU complained, and in August 2001 another WTO panel rejected the ET as an export subsidy scheme. The United States appealed but lost and now faces trade sanctions, amounting to $4 billion per year.

[12]Not all goods qualified for FSCs. For example, Desai and Hines (2000) point out that horses for slaughter shipped by air were eligible, but horses for slaughter shipped by sea were not.

[13]The United States defended FSCs in part as a measure to prevent double taxation of foreign source income earned outside the U.S. To prevail, it had to show that FSCs were indeed "foreign" entities, a task made difficult by their location in U.S. overseas possessions. Moreover, it was difficult to defend against the charge that the intent of FSCs was to support and expand exports. The Treasury Department in reporting on the legislation calculated and published the additional exports attributable to FSCs (Stehmann, 2000).

The economics of DISC and FSC are as tangled as the legal disputes. Mutti and Grubert (1984) present a carefully constructed general equilibrium model of DISC. In one version, capital is perfectly mobile among industries within a country but imperfectly mobile internationally. In the second version, capital is industry-specific so that after-tax rates of return do not equalize within the country. The empirical analysis is based on DISCs in operation in 1979. While the results are sensitive to the parameter values chosen, they remain of interest. The authors found that with homogenous capital, production of U.S. export goods expanded, production of import-competing goods and nontradeables declined, the after-tax rate of return to capital rose, and on the margin world capital was reallocated to the United States. Skilled labor wages rose and unskilled labor wages fell. The net effect on U.S. welfare was negative, in large measure because of adverse terms-of-trade effects, but the magnitude of the welfare loss was small.

The effects of FSCs on exports and tax revenue is of considerable interest. The calculation is complicated, however, as firms were offered a second, separate tax incentive, and it was possible to use both simultaneously. This second tax provision allows multinational corporations to treat certain earnings from exporting as foreign source income. MNCs with excess foreign tax credits can then shield those earnings from U.S. taxes by using their excess foreign tax credits to offset their U.S. corporate profits tax liability.[14] The U.S. Office of Management and Budget and Treasury estimated the loss of tax revenue (the "tax expenditure") from FSCs to be $1.6 billion in 1997 and the loss of revenue from the second incentive just described to be $1.5 billion. It then used these subsidy estimates in a standard trade model to calculate additional exports. The results for 1992 showed that the FSCs accounted for an additional $1.5 billion in exports

[14]Without delving into unnecessary detail, the U.S. taxes the foreign and domestic income of its residents. However, to prevent double taxation, it permits a credit for taxes paid to foreign governments on foreign source income when calculating U.S. tax liability. If a firm operates in a high-tax country, the credit may exceed its U.S. tax liability, and the firm has excess tax credits, of no immediate use. By allowing MNCs to treat some export earnings as foreign source income, the law allows the firm to utilize its excess tax credits to shield that income from U.S. taxes. The net effect is to lower U.S. tax payments with no change in tax payments to foreign governments. Desai and Hines (2000) provide clear numerical examples.

and that the second incentive accounted for another $2.1 billion in exports in 1990 (Desai and Hines, 2000).

Desai and Hines argue that the Treasury estimates of the subsidies and by implication the export stimulus are too low. By analyzing the interaction for the two incentives, they estimate the total subsidy for 1996 to be $5.8 billion, about twice the Treasury estimate. If correct, this represents about a 1 percent export subsidy, but of course it was concentrated on those firms that utilized the two tax incentives. In a separate analysis, based on regression analysis, they estimate that the repeal of DISC in 1984 reduced exports by 3.1 percent but that this was subsequently moderated as the replacement FSCs were phased in.

While the last chapter of this tax feud has yet to be written, it is clear that the U.S. business community has successfully obtained export subsidies through the tax system for three decades. Despite U.S. opposition to export subsidies in the abstract, despite questionable economic benefits, and despite their conflict with GATT and now WTO obligations, successive administrations worked diligently to preserve these tax breaks for exporters.

Agricultural Subsidy Skirmishes and the Wheat Wars

As is well known, agricultural trade policies escaped GATT discipline for many decades. Although Europe bears much responsibility, early actions by the United States also contributed. When GATT was created, the United States was using both import quotas and export subsidies for agriculture, and these illiberal features found their way into GATT. Somewhat later, in the mid 1950s, the United States wished to maintain import restrictions on certain agricultural products. It sought and obtained a waiver from its GATT obligations for this purpose.[15] This waiver set a precedent for similar agricultural trade protection measures by other countries (Jackson, 1997). Moreover, in 1955, with U.S. approval, GATT clarified export subsidy rules, prohibiting such subsidies for manufactures while permitting export subsidies for primary products as long as they were applied "in a manner which results in that Contracting Party having no more than an equitable share of world export trade in that product. . . ." (Trebilock and Howse, 1999, p. 249). It was not until the conclusion of the Uruguay

[15]The products the Unites States restricted were sugar, peanuts, and dairy products.

Round that some discipline was imposed on agricultural trade policies and effective caps were placed on export subsidies.

Although the United States actively pressed for a complete elimination of agricultural export subsidies in the Uruguay Round, it has not hesitated to employ such subsidies itself. At first glance the attraction to subsidies is curious. The United States is a major exporter of temperate zone agricultural products. It appears to have international market power that could be exercised by restricting rather than subsidizing exports, thus securing terms of trade gains. On reflection, however, the putative market power may have a short shelf life. Countries such as Argentina, Australia, Brazil, and Canada have the capacity to expand output and displace the United States in third country markets, should the United States attempt to act as a dominant oligopolist. Moreover, since the establishment of the EC's Common Agricultural Policy, the United States has confronted subsidized EC agriculture in world markets. Restricting U.S. exports to obtain a price increase when competitors are subsidizing is a sure recipe for losing foreign overseas market share. The postwar experience with temperate zone agriculture has been a subsidy story, not an export-restraint story.

Sparring between the United States and the EC over wheat subsidies began in the mid-1970s and intensified in the mid-1980s.[16] In 1975 the U.S. Wheat Millers' National Federation filed a complaint under Section 301 with USTR against the EC's wheat flour export subsidies. The government delayed action until the completion of the Tokyo Round, and the new GATT subsidies code was in place (1979). With no real progress in reining in EC subsidies, the 301 complaint was resurrected and the dispute taken to the GATT. The GATT panel report was delayed, and in the interim the United States responded by subsidizing wheat flour sales to Egypt, a traditional U.S. export market in which the EC was making inroads. When the panel report was finally issued in 1983, the decision went against the United States and concluded that the EC had not taken more than an equitable share of the world wheat flour market. The United States responded to this setback by filing a complaint against EC exports of a downstream wheat product, pasta. This time the GATT panel sided with the United States, finding that pasta was not a primary product and that the EC practices were inconsistent with their GATT obligations. This acrimo-

[16]Rhodes (1993); Trebilock and Howse (1999).

nious history of trade in flour and pasta was the backdrop to an escalation of the wheat wars in the middle of the decade.

The first half of the 1980s, which had been hard on U.S. manufacturing, did not spare U.S. agriculture. Wheat exports, which had soared in the late 1970s, plummeted from 1.8 billion bushels in the crop year 1981–1982 to 0.9 billion in 1985–1986. The market price, which had peaked at almost $4/bu in 1980, fell below $2.50 in 1986. U.S. government stocks had risen from less than 0.4 billion bushels in 1973 to over 1.7 billion bushels in 1985.[17] Moreover, the EC, which had been a net importer of wheat until 1974, had become a major competitor, selling subsidized wheat in world markets.[18]

It was in this distressed situation that the United States in 1985 established the Export Enhancement Program (EEP). The ostensible objectives were (1) to increase export sales over what they otherwise would be (additionality), (2) achieve budget neutrality, and (3) target subsidies most heavily in markets where the EC actively subsidized sales. The underlying purposes were to help U.S. farmers and to contest EC subsidies. Like the DISC, the EEP appeared to be an almost ideal policy. In its initial operation, government-owned surplus commodity stocks were to be paid as bonuses to agricultural exporters, allowing them to lower prices and meet competition in targeted foreign markets. (After 1989, government stocks were depleted and cash subsidies were paid). The purported advantages of EEP were threefold. First, the subsidies would be for incremental exports and not displace normal commercial exports. Second, because the subsidies were to be paid "in kind" out of existing stocks, they would be budget-neutral or, indeed, save government storage costs. Third, by targeting markets where EC subsidies were substantial, the United States would up the stakes in the subsidies war and hopefully engineer a cease-fire.

In practice, the EEP did not work exactly as planned. When excess stocks ran out in 1989 and cash payments were made, the budget neutral-

[17]Under the policy in place at the time, the U.S. government set a target price for wheat, called the loan rate. The Commodity Credit Corporation then bought wheat at this rate in amounts sufficient to keep market prices at least as high as the loan rate. Thus, the loan rate was a floor for U.S. prices and could be well above world market prices.

[18]Under the CAP, minimum internal prices were set. If excess EC production was sold for a lower price in world markets, the difference was made up by the EC in the form of restitution payments to exporters. Preeg (1995, p. 95) shows EC exports of grains to be 18.6 million tons and grain export subsidies to be $1.7 billion in 1986.

ity objective was compromised. Moreover, some studies show that the release of stocks under EEP depressed U.S. wheat prices, forcing the government into higher payments to maintain the loan rate, further eroding budget neutrality. The ability of the United States to discriminate through selective subsidies was challenged by China and the Soviet Union. Both were initially excluded from EEP, and both responded by aggressively shifting their imports to U.S. competitors, including the EC. The U.S. backed down in 1987, making both countries eligible for the EEP subsidies. Indeed, China and the Soviet Union negotiated some of the highest per ton subsidies (Goldberg and Knetter, 1997).[19]

The impact on EC subsidy policy is open to debate. Between 1985 and 1988, EC wheat export subsidies increased from $365 million to $1.8 billion (Goldberg and Knetter, 1997, p. 282). In the long run, of course, the completion of the Uruguay Round in 1994 brought some discipline to agricultural export subsidies, but the role of the EEP in forcing compromise remains controversial.There was a recovery in prices, production, and exports in the latter half of the 1980s. But separating the effects of EEP from other factors and especially the depreciation of the dollar is difficult. Three studies of the wheat subsidy war are of interest. Goldberg and Knetter (1997) conclude on the basis of regression analysis that (1) the collapse of the wheat market in 1981–1985 was caused by the overvaluation of the dollar, not European export subsidies, (2) the EEP had little effect on the U.S. world market share subsequent to 1985, and (3) the effect of the EEP on the domestic price of wheat, the variable of most interest to U.S. farmers, was negligible.

Anania, Bohman, and Carter (1992) are if anything harsher in their analysis of the program. They conclude that the EEP failed to meet its criteria, that the increase in U.S. exports attributable to the EEP was in fact less than the release in stocks, and that other wheat-exporting countries were harmed more than the EC by the program.

A final study by Bagwell and Staiger (2000) takes a novel and interesting approach to explaining the wheat subsidies war. They build a theoretical model along the lines of the Brander-Spencer rent-snatching model. The obvious difficulty in borrowing this model from the strategic trade literature is that the international wheat market does not appear to have oligopolistic

[19]In the end, Japan, Korea, and Taiwan were the only wheat importers excluded from the program.

rents that can be snatched from competitors with strategic subsidies. They attempt to overcome this difficulty by assuming that governments (in this case, the United States and the EC) give disproportionately high weights to the welfare of their agricultural sectors. It follows from the model that an export subsidy can be welfare-enhancing even if it leads to a decline in export prices and a terms of trade loss. Within this framework they go on to investigate the trilateral "game" played by the two principal wheat subsidizers, the United States and the EC, and the wheat importing countries that benefit from cheaper wheat. One conclusion is that the United States and the EC gain from cooperating (limiting but not eliminating subsidies), as compared to higher-level, unrestricted subsidies (the Nash solution). This is of course what ultimately came about in the Uruguay Round Agreements, but it took a decade for the game to be played out.[20]

The agricultural subsidy issue flared again in 2002. In May, Congress passed and President Bush signed a farm bill that reversed free market policies in agriculture and revived a target price support system that was abolished in 1996. The ten year cost of the bill was estimated at $190 billion, an 80 percent increase over the cost of existing farm programs, with two-thirds of the subsidies to go to the largest 10 percent of farmers. Products include grain and cotton, but also honey, milk, peanuts, lentils, and dried peas. At almost the same time the U.S. proposed sweeping changes in agricultural trade in the Doha Round. These included the elimination of agricultural export subsidies over five years, a worldwide reduction in domestic subsidies of $100 billion by 2010, lowering average world tariffs on farm products from 62 percent to 15 percent, and reform and liberalization of tariff-rate quotas. (Tariff-rate quotas allow a certain quantity of imports at a low tariff rate while charging a higher rate for over-quota imports. The United States uses tariff-rate quotas to control imports of beef, dairy, peanuts, sugar, tobacco, and cotton.) Foreign reaction to the farm bill and the liberalization proposal ranged from skeptical to negative.

How are these apparently inconsistent policy initiatives to be explained? One answer is that the farm bill was almost purely domestic poli-

[20]Bagwell and Staiger claim that agricultural trade disputes involving competitive markets may be the most important example of strategic trade theory. Their assumption that governments weight the welfare of various sectors differently in determining policy is certainly convenient. But it risks the Panglossian view that all policy is rational and welfare-enhancing.

tics, much like the steel tariffs earlier in 2002, while the trade liberalization proposal reflected core liberal trade values—an example of U.S. trade policy being "unfaithful but not disloyal to liberal trade principles." At a slightly more sophisticated level, one could interpret the new domestic subsidies as providing stronger negotiation leverage in multilateral talks, a modern variation of the "bargaining tariffs" the United States had created in the late nineteenth century in pursuit of reciprocity. The administration itself chose to point out that under WTO rules negotiated in the Uruguay Round, U.S. domestic and export subsidies were capped at levels well below EU caps. Thus according to the official line the new subsidies merely "leveled the playing field" in the agricultural subsidies "game."

Subsidizing Export Financing: The Ex-Im Bank

Credit is the lifeblood of trade, and subsidized credit has been a popular tool to subsidize exports. The United States joined the ranks in 1934 with the creation of the Ex-Im Bank.[21] But subsidized credit can be expensive for governments and can distort trade. The year 1934 also marked the creation of the Berne Union, whose initial purpose was to exchange information on credit risk among export credit organizations but in the 1950s took on the task of disciplining the terms on which governments offered export credit. That task was subsequently taken over by the OECD. The tension between matching foreign financing subsidies and finding international agreement of curtailing such subsidies persists to this day.

The Ex-Im Bank operates at a modest scale. In fiscal year 2000 it authorized $12.6 billion in loans guarantees and export credit insurance, supporting $15.5 billion of U.S. exports.[22] But it has not been free of controversy. It was almost axed in the 1950s for budget reasons but was rescued

[21]A principal purpose at the time was to expand exports to the Soviet Union, a market for which private commercial financing would have been difficult to obtain. Moravcisk (1989) dates the first modern government export finance scheme to 1919 and the British Export Credit Guarantee Department.

[22]Ex-Im Bank Annual Performance Report, 2000. The Bank offers four "products": (1) fixed rate loans up to 85 percent of export value to foreign buyers of U.S. goods and services; (2) guarantees to export lenders for repayment of interest and principal, should the foreign buyer default on his debt obligations; (3) short-term guarantees to lenders making working-capital loans to exporting firms; and (4) export credit insurance to protect U.S. exporters against foreign debtor default for political or commercial reasons.

by Congress. In the 1990s it was accused of being a prime example of "corporate welfare," a charge given some credibility by the concentration of its services to a small number of large United States–based multinational firms.[23] More broadly, with the increasing sophistication and deepening of private international capital markets, one can question why a government export credit agency is needed at all.

Any evaluation of the Ex-Im Bank must recognize its twofold mission: to provide export financing and guarantees where there is private capital market failure and to meet the competition (level the playing field) *vis a vis* other countries' financing agencies.[24] The first mission is legitimate in principle and can be supported by economic argument. The delicate task, however, is to accurately identify private market failures. The mere lack of commercial export financing on reasonable terms is insufficient evidence. The private markets continually and correctly judge certain loans as too risky to undertake. The Ex-Im Bank itself does not have a free hand in selecting transactions for support. On the one hand, it is constrained not to compete with private financing. On the other hand, it is enjoined not to lend unless there is reasonable ensurance of repayment. Thus, in fulfilling its first mission, the Bank operates in a rather narrow range where risk is too great for private lenders but not too great for the Bank.

The second mission, to meet the competition, has been addressed in two ways. First, the Bank states it is fully prepared to assemble a financing package for an export sale at least as attractive as any offered by another government export credit agency. This covers the traditional loan terms: interest rates, risk premiums, repayment terms, etc. The Bank claims it is successful in providing finance that meets the competitors on qualified loan and guarantee transactions, yet it operates under certain handicaps not always encountered by the competition. These include denial of Ex-Im financing as part of unilateral U.S. sanctions, adherence to anticorruption and environmental standards not always met by competitors, strict rules on the domestic content of exports financed or guaranteed, and the require-

[23]Cline (2001) notes that in fiscal year 1999, some 47 percent of the Ex-Im Bank's authorizations for finance supported aircraft exports. This has led some critics to dub it "Boeing's Bank."

[24]A failure in the export market itself, for example, positive externalities in producing the export good, raises the question of whether financing subsidies are the most appropriate response.

ment (subject to waiver) that Ex-Im Bank–financed exports be shipped in U.S. flag vessels (Mendelowitz, 2001; Evans and Oye, 2001).

The second approach taken by the Bank to meet the competition has been to level the playing field by negotiating with other major trade finance agencies in the OECD to establish strict regulation of trade financing practices. The United States–led effort to discipline pernicious competition in financing subsidies has had some success. Summers (2001) estimates the annual budget savings from the OECD effort to be more than $500 million.[25] But again, indirect or unregulated channels for favorable export financing have sprung up. Among these, the most serious appears to be the so-called market windows opened by U.S. competitors.[26] Whether these windows in fact offer subsidies is disputed.

To summarize, the U.S. has been in the export finance subsidy game for two reasons: to compensate for private financial market failure and to level the playing field by either matching foreign subsidies or, preferably, harmonizing financing practices toward commercial norms. Underlying this activity, of course, is the basic assumption that supporting exports and export-related jobs brings benefits in excess of subsidy costs.[27]

▶ RESTRICTIONS ON EXPORT: AGAINST THE (COMMERCIAL) GRAIN

We now turn to the other face of export policy: restrictions and disincentives. Setting aside their infrequent use to conserve domestic short supply, U.S. export controls can be arrayed along a continuum. At one end are controls designed to maintain or enhance national security, quite narrowly conceived. These are often termed strategic export controls and include, importantly, nonproliferation of nuclear weapons and materials. The central grouping also may have a national security dimension—for example, the destabilization of unfriendly governments—but the goals are often much broader, including changing the behavior of foreign governments.

[25]The OECD agreement is known as the Arrangement on Guidelines for Officially Supported Export Credits and dates to 1978.

[26]Market windows are government-sponsored finance institutions that ostensibly follow the same norms as private financial markets.

[27]For theoretical treatment of the benefits and costs of export subsidies, see Fleisig and Hill (1984).

These goals range from altering their racial and human rights policies to obtaining their assistance in controlling trade in illegal drugs. This central grouping might be called foreign policy–motivated controls, and restrictions on exports in this group are generally part of a larger package of economic sanctions. These sanctions are the "sticks" in carrot-and-stick diplomacy. The last (smaller) group of controls on exports has ethical foundations but with self-interest mixed in. Examples would be controls on the export of pharmaceuticals that are restricted in the United States, similar controls on pesticides, and restrictions on trade in ozone-depleting substances, endangered species, and hazardous wastes. The Foreign Corrupt Practices Act (FCPA), which prohibits U.S. firms from engaging in egregious acts of corruption, might also be mentioned, although it serves foreign policy interests as well.[28]

These three categories of controls raise similar questions. Under what conditions are they effective, and how is effectiveness to be measured? Additionally, they all face opposition from thwarted commercial interests. Finally, while all can be implemented unilaterally, they generally are more effective (less costly) if agreed to multilaterally. Economic statecraft in obtaining cooperation plays a central role.

Strategic Export Controls

The foundations of U.S. controls over the export of military and dual-use products and technology were laid in World War II.[29] The wartime controls were administered by the Commerce Department and coordinated with principal allies, notably, Britain and Canada. In the immediate postwar period, government decontrol legislation was enacted and the number of items subject to export controls was dramatically reduced, although the authority to restrict exports was never repealed. The rise of the Soviet and

[28]The FCPA was passed in 1977 following revelations that many U.S. companies were making illegal payments to foreign government officials. The law prohibits corrupt payments to foreign officials for the purpose of obtaining or retaining business. In response to business complaints that the law placed them at a competitive disadvantage, the United States steered an antibribery convention through the OECD in 1997.

[29]Dual use refers to goods and technology that have civilian and military uses. U.S. export controls, of course, predate World War II. During the interwar period, the 1935 Neutrality Act authorized the president to ban export of military goods to belligerents in a war in the belief that we would be less likely to be drawn into foreign conflicts.

communist threats soon brought this liberal period to an end, although not without some dissent. Early echoes of an argument that persists to this day were advanced: maintaining open trade relations improves leverage over potential adversaries. But by the time of the Marshall Plan in 1947, disturbing memories of shipping war materials to Japan in the 1930s were still fresh, anticommunist attitudes had hardened, and U.S. exports to Soviet Bloc countries were progressively curtailed.[30] The effects of the controls were quite dramatic. Exports to Eastern Europe and to the Soviet Union fell 70 percent and 97 percent, respectively, between the first quarter of 1948 and the third quarter of 1949 (Cupitt, 2000, p. 69).

Controls on strategic exports have to be multilateral to be effective. But not all countries capable of supplying the goods and technology were equally convinced of an imminent Soviet threat, and moreover the trading pattern of European countries differed from that of the United States. Despite these difficulties, a multilateral control body was established in 1950, the rather secretive Coordinating Committee for Multilateral Export Controls (COCOM), and work on developing harmonized lists of sensitive exports commenced.[31] Following the communist takeover of China in 1949 and the start of the Korean War in 1950, the United States embargoed exports to North Korea and China, and COCOM extended its controls to China.

Three general points concerning strategic export controls in the postwar period can made. First, they became the source of considerable tension between the United States and its allies. This was partly the result of the dual system, with separate U.S. and COCOM controls. From the U.S. business perspective, foreign firms operating under less-strict controls enjoyed a competitive edge and U.S. export sales were sacrificed. European allies interpreted the dual system as a lack of trust in their efforts. Equally divisive were U.S. attempts to influence European strategic export policies and practices. These efforts took several forms. Even before U.S. policy

[30]Part of the motivation for export controls in the immediate postwar period was shortages of critical materials such as locomotives and rail cars. This short-supply rationale faded within a few years.

[31]COCOM was located in Paris rather than London to avoid publicity (Cupitt, 2000). The three lists were (1) embargoed items, (2) items subject to quantitative controls, and (3) items subject to government scrutiny. Harmonization did not mean identical lists. Throughout the postwar period, the United States kept its own, stricter lists.

was formalized in the 1949 Export Control Act, the United States used its foreign assistance under the Marshall Plan to pressure Western European countries to tighten controls on trade with the East (Cupitt, 2000, p. 67). More generally, U.S. regulations reached well beyond U.S. borders. Under the Export Administration Act, controls were extended to re-export of U.S.-origin goods or technology by a foreign company and to exports of foreign-origin goods if they contained U.S. components or were the products of U.S.-origin technology. These requirements were implemented by assurances obtained from U.S. foreign subsidiaries, foreign licensees, and wholly unaffiliated foreign firms (Moyer and Mabry, 1988, pp. 108–109).

It was the so-called pipeline controls imposed by the Reagan administration, however, that created the greatest ill will between the United States and Western Europe. In 1981 the United States imposed trade sanctions on the Soviet Union for its repression in Poland and the crackdown on the labor movement Solidarity, and these were tightened a year later. Exports of oil and gas equipment and technology to the Soviet Union by foreign subsidiaries of U.S. firms were embargoed even if the products were wholly of foreign origin, and unaffiliated foreign firms were barred from exporting these products and technology if such exports were manufactured with technology acquired through licensing agreements with U.S. firms.[32] This bold assertion of extraterritoriality was angrily rejected in Europe, with some governments ordering their firms to ignore U.S. restrictions and honor their export contracts. The United States responded by creating a blacklist of offending companies. In the end, there was little foreign compliance with the restrictions (and a backlash in the United States), and the extraordinary measures were lifted five months later.

The second point is that the severity and implementation of strategic export controls has been contentious in the United States itself. While the need to control exports that would contribute to the military potential of adversaries was not challenged, the means by which this is done has been vigorously contested. Exports are important to the U.S. economy, and any controls, regardless of purpose, are likely to impair growth. Moreover, strategic export controls have increasingly concentrated on high technol-

[32]The target was a major natural gas pipeline being constructed by the Soviet Union that would increase Western Europe's dependence on Soviet gas supplies (Moyer and Maybry, 1988).

ogy sectors and especially information technology, which are thought to be the engines of productivity and prosperity.[33] Economic and commercial interests were also undermined by excessively rigid or poorly administered controls.[34] More broadly, as previously noted, trade is often touted as a vehicle for better relations with potential adversaries, and overly strict controls sap this opportunity. Indeed, the severity of U.S. controls has fluctuated with the international strategic and political climate, with pressure for relaxation immediately after World War II, during the detente period of the 1970s, and more recently after the collapse of the Soviet Union. Finally, as the role of information and disembodied technology replaced traditional manufactures in military uses and the sources of this technology have broadened, the ability of the United States to exercise effective control has weakened (Macdonald, 1990). For all these reasons, plus the usual commercial interests of export firms, strategic export controls have encountered resistance.

The third general point is that export controls have mutated over the years. As mentioned above, the emphasis has shifted from tangible goods—machinery and equipment—to information and know-how.[35] As compared to goods, information has special economic attributes that make it especially difficult to control (for example, the purchase of information does not reduce the quantity available; it multiplies it). Controls have also shifted in purpose away from narrow military security to broader foreign policy objectives. Examples are the 1979 grain embargo on the Soviet Union in response to its invasion of Afghanistan, sanctions on Poland following the declaration of martial law in 1981, and the sanction on Iran at the time of the hostage crisis in 1979. While military security interests were in the background, larger foreign policy objectives were in play. Finally, with the collapse of the Soviet Union, the purpose of controls switched

[33]Recall that limiting sales in declining-cost industries is especially costly.

[34]Principal responsibility for administering the controls rested with Commerce, but the Department of Defense has played a large role. Macdonald (1990) reports much bureaucratic infighting. More mundane criticisms involved excessive documentation, delays, and opaque criteria.

[35]The generally liberal 1979 Export Administration Act instructed the Department of Defense to compile a "militarily critical technologies list" where technology is defined very broadly as "information and know-how that can be used to design, produce, manufacture, utilize, or reconstruct goods. . . ."

toward the objectives of nonproliferation, antiterrorism, and limiting the production of weapons of mass destruction.[36]

With the end of the Cold War, COCOM was disbanded. A new agreement, the Wassenaar Arrangement, was established in 1996 to oversee trade in conventional weapons and dual-use technology. It has no independent authority. Under the new arrangement, which includes Russia, all measures are based on members' national legislation and implemented on the basis of national discretion. The United States, of course, maintains a significant export control system.

The economics of strategic export controls are rather thin. The political economy literature reminds us that when the benefits of a public policy are diffused and widely shared, as they are with national security, and when the costs are concentrated on a small number of firms, as they tend to be with export controls, the balance of lobbying expenditures should favor those supporting minimal controls. In the case of strategic controls, however, the force of this argument is weakened, at least during the period when anticommunist sentiments were strong.[37] Strategic export controls can also be analyzed with game-theoretic tools as part of alliance theory, with the payoff an international public good, security for the Western world. Unfortunately, two-level (domestic, international), multiple-agent, repeated games do not often lead to strong conclusions.[38]

The more-straightforward economic analysis has attempted to put the policy in a cost-benefit framework, in which the costs of controls are set against some measure of the benefits. Measuring the benefits, in practice, amounted to estimating the additional costs to the Soviet Union of countering U.S. and allied export controls. In some studies, an attempt was

[36]Economic sanctions directed at countries supporting international terrorism have been an important component of U.S. antiterrorism policy (e.g., Iran, Iraq, Libya, Sudan). Trade restrictions are a component, but sanctions extend to finance, foreign assistance, and other tools. After September 11, 2001, the United States removed or relaxed economic sanctions on a number of countries, including Pakistan and India, presumably as a reward for their cooperation.

[37]An interesting test of whether money or policy stance delivers more votes to politicians.

[38]But Drezner (1999) and others use game theory to investigate the related question of economic sanctions.

made to measure the benefits as the costs to the United States avoided by not having to catch up to improved Soviet technology (Macdonald, 1990). Such studies fall short of ideal, not the least because they fail to examine marginal costs and marginal benefits.

A study by J. David Richardson (1993) remains one of the most sophisticated attempts to size up the effects of broad-range export controls on the United States.[39] The focus is on "lost" exports, not welfare. Three approaches were used: surveys of experts; numerical simulations in which imperfect market structures were calibrated to real world data and then "shocked" by various export disincentives, including controls, to observe the export effects; and regression analysis. This last, statistical exercise took two forms. The first used a gravity model to estimate exports lost due to strategic and foreign policy export controls.[40] Richardson concludes that the full range of export disincentives may have cost the United States between $21 and $27 billion in lost exports in the mid-1990s, with national security and antiproliferation controls accounting for two-thirds to three-quarters of the total.[41] For comparison, total exports of goods and services were $576 billion in 1995, but of course the export controls were disproportionately harsh on a fairly narrow range of high-technology goods.

Trade Sanctions for Foreign Policy Purposes

There is no bright line between trade controls taken for national security purposes and controls to promote foreign policy interests. The measures taken against the Soviet Union and Poland after martial law was imposed and the measures against the Soviet Union after its Afghanistan invasion

[39]Richardson wisely prefers the term "sizing up" rather than "measure" or "estimate," as the latter would suggest a false degree of precision.

[40]More accurately, Richardson used a gravity model to identify unusually low exports to particular countries. He then carefully examined these cases to determine if export controls offered a plausible explanation. His second regression exercise used cross-state variations within the United States in variables such as export promotion expenditures and environmental control costs to assess the effects of these variables on state-level export performance.

[41]This is the likely range. The high estimate is $40 billion.

had national security overtones but were essentially punishments for specific actions by the Soviets. In similar fashion, trade measures to slow the development of weapons of mass destruction—chemical and biological agents—have national security objectives but are also undertaken to isolate or destabilize governments that the United States opposes. The prolonged economic sanctions against Cuba have outlived their military security objective but serve foreign policy (and domestic political) objectives. Sanctions in support of human rights and against racial policies (South Africa, the white government of Rhodesia, the Dominican Republic in the 1960s, and currently against Burma) are designed to change policies or force governments from power, and have minimal national security justification.

The Institute for International Economics has compiled a helpful tabulation of economic sanctions over the past 90 years. Figure 8.1 displays the frequency of sanctions by decade and the number of sanctions in which the United States has played a lead role. Two features stand out. First, the number of sanctions cases has increased dramatically. Second, the United States has become active in global sanctions. Neither is especially surprising. Sanctions are an intermediate measure, stronger than diplomatic protests but less forceful than military action. And over the nine decades covered by the data, the United States shed its isolationist stance and has become the dominant world political and economic power.

The growth of sanctions as a tool of foreign policy has stimulated analytical interest in the same questions as strategic export controls: are they effective, and what are the costs? The effectiveness question is most frequently addressed through case studies, although more theoretical work has been done.[42] Work done at IIE illustrates the case study approach. The authors, Hufbauer, Schott, and Elliott (1990), analyzed 116 cases of economic sanctions from World War I through the embargo of Iraq in 1990.

[42]For example, Drezner (1999) uses a game-theoretic approach to build a conflict expectations model of economic coercion and tests the hypotheses with data adapted from IIE's case studies. Key variables are the opportunity costs of sanctions for sender and target and the bilateral expectations of future conflict. Selden (1999) investigates the theoretical point that export and import embargos have differential distributional effects on target countries and concludes that halting the imports from a target country is more effective than halting exports to that country.

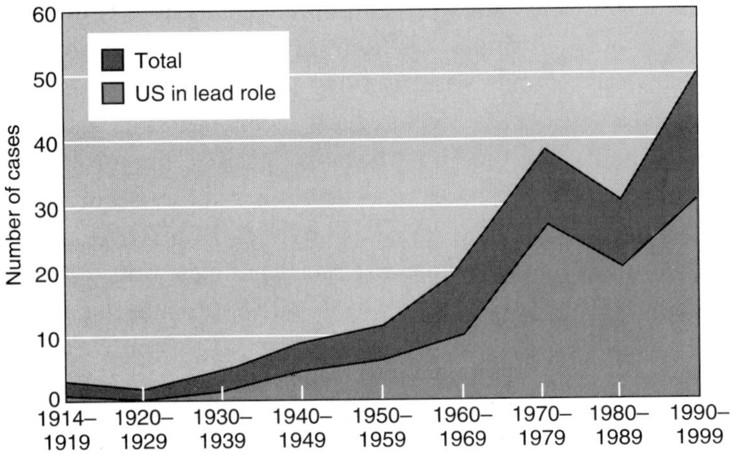

Figure 8.1 Economic sanctions, by decade.
Source: Institute for International Economics, http://www.iie.com/topics/sanctions/sanctions-overview.htm, 9/10/01.

They created an index of "success," measuring the extent to which the sanction-sender's objective was achieved and the contribution to that success attributable to the sanctions. With this framework they calculated a success rate overall of 34 percent but noted that the rate dropped in the more recent years of their study, 1973–1990.

The cost of economic sanctions has aroused more interest as their frequency increases and new evidence on the apparently low success rate materializes. The concern is mostly limited to restrictions on U.S. exports; except for oil, sanctions involving import restrictions do not excite much attention in the business community.[43] Once again, the costs are generally measured by lost exports. But as the more sophisticated studies recognize, lost exports, even if accurately calculated, do not measure welfare effects. Resources that otherwise would be engaged in exporting are available to produce alternative goods and services, although presumably less productively.

[43]In addition, the president has only limited powers to impose broad import limits. He can, however, ban imports from countries that support terrorism.

Hufbauer, Elliott, Cyrus, and Winston (1997) attempt to measure the effects of economic sanctions on U.S. merchandise trade, jobs, and wages in the mid-1990s. The approach is to use a gravity model with dummy variables indicating sanctions to estimate bilateral trade flows. The regressions suggest that U.S. exports in 1995 were \$15–\$19 billion lower because of sanctions (roughly 3 percent of total exports). This method does not adjust for diversion of exportables to other markets following the sanctions. The job content of these "lost" exports is calculated with use of direct and indirect labor-output coefficients (average, not marginal) and is estimated to be 200,000–260,000 jobs in the export sector (this technique is similar to the trade-employment balance studies described in Chapter 5). Because the United States was enjoying generally full employment, these lost export jobs do not imply unemployment or lost output. But the authors argue that export jobs pay higher than average wages—a premium of 12–15 percent. Using data on average manufacturing wage, they calculate the lost wage premium to be \$800 million–\$1 billion for 1995. This is a questionable step. If the wage premium in exporting reflects higher labor-skill levels that can be utilized and compensated in other activities, the lost-wages estimate would be lower or zero.

Ethical Concerns

The United States has a modest number of export restrictions, based on ethical principles mixed with self-interest. For example, it adheres to the Convention on International Trade in Endangered Species, the Montreal Protocol limiting trade in ozone-depleting substances, and the Basel Convention limiting trade in hazardous wastes. The aggregate trade impact of these measures is small, but opposition from thwarted commercial interests is not totally absent. Controls on the export of drugs not approved for use in the United States provide a good example. The relevant U.S. law dates to 1906 and permitted the export of unapproved drugs so long as the drug was not in conflict with the laws of the importing country (U.S. FDA, 1998). A subsequent change in the law (1938) introduced the term "new drugs," and this was interpreted by the courts as *not* permitting the export of unapproved new drugs. Following pressure from the pharmaceutical industry, the legislation was altered in 1986. Under the new law the FDA could permit the export of drugs not approved for use in the United States, provided either that they contained active ingredients for which marketing approval in the United States was being sought and were exported to one of 21 designated developed countries or that the drugs were intended for the treatment of tropical diseases. In the latter case, the exporter must demonstrate to the FDA that on the basis of credible scientific evidence, the drug would be safe and effective in the importing country. Elements of the U.S. industry found both the country restriction and the approval process burdensome. Subsequent legislation in 1996 eliminated the requirement of prior FDA approval of exports of unapproved drugs in most cases and authorized the export of unapproved drugs for use in clinical trials in 25 listed countries. It should also be noted that the Committee on Trade and Environment of the WTO has been actively considering the issue of trade in domestically prohibited goods, but progress has been modest.

CONCLUSIONS

At first glance, U.S. export policy appears to be at cross-purposes—numerous efforts to both promote and restrict exports. This chapter demonstrates that while genuine conflicts in objectives exist, there is no paradox to explain. The many measures designed to promote and facilitate exports derive from commercial objectives and have frequently been "sold" on the basis of export-related jobs. In some cases, export assistance is strategic in the sense of attempting to limit foreign subsidies or establish a "level playing field." While the appropriate analytical approaches to export promotion policies are benefit cost analysis and game theory, the results are often inconclusive.

Restrictions on exports serve different, noncommercial goals—national security, an array of foreign policy objectives—and occasionally reflect ethical concerns. These restrictions inevitably encounter some opposition from firms that are denied export market opportunities, and this tension has been a persistent characteristic of export policy. The degree of enthusiasm for economic sanctions generally and export controls in particular depends on an assessment of their effectiveness. The literature on this subject is generally neutral to negative but is not conclusive. The practical issue is to design and administer effective and efficient controls with the least possible burden to trade.

REFERENCES

Amania, Giovanni, Mary Bohman, Colin Carter. 1992. The United States Export Subsidies in Wheat: Strategic Trade Policy or Expensive Beggar-Thy-Neighbor Tactic? *American Journal of Agricultural Economics* 74(3):534–545.

Bagwell, Kyle, and Robert Staiger. 2000. *Strategic Trade, Competitive Industries and Agricultural Trade Disputes.* Cambridge, MA: Working Paper 7822. NBER.

Cline, William. 2001. Ex-Im, Exports and Private Capital: Will Financial Markets Squeeze the Bank? In: Gary Hufbauer and Rita Rodriquez (eds.). *The Ex-Im Bank in the 21st Century.* Washington, DC: Institute for International Economics.

Cupitt, Richard. 2000. *Reluctant Champions: U.S. Presidential Policy and Strategic Export Controls.* New York: Routledge.

Desai, Mihir, and James Hines. 2000. *The Uneasy Marriage of Export Incentives and the Income Tax.* Cambridge, MA: Working Paper 8009. NBER.

Drezner, Daniel. 1999. *The Sanctions Paradox.* Cambridge, UK: Cambridge University Press.

Evans, Peter, and Kenneth Oye. 2001. International Competition: Competition and Cooperation in Government Export Financing. In: Gary Hufbauer and Rita Rodriquez (eds.). *The Ex-Im Bank in the 21st Century.* Washington, DC: Institute for International Economics.

Ex-Im Bank. 2000. *Annual Performance Report 2000.* Washington, DC: Ex-Im Bank.

Fleisig, Heywood, and Catherine Hill. 1984. The Benefits and Costs of Official Export Credit. In: Robert Baldwin and Anne Krueger. *The Structure and Evolution of Recent U.S. Trade Policy.* Chicago: University of Chicago Press.

Goldberg, Pinelopi, and Michael Knetter. 1997. Causes and Consequences of the Export Enhancement Program for Wheat. In: Robert Feenstra (ed.). *The Effects of U.S. Trade Protection and Promotion Policies.* Chicago: University of Chicago Press.

Hufbauer, Gary, Jeffrey Schott, Kimberly Elliott. 1990. *Economic Sanctions Reconsidered.* Second ed. Washington, DC: Institute for International Economics.

Hufbauer, Gary, Kimberly Elliott, Tess Cyrus, Elizabeth Winston. 1987. U.S. Economic Sanctions: Their Impact on Trade, Jobs and Wages. Working Paper. Washington, DC: Institute for International Economics.

Itoh, M., and K. Kiyono. 1987. Welfare Enhancing Export Subsidies. *Journal of Political Economy* 95(11):115–137.

Jackson, John. 1997. *The World Trading System.* Second ed. Cambridge, MA: MIT Press.

Macdonald, Stuart. 1990. *Technology and the Tyranny of Export Controls.* London: MacMillan.

Mendelowitz, Allan. 2001. The New World of Government-Supported International Financing. In: Gary Hufbauer and Rita Rodriguez (eds.). *The Ex-IM Bank in the 21st Century.* Washington, DC: Institute for International Economics.

Moravesik, Andrew. 1989. Disciplining Trade Finance: the OECD Export Credit Arrangement. *International Organization* 43(1):173–205.

Moyer, Homer, and Linda Mabry. 1988. *Export Controls as Instruments of Foreign Policy.* Washington, DC: International Law Institute.

Mutti, John, and Harry Grubert. 1984. The Domestic International Sales Corporation. In: Robert Baldwin and Anne Krueger. *The Structure and Evolution of U.S. Trade Policy.* Chicago: University of Chicago Press.

Preeg, Ernest. 1995. *Traders in a Brave New World.* Chicago: University of Chicago Press.

Rhodes, Carolyn. 1993. *Reciprocity, U.S. Trade Policy and the GATT Regime.* Ithaca, NY: Cornell University Press.

Richardson, J. David. 1993. *Sizing Up U.S. Export Disincentives.* Washington, DC: Institute for International Economics.

Selden, Zachary. 1999. *Economic Sanctions as Instruments of American Foreign Policy.* Westport, CT: Praeger.

Stehmann, Oliver. 2000. Foreign Sales Corporations Under the WTO. *Journal of World Trade* 34(3):127–156.

Summers, Lawrence. 2001. Continuing the Fight Against International Trade Finance Subsidies. In: Gary Hufbauer and Rita Rodriguez (eds.). *The Ex-Im Bank in the 21st Century.* Washington, DC: Institute for International Economics.

Surrey, Stanley. 1971. The DISC Proposal to Subsidize Exports. In: Commission on International Trade and Investment Policy. *United States International Economic Policy in an Interdependent World.* Papers, Vol. I. Washington, DC: GPO.

Trebilock, Michael, and Robert Howse. 1999. *The Regulation of International Trade.* Second ed. New York: Routledge.

United States Food and Drug Administration. 1998. *FDA Guidance for Industry on Exports and Imports Under FDA Export Reform and Enhancement Act of 1996.* http://www.fda.gov/opacom/fedregister/frexport.html.

Vousden, Neil. 1990. *The Economics of Trade Protection.* Cambridge, UK: Cambridge University Press.

CHAPTER

9

THE 1990s: A SUCCESS, A LULL, AND A DEBACLE

We now pick up a more chronological thread to the story. By the conclusion of the Uruguay Round in 1994, it appeared that the United States had returned to the liberal trade fold and, indeed, had helped bring the entire trade system up to date. True, preferential trade agreements flourished, but they were seen by many practitioners as way stations or stimuli on the road to multilateral liberalization. It was also true that old-fashioned protection lived on, cloaked in the antidumping and antisubsidy provisions of trade law. But set against these blemishes were the accomplishments of the Uruguay Round in addressing new issues, in putting agriculture and the MFA into play, in tightening the dispute settlement process, and indeed in creating the WTO itself.

By the mid-1990s, U.S. trade policy had drawn back from its flirtations with managed trade, VERs were officially out, Section 301 was tamed by new international rules, and Japan-bashing persisted at a much-subdued level. Despite certain eddies, the trade system appeared unusually calm up to the Seattle Ministerial in late 1999, when a new set of challenges broke to the surface. In retrospect the calm was more apparent than real. Many of the Uruguay Round initiatives were incomplete or fragile, and important constituencies in the United States, especially labor and environmentalists, had not bought into the presumed benefits of globalization. And many developing countries came to believe that their Uruguay Round benefits were minimal and the costs they incurred were high.

This chapter starts with a brief summary of Uruguay Round results, continues with an examination of four unsettled or unsettling issues in the latter part of the decade, and concludes with an analysis of the 1999 Seattle debacle and its implications. The recovery from Seattle at Doha in 2001 is examined in the next chapter.

THE URUGUAY ROUND

The Uruguay Round was a substantial but not unalloyed success. By almost any measure the international trade system and U.S. trade policy were in better shape at its conclusion in 1994 than at its start eight years earlier. Still, some of the progress has proved fragile and should not be exaggerated. We need to sketch some of the main results.[1]

In addition to substantial scheduled reductions in industrial tariffs, the agreements prohibited new VERs and phased out existing ones; started to dismantle the MFA; and took the first steps in liberalizing agricultural trade, long excluded from GATT disciplines. VERs and OMAs had become popular in many countries, including the United States, during the 1980s, despite their pernicious effect on the liberal trade system. It took considerable courage to negotiate their demise. The MFA transition period agreed to in the UR was ten years, with true liberalization heavily back-loaded. Strong interim safeguards were established, and even at the end of the transition, tariff rates will remain exceptionally high. Even so, the negotiated demise of the MFA moved textile and apparel trade in a liberal direction. In agriculture the major accomplishments were to start the process of converting nontariff barriers into bound tariffs, to reduce export subsidies by 36 percent (over 6 years), and to reduce domestic farm support by 20 percent. The tariffication of NTBs in agriculture proved "dirty," however, with many countries, including the United States, setting tariff rates in excess of 1994 protection levels and with export subsidy and domestic support commitments subject to large loopholes.[2] In the sensitive area of rice, Japan agreed to import 4 percent of consumption in 1995, rising to 8 percent by 2000. The negotiators recognized that these and other commitments were only a first step and agreed that agriculture would be a central element in the so-called built-in agenda for a new set of negotiations.

[1]For a more complete treatment, see Bhagwati and Hirsch (1998), Martin and Winters (1995), Schott (1994).

[2]Martin and Winters (1995) state that the EU conducted dirty tariffication in six of seven major product groups, and the U.S. in milder form, in five of nine products.

The Uruguay Round agreements also revised trade rules, but with mixed success. Reforming the escape clause (Article XIX) presented a dilemma. On the one hand, there was a desire to make use of the escape clause more attractive to compensate for the loss of VERs and to reduce pressure to pursue antidumping and countervailing duty actions. On the other hand, if it were too liberal or allowed discrimination when applying import relief, the escape clause would subvert the goal of trade liberalization. The result was a compromise. Some discrimination (called "selectivity") against the most rapidly increasing sources of imports is permitted, as are quantitative restraints (both illiberal provisions). On the other hand, the agreement clarifies the standard for serious injury that must be met before trade restrictions can be used and imposes time limits for relief. Also, by eliminating the need to immediately compensate countries whose imports are restricted, the escape clause may be marginally more attractive for U.S. policy-makers.[3] The subsidies code was also reformed, although it remains murky and controversial. Little progress was made on dumping, and this failure came back as a major sticking point at Seattle. Finally, at the United States' insistence, the code dealing with technical barriers to trade (i.e., product standards) was rewritten and a new agreement on sanitary and phytosanitary standards was hived off. The U.S. effort was motivated in large measure by its dispute with the EU over hormone-fed beef (discussed later in this chapter), and the rules are critical to new controversies concerning trade in genetically modified organisms (GMOs).

However, it was the new issues considered in the Uruguay Round—trade in services, protection of intellectual property, and trade-related investment measures—that most directly reflected U.S. efforts to beef up and modernize the trade system and improve its performance. GATT, of course, covered only trade in goods. By the mid-1980s, U.S. trade in services had grown to almost 30 percent of its trade in goods, and U.S. negotiators were under strong pressure from private sector firms to open foreign markets for services in which the U.S. had a presumed comparative advantage (e.g., finance, insurance, telecommunications, consulting/profes-

[3]This needs clarification. WTO's escape clause (safeguard) rules require consultations on compensation. If the consultations are unsuccessful, the affected members may withdraw equivalent concessions but are barred from doing so for three years if the safeguard action was in conformity with WTO rules and if there had been an absolute increase in imports. Compensation for the 2002 U.S. steel tariffs is in dispute.

sional) and to bring services trade within the ambit of WTO rules. The task was both novel and contentious. Unlike trade in goods, trade in services involves multiple forms of delivery (e.g., tourism, with cross-border movement of tourists; and via a foreign commercial presence, as, for example, a branch office of an accounting or law firm). Service trade often requires either some foreign investment or movement of persons to be effective. And trade in services is more often restricted by internal regulations in the importing country than barriers at the border such as tariffs. Key developing countries, especially India and Brazil, had initially opposed any discussion of services, fearing that they were at a competitive disadvantage in too many service sectors. In the end, services were notationally separated from goods trade and negotiated under a parallel track. The result was the General Agreement on Trade in Services (GATS).

The accomplishments of GATS, like the proverbial half glass of water, are in the eye of the beholder. GATS does bring services within the WTO framework and does establish MFN and national treatment principles, albeit with numerous caveats and exemptions. But even the United States, the principal sponsor of GATS, has been unwilling to commit to MFN treatment across all sectors in order to preserve its negotiating leverage. Specific commitments for liberalization of services were very limited, although some "standstill" obligations not to increase restrictions were made. As in agriculture, the tentative and preliminary steps toward liberalization resulted in an agreement for follow-up negotiations, the second element of the built-in agenda that was to be addressed in Seattle.

The other new issue of importance to the United States was improved protection of intellectual property.[4] Like services trade, intellectual property protection was heavily promoted by the U.S. private sector and was a "big deal" for the negotiators. Owners of intellectual property, be it pharmaceutical companies with drug patents, entertainment firms with copyrights, or firms with trademarks, made a vigorous case that infringement and piracy is "theft" and causes great loss to U.S. firms. But the economics (and ethics) of intellectual property are not so simple. Advances in knowledge—for example, a potentially patentable innovation or drug—have the attribute of a public good, nonrivalry in consumption. That is, one individual's use of the knowledge does not interfere with use by another individual. This sets up a dilemma. Unless a firm can appropriate a financial re-

[4]The third new issue, trade-related investment measures, resulted in the so-called TRIMs agreement but was of second-order importance.

turn, it will not invest a socially optimal amount of resources in producing the new knowledge or the new drug. Patents, which confer a legal monopoly to the owner of the intellectual property, are one way to reward the creator of intellectual property. But patents and copyrights are monopolies and allow the holder to exploit the market, restricting production and holding price above marginal cost.

Striking the appropriate balance between encouraging the creation of intellectual property through granting legalized monopoly rights and permitting access to that knowledge at reasonable cost is a serious issue for a closed economy. It is considerably more complex in an open international trade system. For example, countries differ in their views on the economics and ethics of patents on living organisms, including seeds and higher life forms. An equally sharp difference characterizes patent protection for pharmaceuticals. If international prices reflect income and demand in rich countries, and if patent protection is rigorously enforced, poor countries are simply priced out of the market. Indeed, differential pricing for AIDS drugs and the right of poor countries to ignore patent protection and manufacture or import generic versions became a hot issue in 2001. More fundamentally, strengthening intellectual property protection, a major objective of the United States in the Uruguay Round, has important international distributional consequences. Countries that are net creators of intellectual property—mainly but not exclusively OECD countries—extend their market power and potential for commercial exploitation. Countries that are net importers of intellectual property, mainly developing countries, pay higher prices for goods and services embodying intellectual property and for the use of the property itself. Although some developing countries may derive long-term economic advantage from stronger intellectual-property protection (e.g., nurturing domestic innovations, higher levels of direct investment and technology transfer), the putative benefits often seem distant and ephemeral.

In any event, the Agreement on Trade-Related Aspects of Intellectual Property Rights (TRIPs) was a significant move in the direction of strengthening the international protection of intellectual property rights.[5] It represents one of the first tangible attempts at comprehensive harmo-

[5]Developing and transition economies were given a 5-year transition period (until 2000). The least-developed countries received an extendable 11-year transition period. In Fall 2001, the United States indicated it was willing to give a further extension to the poorest countries in Africa.

nization of business regulation and, in that respect, is a major movement of trade negotiations beyond border barriers to consideration of ostensibly domestic regulations. Moreover, the enforcement provisions of the TRIPs agreement "constitute a largely unprecedented degree of control by an international regime over domestic civil and administrative procedures" (Trebilock and Howse, 1999, p. 327). Three final points need be made. First, it is not clear whether the full force of TRIPs will stick, or whether some reconsideration and revisions will be made in new trade talks. Second, the aggressive U.S. effort to harmonize intellectual property protection has implications for harmonizing other ostensibly domestic regulations with trade implications—most notably, competition, labor, health, and environmental policies. Third, the TRIPs agreement illustrates the great willingness of U.S. trade negotiators to go to bat for U.S. business interests.

THE HYPE

Completing NAFTA and the Uruguay Round did not exhaust the energies of the first Clinton administration. The time appeared ripe for a redirection of U.S. foreign policy toward more overtly commercial objectives. The Cold War was over and trade interests were no longer subordinate to security concerns. Clinton's campaign slogan, "its the economy, stupid," with its focus on business and jobs, reinforced the shift in direction. And the energetic incoming Secretary of Commerce, Ron Brown, saw major deals to be struck by U.S. firms in the so-called Big Emerging Markets (BEM), identified as Argentina, Brazil, China, India, Indonesia, Mexico, Poland, South Africa, South Korea, and Turkey.[6]

Mr. Brown had a sense of style and a flair for publicity. The Commerce Department boasted a "war room" to track the progress of major export contracts. Brown himself led some 15 overseas trade missions before his death in 1996. These missions, packed with U.S. CEOs, traveled on jets picked from the Presidential fleet. Multibillion-dollar deals were signed for big ticket items such as power stations and telecommunication systems, although in many cases the dollar values were exaggerated and the deals were often Memoranda of Understanding (MOUs) that were never con-

[6]The term has been the source of some derision. After the economic crisis starting in Asia in 1997 and hopscotching as far as Russia and Latin America, these countries have been called "the has-BEMs" or the "Submerging Markets."

summated. President Clinton himself was brought in to flog U.S. exports, calling the Brazilian Prime Minister to support a radar contract for Raytheon, persuading Saudi Arabia to buy U.S. telecommunications equipment from AT&T and to place aircraft orders with Boeing and McDonnell Douglas, and pressing for Motorola's cell phone sales in Japan.[7] Mr. Brown also was said to be influential in persuading Clinton in 1994 to reverse a campaign pledge and delink the MFN trade issue with China from that country's human rights performance.

Ultimately this unprecedented, high-level, controversial thrust into commercial diplomacy subsided. The conservative Congress elected in 1994 raised the issue of "corporate welfare," and some members pressed for dismantlement of the Department of Commerce itself. Questions were raised as to how the CEOs on trade missions were selected and whether these seats were "sold" for campaign contributions. With the death of Brown, the new Commerce Secretary, William Daley, kept a much lower profile. And the 1997 Asian crisis exposed serious weaknesses in the so-called Big Emerging Markets initiative.

▶ THE LULL

After the bruising domestic battle for NAFTA and the protracted struggle to complete the Uruguay Round, after the long period of Japan-bashing had abated, and after the hype of a new commercial diplomacy and of cracking open the Big Emerging Markets that characterized the first Clinton administration had subsided, the period between 1995 and the end of 1999 appeared on the surface to be relatively calm. Several factors contributed. As noted, new negotiations on agriculture and services had been postponed to the end of 1999, and a nine-year peace clause immunizing certain agricultural subsidies from countervailing duty actions was in effect. Japan was down and out throughout this period, and U.S. dialogue (hectoring?) with that country emphasized deregulation, domestic reform, and macro-policy over trade. And Clinton's failure to obtain fast-track authority delayed serious negotiations to extend NAFTA southward. More fundamentally, U.S. prosperity—low inflation, full employment, rising pro-

[7]The CIA helped out by providing "defensive intelligence" about competitors' efforts to edge out U.S. firms from obtaining overseas contracts (*Christian Science Monitor*, 3/28/95).

ductivity, and booming financial markets—took the edge off earlier trade concerns.

This period was not without interest, however. The failure to obtain fast-track authority, two bitter disputes with the EU over beef and bananas, the collapse of the Multilateral Agreement on Investment (MAI), and the trade policy response to the Asian crisis all deserve attention.

Fast Track

Fast-track legislation was first adopted in 1974 and subsequently renewed or expanded five times. It lapsed in 1994 after the legislation implementing the Uruguay Round was passed. Despite periodic efforts by the President and Congress, it had still not been renewed by early 2002. The failure to acquire this authority illustrates several features of U.S. trade policy: the long-standing struggle between Congress and the President over control of trade policy; the central role of domestic politics; and the emergence of labor and environmental standards as new critical issues in trade.

The Constitution grants Congress the authority to regulate international trade. From 1934 through the 1960s, Congress removed itself from line-by-line tariff setting and authorized the President to negotiate tariff reductions within specified limits. This arrangement was judged inadequate to accommodate the negotiated reduction in nontariff barriers contemplated in the Tokyo Round.[8] As an alternative, fast-track provisions were included in the 1974 legislation. In this arrangement the President was required to state negotiating objectives and a timetable, consult with Congress during negotiations, and submit implementing legislation at the conclusion. In return, Congress bound itself to vote up or down on the legislation without amendment and within a specified time frame. The idea was to give the Executive credible negotiating authority while maintaining the constitutional authority and guidance of Congress.

This sharing of responsibility for trade policy was in disarray after 1994. There are two related reasons. First, fast-track authority fell victim to domestic politics. Second, it became entangled in the contentious trade/

[8]In the Kennedy Round (1964–1967), U.S. negotiators had agreed to scrap the "American Selling Price" system for customs valuation of selected products, an NTB. Under ASP, the United States assessed duties on the basis of a competitive U.S. product and not on the generally lower value of the imported product. When presented with the final results of the round, Congress refused to change ASP, causing considerable ill will abroad.

environment/labor standards issue. Both can be traced to the sharp debates over NAFTA earlier in the decade. A quick sketch is sufficient. In submitting implementing legislation for the Uruguay Round in 1994, the Clinton administration wished to include new fast-track authority to replace the expiring authority. The draft language included labor standards and environmental objectives, both the subjects of earlier side agreements to NAFTA. These were unpopular with various constituencies, especially certain business groups and conservative Republicans, who wished to keep trade matters clean of environmental and labor strictures. In the end the implementing legislation was simply stripped of new fast-track authority. At this point domestic politics became crucial.[9] By and large, Republicans supported new fast-track authority but with minimal commitments with regard to labor and environmental standards. President Clinton also wanted fast track but was stymied by many in his own party, who wished to see a strong link between new trade-negotiating authority and environmental and labor protections. No compromise was reached, and at the end of 1997 Congress adjourned without voting on new fast-track authority. The second Bush administration continued to seek the authority and was able to obtain a positive vote by the House in 2001, although the margin was only one vote.

In the summer of 2002 President Bush was successful in obtaining fast-track (trade promotion authority) as part of the Trade Act of 2002. He promised to move ahead multilaterally (the Doha Round), regionally (the Free Trade of the Americas initiative), and bilaterally through new FTAs with Chile, Singapore, and Morocco. A compromise was reached with regard to the environment, which was elevated to one of several overall negotiating objectives. More specifically, the president was instructed to ensure that our trade partners do not fail to enforce their environmental laws in order to gain an unfair trade advantage, and that environmental reviews of trade agreements, as established in the Clinton administration, be continued. The first instruction, however, was immediately weakened by the statement that the United States cannot use punitive trade measures if a foreign government fails to enforce its environmental laws, and that failure was the result of a reasonable decision to prioritize other policies ahead of environmental enforcement. In short, the United States is loathe to use trade sanctions to enforce foreign environmental laws.

[9]The Mexican peso crisis and the rocky start for NAFTA did not help.

Beef and Bananas

The disputes between the United States and the EU over hormone-fed beef and banana trade have long and complicated histories. The beef dispute, which predates the establishment of the WTO, is of particular interest as a cutting edge case in food safety and product standards. The banana dispute illustrates the extent to which government officials were willing to go to protect United States–based multinational corporate trade interests (the U.S. is not a banana producer, nor is continental Europe). Both disputes illustrate weaknesses in implementing WTO dispute panel decisions.

In 1989 the EC banned the importation and domestic sale of hormone-treated beef.[10] The ban responded to public pressures in Europe and was an effort to harmonize conflicting regulations among EC members. The United States was caught in an awkward position. Its beef and beef product sales to the EC were modest (around $120 million) and consisted mainly of varietal meats (e.g., livers, hearts, and tongues). As most U.S. beef was hormone-treated and as the exports to Europe were in the nature of a byproduct, it was difficult to give up the clear economic advantage from hormone treatment of greater weight gain in a shorter time just to maintain a market for the byproduct. Unable to reach a compromise, the U.S. initiated a Section 301 case. We need not follow the twists and turns in the dispute except to say that it was partly responsible for the new language in the Uruguay Round agreement on sanitary and phytosanitary measures. Among other provisions, this agreement requires that measures must be "necessary" and be based on scientific principles and evidence. In the subsequent history of the dispute, the EU has had difficulty in demonstrating the scientific basis for its ban. In 1997 a WTO panel found the EU not in conformity to WTO rules. The EU then lost an appeal in 1998 and was given until May 1999 to comply. When it did not do so, the United States, with WTO authorization, retaliated and imposed 100 percent *ad valorem* duties on certain imports from the EU. The products were selected to put maximum pressure on the EU while avoiding damage to U.S. industries. They included certain meat products, Roquefort cheese, truffles, goose liver, prepared mustard, and (for France only) lingonberry and raspberry jams.

The banana case is no less convoluted but involves more straightfor-

[10]For a good early account, see Vogel (1995). Hormones in animal feed accelerate weight gain.

ward commercial interests, untainted by food safety considerations.[11] Some European countries had long used quantitative restrictions that gave preferred access for high-cost banana growers in certain African, Caribbean, and Pacific countries, mainly territories and former colonies. In 1993 the EU created a unified policy consisting of quotas and tariff-rate quotas that was both more restrictive and, arguably, more discriminatory *vis a vis* Latin America suppliers. The ostensible reason was to give aid to some poor countries in Africa and the Caribbean, although the existence of marketing boards in several of these countries makes it questionable how much the farmers themselves benefited. A simple cash payment would have been far more efficient.

The U.S. government's interest was the interest of its multinationals, especially Dole and Chiquita, who produced and distributed bananas from nonfavored Latin American countries. The United States and other Latin American countries challenged the EU's 1993 banana scheme, and in 1997 a WTO panel found it to violate WTO obligations. A revised scheme was implemented in January 1999, and that, too, was found in violation. In view of the EU's delays and failure to reform its banana regime, in Spring 1999 the United States retaliated by imposing 100 percent *ad valorem* tariffs on $191 million of imports from the EU. This time the products were eclectic and included bath preparations other than bath salts, felt paper, cotton bed linen (not embroidered), and electric coffee makers. To tighten the screws further, the United States considered a "Carousel" retaliation system, which would have rotated products subject to the sanctions every 6 months. Under consideration for the carousel were Pecorino cheese from sheep's milk, not suitable for grating; cashmere sweaters; electric hair clippers; and canned corned beef. The carousel approach was challenged by the EU in the WTO. Despite the rather small value of trade involved, these two disputes illustrate a weakness in the WTO's dispute settlement procedures in that the EU refused to comply with WTO rulings and ultimately trade sanctions had to be employed. The disputes also soured broader relations with Europe and were unhelpful when trade ministers met in Seattle.[12]

[11]The banana dispute was finally resolved in 2001. Following a five-year transition period, during which quotas based on prior trade will be used, the EU will switch to a tariff-only system.

[12]There is some speculation that Europe pressed its tax subsidy case (FSC) against the United States out of spite arising from the beef and banana brawls (Kahn, 2000).

Multilateral Agreement on Investment (MAI)

While fast track and beef and bananas captured most of the trade headlines in the second half of the 1990s, trouble that foreshadowed the Seattle debacle was brewing in negotiations concerning investments. Recall that in the early postwar period, rules and institutions governing trade (the GATT), monetary affairs (the IMF), and development assistance (the World Bank) were established. International investment, in particular, investment by multinational corporations, was outside this institutional framework. This proved to be a significant omission. By the end of 1998, the book value of world foreign direct investment exceeded $7 trillion.[13]

This book is primarily concerned with U.S. trade policy, but there are intimate connections between trade and investment policy. At a high level of generality and with certain restrictive assumptions, it can be shown that liberal investment policy, like liberal trade policy, improves efficiency in resource allocation and increases world welfare. The United States, as a major participant in international direct investment, has long had an interest in liberalizing international capital markets and securing protections for its foreign direct investment.[14]

In the early 1990s the United States put forth the idea of a multilateral agreement to protect and promote foreign direct investment. The initiative was pressed at the OECD under the belief that in a larger forum such as the WTO, developing countries would block a meaningful agreement. The idea has a parallel in trade negotiations; a group of so-called like-minded countries might achieve greater liberalization than full multilateral negotiations might achieve. The basic concept was a freestanding agreement that would liberalize government barriers and controls on foreign investment, much as the WTO limits and proscribes government intervention in trade. As it evolved, the draft MAI adopted two fundamental principles from the international trade system. The first was "national

[13]Graham (2000) estimates that the total asset value of foreign direct investors, including their home investments, to be about $36 trillion, which exceeds world GDP. The investment figure is, of course, a stock concept, and GDP is a flow concept.

[14]Bhagwati (2000) argues that much of the 1997–1998 Asian financial crisis was the result of premature liberalization of capital markets under pressure from what he calls the Wall Street–Treasury complex. But the issues surrounding portfolio and foreign direct investment are quite different.

treatment," in which governments would treat foreign investments no less favorably than domestic investments.[15] The novel feature was that national treatment would have applied to preinvestment as well as postinvestment situations. That is, laws and policies that discourage new investments by foreign firms would be disallowed unless they were applied equally to new investments by domestic firms. The more traditional practice of national treatment has been to treat foreign and domestic firms equally *after* they have been established.

The second principle was most favored nation (MFN) treatment, long the norm in trade, but not applied to investment. The idea is that investors from country A should have equal rights and opportunities with investors from country B in investing in country C. While we have seen that MFN is given lip service in the GATT, the tolerant attitude toward partial free trade agreements undermines the MFN principle. It is interesting to note that when the MAI collapsed in 1998, the issue of whether regional preference in investment—for example, by and among EU countries—could trump the MFN principle was unresolved.

The mindset appears to have been that investment liberalization was a clone of earlier trade liberalization. But a thoughtful analysis would have seen three obstacles. First, trade rules have stumbled repeatedly over subsidies. The investment counterpart of trade subsidies is investment incentives offered by governments to attract and retain foreign investment. Nothing in the MAI would have been effective in reining in these distortive and inefficient practices. Second, the draft MIA did not address national tax policies and their effects on the location of investment and competitive position of firms. As is now widely recognized, the decline of tariffs has increased the saliency of national tax policy for trade, and surely tax policy affects investment decisions as well.

It was, however, the blind eye that the MAI negotiators turned toward environmental concerns that was most conspicuous. No one can doubt that direct investment has a profound impact on the environment. One would have thought that after the energetic interventions of the environmental community in the Uruguay Round negotiations and more decisively in the NAFTA debate, the MAI negotiation process would have anticipated environmental concerns. Apparently it did not. The draft preamble contained

[15]In trade, national treatment means that imported products, once they have cleared customs, should receive the same regulatory and tax treatment as domestic products.

(bracketed) hortatory language regarding environmental protection, but this is of course nonbinding. A rather weak provision to prevent lowering environmental standards to attract investment was suggested but not agreed to (Graham, 2000).

The entire MAI processes collapsed in 1998, and a new effort is unlikely. One can argue that the collapse was internal—the so-called like-minded OECD countries in fact had fundamental differences—or that external forces, mainly NGOs with labor and environmental agendas, pulled the plug. Alternatively, one can argue that the entire exercise was unnecessary. Foreign direct investment continues to flourish without a GATT-like institutional and regulatory apparatus. The lesson for the trade system, our principal concern, is that segments of the environmental community, still smarting from the tuna–dolphin dispute and having tasted some success in the NAFTA debate, were energized by their role in the collapse of the MAI to take on the WTO in Seattle.

▶ THE GOOD NEWS

Perhaps the most encouraging trade development in the latter part of the 1990s was the dog that did not bark: the absence of significant new protectionist pressure in the wake of the Asian economic crisis and the dramatic increase in the U.S. trade deficit. The trade numbers were quite remarkable. The balance on goods and services, which had stabilized at a deficit of about \$100 billion in 1994–1997, rose to \$265 billion in 1999 and \$376 billion in 2000, or about 3.8 percent of GDP, a record for the 20th century. And yet there was no discernable surge in serious protection measures. One could explain this as an enlightened and intelligent response to widespread economic distress in Asia and elsewhere; open markets in the United States were crucial to limiting economic damage abroad. And indeed the need to maintain an open market was recognized and acknowledged by policy-makers. In this instance, the United States' passion for consumption served global interests. But a second explanation is equally compelling. For the 1993–1999 period, U.S. real GDP growth averaged 3.8 percent annually, a remarkable achievement, and the unemployment rate fell from 7.5 percent in 1992 to 4 percent at the start of 2000. Full employment tends to blunt protectionist pressure. Moreover, unlike previous decades, the United States itself became a major destination for foreign direct investment, which rose from an inflow of $21 billion in 1992 to $283 billion in 1999. The MNC job threat had lost some credibility. There is a third reason. The Uruguay Round reforms and especially the prohibition on VERs and general tightening of trade rules made *ad hoc* protection more difficult. This last explanation should not be pushed too far. A residual concern for import surges remained and was met in part by active use of the unfair trade laws. The United States did initiate 136 new antidumping cases in the 1995–1999 period. Moreover, the 1999 bilateral agreement with China contains a special escape clause (safeguard) procedure, which is far easier to invoke then the standard escape clause.[16] And as noted elsewhere, when the 2001 recession arrived, President Bush himself initiated protection in steel.

▶ THE SEATTLE DEBACLE

We do not present a full account of what went wrong in Seattle. The jumble of competing interests, expectations, and misjudgments was too intricate, too snarled for easy interpretation. Still, it seems clear that there were three levels to the tangle. First, there was the external attack on the WTO, the international trade system, and globalization broadly construed. Second, there was poor preparation in the face of sharp differences among WTO members, North vs. South but also among the major industrial countries. Third, the meeting revealed that the WTO's internal structure, including its *modus operandi* and its external relations, needed reform.

The external attack is difficult to parse because the demonstrators came with diverse objectives and because the targets were fluid and diffuse.[17] The environmental, labor, and human rights communities were all represented. While the proximate target was the WTO and the Millenium

[16]The United States–China agreement creates a safeguard mechanism that departs from WTO rules. It allows the United States to address imports solely from China rather than from the whole world and allows restrictions if imports are a "significant cause of material injury," a weaker standard. This special safeguard will remain in place for 12 years after China's accession to the WTO. Moreover, the United States can impose special restrictions on China's textile exports for up to four years after the deadline for the phaseout of the MFA set by the WTO.

[17]For an account from the demonstrators' perspective, see interview with Lori Wallach, Director of Public Citizen's Global Trade Watch, in the Spring 2000 issue of *Foreign Policy*.

Round, earlier targets had included the MAI and would be followed-up in Spring 2000 by well-publicized demonstrations at the joint World Bank/IMF meetings and at subsequent international meetings. Indeed, the roots of protests in the United States stretch back to the divisive fight over NAFTA, surfaced in the long struggle over fast track, and foreshadowed the then-pending PNTR debate concerning China. The core allegations against the WTO were that it lacks democracy, transparency, and accountability and that it has set trade as an end, not a means, to the exclusion of other social goals. The overlay to these allegations was suspicion and distrust of globalization.

The demonstrations were disruptive but not decisive in scuttling plans for the new trade round. That failure occurred as a result of poor preparation, an overloaded agenda, and sharp divisions among the countries represented. Preparatory meetings in the WTO had failed to reach agreement on important substantive issues. The customary "quad" meeting between the United States, Canada, EU, and Japan to plot strategy was not held. At Seattle, the United States Trade Representative, Charlene Barshefsky, both led the American delegation and served as Chair of the Conference, potentially conflicting roles.

Areas of conflict at Seattle included agriculture, dumping, investment, and competition policy. Developing countries were reluctant to entertain new issues and sought to slow implementation of their obligations under the prior TRIPs and TRIMs (Trade Related Investment Measures) agreements; to accelerate the phase-out of the MFA; and to avoid any consideration of labor and environmental standards. The United States pressed for substantial new liberalization in agriculture; others, including the EU and Japan, resisted and stressed agriculture's "multifunctionality" (unique characteristics). Japan and others looked for reform of dumping regulations, and the United States resisted. Europe wanted new rules concerning investment and competition policies, and the United States was wary. These conflicts were not eased by the United States' desire to have a short initial negotiation with limit agenda and with an "early harvest" of agreements in areas of particular interest to the United States, such as e-commerce and information technology products.

The so-called social issues, environment and labor, were especially divisive, as they had been within the United States since NAFTA. The trade-labor standards issue is considered in the next chapter and is only briefly summarized here. Labor unions in the United States and other industrial countries have argued standards are weak or unenforced in many developing countries, harming workers there but also threatening jobs and wages in industrial countries. Labor was joined by other groups in civil society with humanitarian concerns: improving the plight of poor workers in poor countries. Both argued that international recognized labor standards be included in trade agreements. Two groups opposed this. Governments in developing countries viewed this as a protectionist ploy that would undercut their competitive advantage based on low labor costs. Many in the trade policy community, eager to protect the liberal trade regime, also opposed WTO's move into social issues.[18]

Official U.S. policy prior to Seattle was that WTO should establish a formal working group on trade and labor to examine issues such as core labor standards and child labor.[19] This moderate position was thrown into confusion when President Clinton, in an interview immediately before speaking at the conference, stated he ultimately would support sanctions against countries violating labor provisions of a trade agreement. This raised hackles in developing-country governments and among some business groups. It also left the impression that the President was using the demonstrations to advance the position of the United States at the meeting.

The final knots in this tangle arose from WTO's defective internal procedures and external relations. The internal problem centered on decision-making. The GATT and then the WTO have traditionally operated on a consensus basis. This procedure works increasingly poorly. At its origin, nine members of GATT accounted for 80 percent of world trade. By Seattle, membership had expanded from GATT's original 23 members to WTO's 137, with some 30 others seeking entrance. What worked with 9 can fail with 137. Also, WTO decisions are increasingly important for all members. In the old GATT system a country could sign a code—for example, the subsidy agreement—or refuse to sign as it saw fit. Under the WTO, all members are bound by all decisions. Moreover, agreements are increasingly intrusive in regulating domestic policy, and hence members are more sensitive to results. The agreement on intellectual property is a good example. Developing countries, which had been invited to be active

[18]The trade-environment issue led to similar conflicting interests. Recall from Chapter 7 that environment was shunted to a side agreement in NAFTA.

[19]For discussion, see Kimberly Elliott (2000).

participants in the WTO, were given a secondary role in decisions.[20] The internal procedures lacked participation and transparency. The WTO itself had been weakened by an earlier bitter dispute, partly along North–South lines, over who should be its new Director-General.

The external relations problem centered on accessibility and transparency and has been particularly irritating to the environmental community.[21] The WTO was slow in recognizing the need to listen to the environmental NGO (Nongovernmental Organization) community but had attempted to mend relations in recent years. The U.S. government also supported the idea of greater accessibility and transparency, although the modalities remain elusive. Some procedural steps had been suggested with regard to the dispute settlement process. These include opening panel hearings to the public; publishing briefs, position statements, and panel decisions as rapidly as possible; and encouraging NGOs to submit materials to the panels. At a broader level, the issue of whether and how dispute settlement panels acquire the scientific and technical expertise to evaluate the environmental component of trade disputes had not been resolved.

In the end, the meeting failed to reach any agreement, and delegates went home empty-handed.

▶ A SHORT SUMMARY OF THE 1990s

The completion of the Uruguay Round and the economic boom of the 1990s rebuilt support for liberal trade in the United States. There was progress on issues dear to the business community: trade in services, protection of intellectual property, and a new agreement on telecommunications trade. Aggressive commercial diplomacy was a hallmark of the first Clinton administration. The perceived threat from Japan Inc faded over the decade. Under the surface, however, trade tensions remained and erupted at the failed Seattle meeting. Some tensions stemmed from the bruising fight over NAFTA. The issues of labor and environmental standards had not been resolved. The failure of the Multilateral Agreement on

[20]The Seattle meeting continued the so-called green room process. In this arrangement a self-selected subset of members retires to a separate location, works out a consensus, and returns to present the results to full membership.

[21]Trade officials and environmental officials within national governments have only recently started a dialogue.

Investment talks signaled trouble, as did the failure of the President to gain fast-track authority. Many developing countries felt shortchanged by the trade system generally and the Uruguay Round in particular. These tensions, together with the post-Seattle shocks of global slowdown or recession and the new war on terrorism, provided the context for liberal trade policy as it entered the first years of the new millennium.

▶ REFERENCES

Bhagwati, Jagdish. 2000. *The Wind of the Hundred Days: How Washington Mismanaged Globalization.* Cambridge, MA: MIT Press.

Bhagwati, Jagdish, and Mathias Hirsch. 1998. *The Uruguay Round and Beyond.* Ann Arbor: University of Michigan Press.

Elliott, Kimberly. 2000. Beyond No . . . !: Promoting Worker Rights and Trade. In: Jeffrey Schott (ed.). *The WTO After Seattle.* Washington, DC: Institute for International Economics.

Graham, Edward. 2000. *Fighting the Wrong Enemy: Antiglobal Activists and Multinational Enterprises.* Washington, DC: Institute for International Economics.

Kahn, Joseph. 2000. U.S. Loses Dispute on Export Sales. *New York Times* February 24.

Martin, Will, and Alan Winters. 1995. *The Uruguay Round: Widening and Deepening the World Trading System.* Washington, DC: The World Bank.

Schott, Jeffrey. 1994. *The Uruguay Round: An Assessment.* Washington, DC: Institute for International Economics.

Vogel, David. 1995. *Trading Up: Consumer and Environmental Regulation in a Global Economy.* Cambridge, MA: Harvard University Press.

CHAPTER

10

THE WAY AHEAD

The purpose of this book is to illuminate the paths that U.S. trade policy has followed, not to provide a road map for the future. But the effort spent in following past twists and turns would be unnecessarily barren if we did not take the opportunity to collect our thoughts and look ahead.

There is no question that for all its hesitations, lurches, and missteps, U.S. policy in the postwar period has had a distinctly liberal cast. One can go further and make a strong case that the United States has been a major force in leading (or bullying) the international system toward freer trade. It is easy to be an armchair critic of one false step or another, and we have been guilty here, but the basic liberal thrust of policy is clear. This is a substantial accomplishment considering our long history of fluctuating protectionism, the persistent opposition to freer trade from various domestic interest groups, and the frequent reluctance of our trade partners to march at the precise cadence set in Washington.

TESTING THE SYSTEM

How firmly rooted is this commitment to liberal trade? How strong are the antiglobalization forces? Economic historians are fond of pointing out that the current wave of globalization, which is both a measure of and the fruits of a liberal trade system, is not altogether novel. The international system from the last half of the 19th century up to 1914 reached a level of globalization in many respects comparable to that of today, although the United States was not a full participant.[1] Like the current era, that wave of global-

[1]For example, O'Rourke (2001) provides data showing remarkable convergence of international commodity prices in the earlier period, a measure of market integration: the Chicago–London price gap in wheat, falling from 58% in 1870 to 16% by 1913; the cotton price spread between London and Bombay, falling from 57% in 1873 to 20% in 1913; and the London–Rangoon price spread for rice, falling from 93% to 26%. See also Frankel (2000).

ization was driven by improvements in transport and communication technology, especially the railroad, steamship, telegraph, and refrigeration. But the international economic system crashed in the early and middle decades of the 20th century under the suffocating weight of two world wars and the Great Depression. Much of the postwar trade policy effort was simply to reconstruct an earlier system left in tatters by political, military, and economic firestorms. Postwar reconstruction itself was greatly influenced by two new major world forces, the Cold War and the difficult process of decolonization. Although once again technological change is the driving force in globalization (i.e., telecommunications, computers, etc.), the lesson from the past is that military, political, and economic circumstances can derail liberal trade for long periods of time. In this sense, continued globalization is not inevitable.

Still, the vision of liberal trade has shown considerable resiliency in the postwar era, suggesting the roots are firmly established. It has quashed three challenges that appeared serious at the time. The first is well known and needs little elaboration. The formation of a rich, powerful, regional economic bloc, the European Community, could have resulted in a very different trade system, one composed of inward-looking regional economic and trading arrangements. In that event the basis for liberal trade, multilateralism and nondiscrimination, would have been fatally compromised. This did not happen. Fortress Europe did not materialize. The United States did not retreat to exclusive trade relations with Latin America. And Japan chose to remain aloof from all preferential trade arrangements, regional or otherwise.

We acknowledge that resurgent PTAs may yet create a bloc-based trade system, but the concern seems a bit overblown. Trade barriers at the border are at historically low levels, and most tariffs are bound in the GATT/WTO. Unless countries take the extreme step of repudiating their GATT obligations, the scope for bloc-based trade discrimination has been greatly reduced. This benign view of PTAs should not be interpreted as an endorsement for any and all new arrangements. At the micro-level, they can create substantial trade distortions through opaque and restrictive rules of origin and through overlapping membership. And tariffs, while low, can still divert trade in the classic Vinerian sense. At a more political level, PTAs shelter firms by granting preferential market access, thus creating opposition to multilateral liberalization and diverting energies from pushing forward on the multilateral track. But the main point seems clear.

A deterioration of the trade system into inward-looking regional blocs, a valid cause for concern in the 1960s, is much less likely today.

The vision of liberal trade also survived the intellectual and policy challenge of import substitution (IS) as a viable development strategy. As James Riedel (1991) correctly observes, IS did not fall to the force of ideas—neoclassical trade theory—but to the exemplary economic performance of those East Asian economies that choose an export-oriented development path. This was trade liberalization by example, a technique that the United States might still find useful today. The point here is not that governments in East Asia were uninvolved in trade matters. Indeed, the experience of Japan, which in earlier years was heavily engaged in allocating resources and guiding market outcomes, was something of a model. Instead, the point is that these governments saw exports as an engine of growth and nudged the structure of incentives toward exporting. This took some courage. They ignored the then-popular export pessimism and instead saw a world market for their manufactures. In this fashion, East Asia escaped the trap that IS was designed to remedy—a permanent trade structure in which the role of developing countries was as natural resource exporters, or hewers of wood and drawers of water, in the trade system. Virtually all developing countries, sooner or later, have come to realize that trade liberalization trumps IS as a development strategy.

The United States played an important but mostly passive role here. By refraining from draconian restrictions on labor-intensive imports, it provided a vital market for developing-country exports. Between 1970 and 1980, developing countries' share of U.S. consumption of manufactures more than doubled, and the share from Asian NICs more than tripled. Later, in the Asian economic crisis of 1997–1999, the United States tolerated very large trade deficits, moderating GDP losses in Asia and elsewhere. The open market was not always an easy policy to maintain, and there has been occasional backsliding into *ad hoc* protection. Workers displaced by imports bore real economic costs. Remedies through the escape clause and trade-adjustment assistance were incomplete at best. But by and large, the United States correctly saw the demise of IS and the rise of export-oriented development as consistent with and supportive of its vision of the trade system. Liberal trade survived the IS challenge.

The third challenge, occurring in the 1970s and 1980s, is described in Chapters 2–4 and need not be repeated here in detail. A pernicious combination of internal and external forces was at work. The overvalued dollar, the seemingly formidable economic clout of Japan Inc, the lure of strategic trade policy, the weakness of GATT and its failure to address issues of deep concern to the United States—agriculture, services, intellectual property—all conspired with residual protectionism to erode support for liberal trade. We do not wish to overdramatize this loss of support, but in hindsight it is clear that liberal trade has stalled and even slipped backward. The solution came through fundamental economic forces (e.g., the depreciation of the dollar, starting in 1985), political statesmanship (the ultimate completion of the Uruguay Round), and the collapse of Japan in the 1990s as a viable model for industrial and trade policies.

NEW CHALLENGES

As it turned out, the debacle at Seattle in 1999 had a positive effect in underscoring the need for advanced preparation and a spirit of compromise when launching multilateral negotiations. The unlikely coalition of environmental, labor, and human rights demonstrators gathered there succeeded in sharpening the debate over the distributional effects of globalization and its handmaiden, liberal trade. Seattle also brought into focus the simmering controversy over the use of the trade system for noncommercial social objectives. At the same time, the Seattle meeting made clear that the developing countries were no longer passive in negotiations to restructure the trade system. They were uniformly adamant that the WTO stay out of the business of setting labor standards. They also insisted that benefits promised to them in the Uruguay Round actually materialize, if they were not to sour on liberal trade. Specific complaints from the South centered on foot-dragging in phasing out the MFA, agricultural protection in industrial countries, abusive use of antidumping legislation, and onerous and expensive obligations regarding intellectual property protection (the TRIPs agreement).

These contentious issues were not resolved in the two years between Seattle and the 2001 Ministerial meeting in Doha. But the shadow cast by the failure in Seattle and, arguably, the unifying effects of the terrorist attacks on the United States in September 2001 produced a new realism and sufficient compromise to launch a new round of trade talks. On the surface at least the compromises appeared to favor developing countries, not the antiglobalization coalition. What had originally been termed the Millennium Round was renamed by some as the Development Round.[2] Liberalization of trade in agriculture, long a goal of the United States, was touted for its benefits to developing countries.[3] On the sensitive issue of exempting pharmaceuticals from full patent protection and allowing generic alternatives, a separate "declaration" extended the phase-in period for poor countries and confirmed flexibility in the interim (the United States, under heavy public pressure, had agreed to flexibility before the Doha meeting). Most significantly, on the critical issue of linking labor standards and trade in the WTO, the United States backed away from its earlier position. Specifically, the Doha Declaration merely reconfirmed the WTO's position taken five years previously in Singapore, that the ILO is the competent body to deal with such standards, not the WTO. The trade-labor issue, which doomed the Seattle meeting, was off the table for the time being.

The environmental "camel's nose" had been in the WTO tent since the creation of the Trade and Environment Committee at the end of the Uruguay Round. But the delegates were wary of further intrusions. The Doha Declaration did agree to negotiate disciplines on fisheries subsidies (a much-needed conservation measure) and to limited negotiations on the relation between WTO rules and the trade provisions of MEAs. The Doha declaration "noted" the efforts by some countries to undertake environmental reviews of trade agreements but did not applaud such efforts, make them mandatory, or commission such studies itself.

Along with others, the United States showed greater flexibility at Doha than at Seattle but was still able to secure much of its wish list. The United States obtained a (qualified) commitment to phase out agricultural export subsidies (but see footnote 3) and agreements to place trade in services (now 26% of merchandise trade) and reductions in barriers to manufac-

[2]Immediately before the Doha meeting, USTR released a background paper titled "10 Ways Global Trade Negotiations Would Benefit Developing Countries." A certain déjà vu is inevitable. The first agenda item in the preparatory meeting for the Kennedy Round (1964–1967) was expanding trade for developing countries. Christian Herter, head of the U.S. delegation, asserted "no task this meeting faces is more important than finding ways to improve the export opportunities of less developed countries" (Preeg, 1970, p. 6).

[3]Clearly a benefit for agricultural exporters in the South; less clearly a benefit for the numerous net food importers that enjoyed subsidized imports. The sincerity of U.S. commitment to free trade in agriculture can also be questioned. As explained in Chapter 8, the United States passed new agricultural legislation reversing earlier market-oriented reforms and granting massive subsidies to U.S. farmers.

tures on the negotiating agenda. It deflected pressures to reopen previous agreements on textiles and on dumping, although work on clarifying and improving the rules will continue. Negotiations on harmonizing trade and competition policy were put off until after the next Ministerial meeting. Negotiations on trade and investment were also put off.

It should be remembered that at the time of the Doha meeting, Congress still had not granted President Bush Trade Promotion Authority (TPA, the old fast-track authority). As noted, the House subsequently approved TPA by a margin of one vote.[4] Moreover, the legislation granting TPA was replete with admonishing references to labor and environmental laws and practices, implying these issues were far from settled within the country, let alone internationally.[5] One objective in the authorizing legislation is that other countries effectively enforce their environmental and labor laws. At the same time and out of concern that other countries might challenge the United States, the legislation recognized that countries, including the United States, can exercise discretion in enforcing their labor and environmental laws. No retaliation can be taken against countries exercising such discretion. All in all, this is an obfuscating provision.

THE LARGER PICTURE

We do not wish to be bogged down in the minutiae of trade negotiations, but we do wish to understand at a broader level the current challenges to liberal trade. Why is it under attack in many quarters and why is it often on the defensive? It would be easy to put most of the blame on mindless antiglobalization, but this would be incorrect. The more sensible critics of unfettered free trade raise legitimate questions and deserve reasoned replies. It would also be easy to assert that the current backlash is simply a new strain of the old protectionist virus, but this too would be incorrect. Old-fashioned protectionism is not dead but is crippled and not a sufficient explanation. Instead, we suggest that there are two interlocking forces at work, which although not totally absent in the past, have gained new im-

[4]Securing the votes was made easier, as Bush was in the process of deciding on major import relief for the steel industry under the escape clause proceeding that he himself had initiated.

[5]The TPA legislation sets out the principal objectives to guide U.S. negotiators.

portance. Accommodating these forces will occupy much of trade policy over the next decade. The first is finding the appropriate balance between harmonization and diversity of domestic economic and social policies among countries, and the second is the use of the trade system for noncommercial objectives. Both involve questions of "fairness," and both involve national sovereignty. Finding agreement will be especially difficult, as developing countries are (finally) asserting their rights in restructuring the trade system.

Harmonization

With traditional tariffs on a downward trend in most countries and with the most egregious nontariff trade barriers tamed, if not eliminated, by WTO disciplines, the international pattern of production and trade is increasingly influenced by ostensibly domestic policies, standards, and practices. The obvious ones are labor, environment, competition (antitrust), intellectual property protection, tax, health, and social welfare policies. Research and development and education policies are also relevant. That these policies affect cost structures and hence trade is well known. Recent technological changes that facilitate foreign direct investment and the practice of outsourcing production simply amplify the production-location effects of these policies. This shift in the determinants of trade patterns, from tariffs to NTBs and from NTBs to domestic policies with trade effects, has reinvigorated the debates on fairness and national sovereignty.

Broadly speaking, one response to diversity in domestic policies and practices has been to call for harmonization, or at least some convergence, to mute the trade effects. Thus, environmental, labor, intellectual property, and competition policies are now, or may come to be, thrashed out in trade negotiations. Some types of harmonization are clearly beneficial on efficiency grounds. For example, setting internationally uniform standards for the size of credit cards makes them acceptable in ATMs worldwide. The International Standards Organization has long been engaged in developing *compatibility standards* for products. By and large, one can rely on markets and private sector institutions to accomplish this. Harmonization of disclosure rules in the financial sector or of tax laws to limit tax havens may also improve the efficiency of international financial markets. The harmonization of financial regulation is a task for governments. Harmonizing conservation measures for international resources such as ocean fisheries also contributes to efficiency, although there can be bitter fights over the distribution of the rents.

In short, some efforts at harmonization improve efficiency and promote trade. But to the extent that the economic and social policies listed previously accurately reflect real differences among countries in income, economic structure, social values, and physical environmental characteristics, forced or coercive harmonization can be a source of inefficiency. The value of *diversity* in policy is that it can more accurately reflect local conditions and preferences (Bhagwati, 1996). It is of course diversity in natural resource endowments, labor skills, technology, and preferences that are the sources of gains from trade. Moreover, coercive harmonization of domestic standards and policies can create a "forced rider" problem. Large countries with market power may attempt to influence social and economic policies in other countries by the threat or use of trade restrictions. This may be done under the guise of creating a "level playing field" or eliminating "unfair" competition. Under the peculiar calculus with which trade is assessed—exports always a benefit, imports questionable—forced rider countries bear the costs of harmonization, and coercing countries enjoy the benefits. In such circumstances, the exercise of unequal market (bargaining) power is an unwelcome infringement on national sovereignty and results in the establishment of inappropriate standards.

The competitive effects of differential standards and policies and the "level playing field" argument for harmonization are sometimes accompanied by a "race to the bottom" argument. Countries compete for investment and economic activity. There is a concern that regulatory competition will favor countries that impose minimal obligations on industry. As a consequence, all countries may feel obliged to establish inappropriately low social and environmental standards, the race to the (regulatory) bottom. If this argument is valid, there may be a case for harmonized or at least minimum international standards.

Humanitarian Interests

The elimination of perceived unfair trade and the prevention of a possible race to the bottom in regulatory standards are not the only reason that internationalization or harmonization of standards is pursued. Residents of one country may have a global perspective and thus an interest in conditions in other countries—securing human rights, environmental protection, and religious freedom and ending child labor abuses. In some cases the interest can be quite direct, as, for example, transboundary pollution or curtailing the international drug trade, and in others the interest is altruistic and ethically based. A proper concern for human welfare does not stop at the border. The catch is that there are neither effective international markets nor international political structures in which citizens can express these preferences. Environmentalists in the United States or Europe do not vote in Asia and cannot directly "buy" clean air in Manila or clean water in Jakarta. Under these circumstances, the international trade system appears to offer a convenient and potentially effective instrument for securing noncommercial objectives abroad. In this fashion the competitive effects of different economic, social, and environmental policies are joined to the issue of using the trade system for noncommercial objectives.

It would be tedious and unproductive to analyze the prospects for harmonization over the full range of policy areas, from competition to the financing of health care. Fortunately, many of the basic issues are present in the debate on linking trade and fair labor standards, and we concentrate on this as an illustration of the new challenges to U.S. trade policy and to the liberal trade system.

▶ FAIR LABOR STANDARDS AND TRADE

Labor standards and trade have in fact been entwined since the early decades of the Industrial Revolution (Leary, 1996; Charnovitz, 1987). The concern, then as now, was that costly regulations protecting labor would be undermined by international competition.[6] As explained in this section, this can be thought of as an international collective-goods problem in which the "supply" of labor-protection regulation by governments itself needs protection. The principal response to this dilemma was the creation of the International Labor Organization in 1919, designed to establish min-

[6]The 19th century concern was intra-European competition; the current concern is mainly between the industrial North and the developing South.

imum levels of labor protection through the voluntary adoption of international conventions.[7]

The trade-labor issue was present in the NAFTA debate. Many were wary of any connection, but in the end a side agreement, the North American Agreement on Labor Cooperation (NAALC), was signed. NAALC does not commit members to harmonize labor standards but they do pledge to promote effective compliance with their own labor laws. Dispute settlement is restricted to matters involving worker health and safety, child labor, and minimum wages and not controversies involving freedom of association and collective bargaining. Minimal trade sanctions are possible if a convoluted dispute settlement procedure fails, but the clear intent is to resolve problems before that point.

In recent years there has been increasing pressure to incorporate labor protection obligations in the WTO itself—in short, establishing a base level of fair labor standards internationally. The rights most frequently mentioned are (1) freedom from forced labor, (2) abolition of child labor or the less-demanding prohibition of exploitative child labor, (3) freedom from discrimination in employment, and (4) freedom of association and collective bargaining. These parallel the ILO's Declaration of Fundamental Principles and Rights at Work.

Three arguments for inclusion can be advanced. First, trade based on grossly deficient labor standards is unfair trade and relies on an implicit subsidy (i.e., firms escape costly labor protections). The antidumping and countervailing duty provisions of the WTO are already concerned with limiting unfair trade, and it would seem logical to extend protection to goods and services unfairly traded through implicit labor standards subsidies. Second, the lack of international labor standards creates a "prisoner's dilemma" situation. Minimum standards have the attributes of a public good (collective good), but the desire of countries to attract investment and industrial activity leads to a regulatory race to the bottom. Govern-

[7]The competitiveness concern was nicely captured in a 1917 observation by a French official and quoted by Leary (1996, p. 186): "In questions such as hours of work, the regulation of dangerous trades, the prohibition of certain work for women and children, international competition may for a long time favor those countries which do not accept the highest standards of human conditions, to the serious detriment of more generous nations."

ments are forced into pernicious regulatory competition. Unlike product competition, which leads to lower prices and improved quality, regulatory competition lowers worker protection everywhere. Fair labor standards enforced through the WTO would presumably remedy this. Third, fair labor standards should be pursued for humanitarian reasons. It is an ethical obligation to attempt to reduce or eliminate exploitative child labor, gender or ethnic discrimination, unnecessarily dangerous working conditions, and so forth, wherever they occur. The trade system generally, and WTO's ability to authorize sanctions in particular, is a convenient instrument for doing good in the world.[8]

There are theoretical and practical problems with these three arguments. Several theoretical models conclude that establishing better labor standards in the South might increase, not decrease, competitive pressure on labor-intensive manufacturing in the North, thus undercutting the unfair trade argument. For example, if a trade measure forces the elimination of monopsonistic practices in the South's export industries (a classic case of labor exploitation), output and hence competitive pressure would tend to increase in the North.[9] At a more subtle level, the unfair competition/protection justification may conflict with the humanitarian objective (Corden and Vosden, 2001). For example, imposing higher labor costs on a monopsonistic exporter may improve conditions (and real wages) for workers in that sector, but if paid for by squeezing monopsonistic profits, there would be no output effect and hence no competitive relief. Alternatively, if the higher costs are passed forward in price, import competition is indeed reduced. But labor displaced in the declining export sector would tend to depress wages in nontradeable goods and services, harming what is likely to be the poorest and most vulnerable segment of the workforce.[10] This is not what humanitarian groups have in mind.

[8]Similar arguments can be made for including environmental standards in WTO obligations, but there are differences. Transboundary pollution and the protection of international resources complicate the trade–environment debate but have no direct parallels in the trade–labor debate. Also, trade restrictions on products that are environmentally damaging in their consumption are permitted in the WTO, but there is no parallel issue in the labor–trade debate.

[9]See Martin and Maskus (2001) for models in which better labor standards would increase competition in the North.

[10]This assumes, realistically, that in poor countries effective labor-protection standards cannot be initially extended to an unregulated informal sector.

Eliminating child labor provides another example of potentially perverse effects. There are strong ethical reasons to deplore child labor in developing countries. Moreover, child labor may be at the expense of schooling and work against long-run development. But it does not automatically follow that trade measures to coerce the elimination of child labor will improve conditions in poor countries. Maskus (1997) provides a model in which a tariff imposed by importing countries on products incorporating inputs produced by child labor could reduce employment of children to some extent but leave the remaining working children with a yet-lower wage (and depress adult wages at the same time). A variation of this model would in fact increase employment of children and again depress adult wages.[11]

The "race to the bottom" argument also has problems. The underlying premise, that labor suffers an inequality in bargaining power *vis a vis* employers and needs government protection, may be incorrect. Unless we are speaking of compulsory labor, workers have options and employers have an interest in recruiting a stable and productive work force. Moreover, governments are not restricted to compete for investment by lowering labor standards. There is considerable evidence that stable macroeconomic policies, education policies, protection of intellectual property, and generally clean government outweigh labor standards as carrots in competition for economic activity.

This is not the occasion to parade the practical questions that inclusion of labor standards in the WTO would raise. One point, however, is central. GATT and now the WTO have always operated on the principle of proportionate response to violations of obligations (Hudec, 1996). That is, if a country violates its obligations by dumping or export subsidies, or even if it raises a bound tariff in a legal safeguard action, members whose trade is adversely affected can expect proportionate compensation for trade losses to restore the original balance of concessions. The WTO, and GATT before it, is neither punitive nor coercive. The implication of this tradition is that should fair labor standards become a WTO obligation, and should a complaint filed by one member against another be deemed valid, it will be necessary to calculate in monetary terms the trade advantage gained and lost

[11]In the latter situation, children are assumed to provide an input to an import competing sector. A tariff on that country's export good would drive resources into the import competing sector and increase employment of children supplying inputs to that sector.

by the two countries if a proportionate response is to be fashioned. Is this possible? Can the implicit subsidy associated with failure to permit collective bargaining or the implicit subsidy associated with workplace discrimination be quantified? If not, the entire rationale of restoring fair competition evaporates, and labor standards are exposed as either handy tools to advance humanitarian interests, as determined by the North, or covert instruments of protection.

In summary, while the drive to involve the WTO in labor standards has temporarily stalled, the issue nicely captures what appears to be the central challenges for the U.S. and the liberal trade system over the next decade: determining the appropriate limits to harmonizing a wide range of domestic policies while warding off covert protection, avoiding pernicious regulatory competition and a possible race to the bottom in social policies, preserving diversity and national sovereignty in an economically integrated world, and finding the right balance in using trade measures to accomplish noncommercial objectives abroad.

▶ CONCLUSION

United States trade policy remains a work in progress, for which there is no conclusion. Our account of that policy, however, can close with two quotes from David Ricardo (1817) on the virtues of free trade and the folly of government intervention:

> "Under a system of perfectly free commerce, each country naturally devotes its capital and labour to such employments as are most beneficial to each. This pursuit of individual advantage is admirably connected with the universal good of the whole. By stimulating industry, by rewarding ingenuity, and by using most efficaciously the peculiar powers bestowed by nature, it distributes labor most effectively and most economically: while, by increasing the general mass of productions, it diffuses general benefit, and binds by one common tie of interest and intercourse, the universal society of nations throughout the civilized world."

> "The sole effect of high duties on the importation either of manufactures or of corn, or of a bounty on their exportation, is to divert a portion of capital to an employment, which it would not naturally seek. It causes a pernicious distribution of the general funds of the society—it bribes a manufacturer to

commence or continue in a comparatively less profitable employment. It is the worst species of taxation, for it does not give to the foreign country all that it takes away from the home country, the balance of loss being made up by the less advantageous distribution of the general capital."

▶ REFERENCES

Charnovitz, Steve. 1987. The Influence of International Labor Standards on the World Trade Trading Regime. *International Labor Review* 126:565–584.

Corden, W. Max, and Neil Vousden. 2001. Paved with Good Intentions: Social Dumping and Raising Labor Standards in Developing Countries. In: Zdenek Drabek (ed.). *Globalization Under Threat.* Cheltenham, UK.: Edward Elgar.

Frankel, Jeffrey. 2000. *Globalization of the Economy.* Cambridge, MA: NBER Working Paper 7858.

Hudec, Robert. 1996. GATT Legal Restraints on the Use of Trade Measures Against Foreign Environmental Practices. In: Jagdish Bhagwati and Robert Hudec (eds.). *Fair Trade and Harmonization: Prerequisite for Free Trade?* Vol. 2. Cambridge, MA: MIT Press.

Leary, Virginia. 1996. Workers' Rights and International Trade: The Social Clause. In: Jagdish Bhagwati and Robert Hudec (eds.). *Fair Trade and Harmonization: Prerequisites for Free Trade?* Vol. 2. Cambridge, MA: MIT Press.

Martin, Will, and Keith Maskus. 2001. Core Labor Standards and Competitiveness: Implications for Global Theory. *Review of International Economics* 9(2):317–328.

Maskus, Keith. 1997. *Should Core Labor Standards be Imposed Through International Trade Policy?* World Bank Policy Research Working Paper 1817. Washington, DC: World Bank.

O'Rourke, Kevin. 2001. *Globalization and Inequality: Historical Trends.* Cambridge, MA. NBER Working Paper 8339.

Preeg, Ernest. 1970. *Traders and Diplomats.* Washington, DC: Brookings Institution.

Ricardo, David. 1817. *The Principles of Political Economy.* London (1973): J. M. Dent & Sons.

Riedel, James. 1991. Strategy Wars: The State of the Debate on Trade and Industrialization in Developing Countries. In: Ad Koekoek and B. M. Mennes (eds.). *International Trade and Global Development: Essays in Honor of J. Bhagwati.* London: Routledge.

APPENDIX

The following charts provide a visual display of relevant features of U.S. trade.

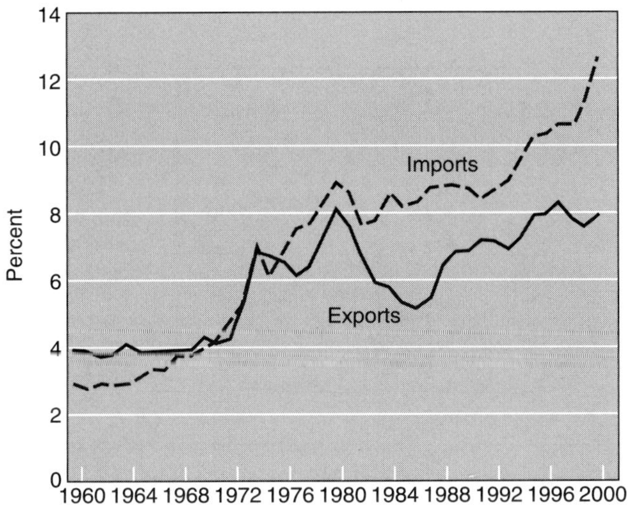

Figure A.1 U.S. exports and imports as a percentage of GDP, 1960–2000.*

*Merchandise trade.

Source: Council of Economic Advisors. *Economic Report of the President*. Washington, DC: GPO, 2002.

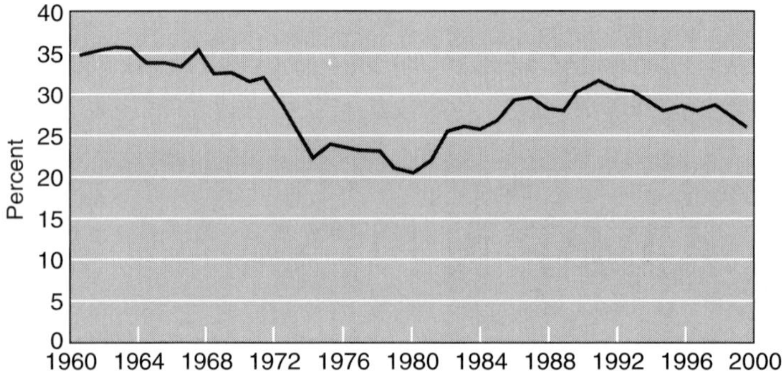

Figure A.2 U.S. services trade as a percentage of merchandise trade, 1960–2000.

Source: Council of Economic Advisors. *Economic Report of the President*. Washington, DC: GPO, 2002.

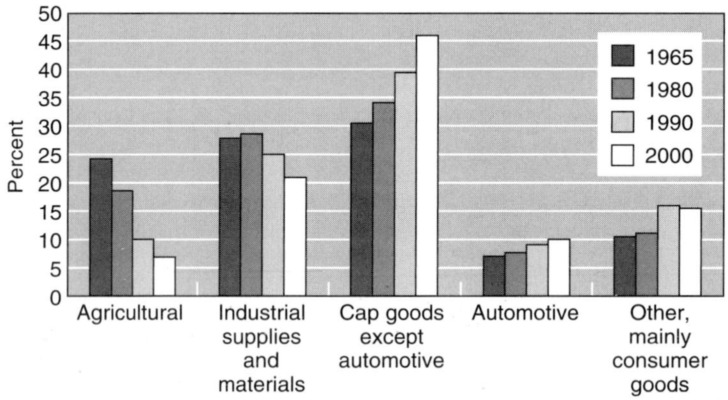

Figure A.3 Composition of U.S. merchandise exports, 1965–2000.

Source: Council of Economic Advisors. *Economic Report of the President*. Washington, DC: GPO, 2002.

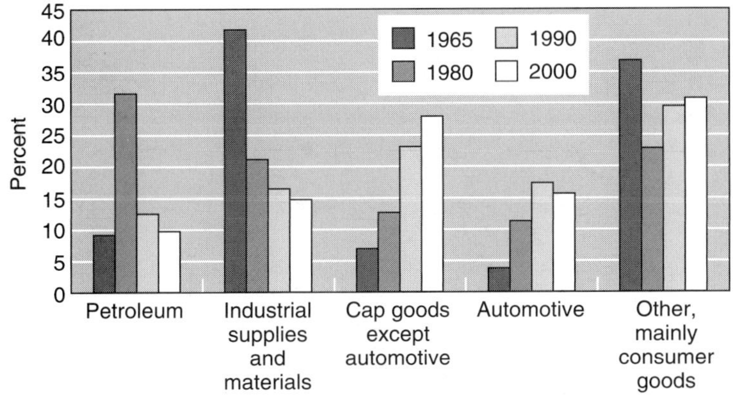

Figure A.4 Composition of U.S. merchandise imports, 1965–2000.

Source: Council of Economic Advisors. *Economic Report of the President*. Washington, DC: GPO, 2002.

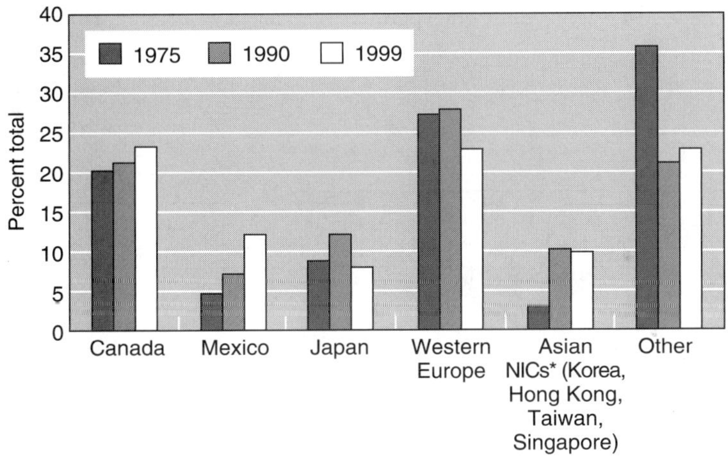

Figure A.5 Direction of U.S. exports.

*Asian NICs in 1975: Korea, Hong Kong, Singapore; in 1990 and 1999: Korea, Hong Kong, Singapore, Taiwan.

Source: IMF. *Direction of Trade Statistics Yearbook*. Washington, DC: 1981, 1997, 2000.

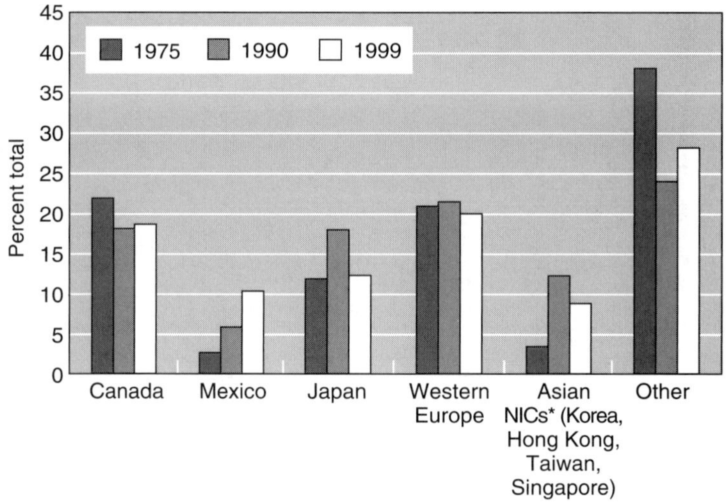

Figure A.6 Sources of U.S. imports.

*Asian NICs in 1975: Korea, Hong Kong, Singapore; in 1990 and 1999: Korea, Hong Kong, Singapore, Taiwan.

Source: IMF. *Direction of Trade Statistics Yearbook.* Washington, DC: 1981, 1997, 2000.

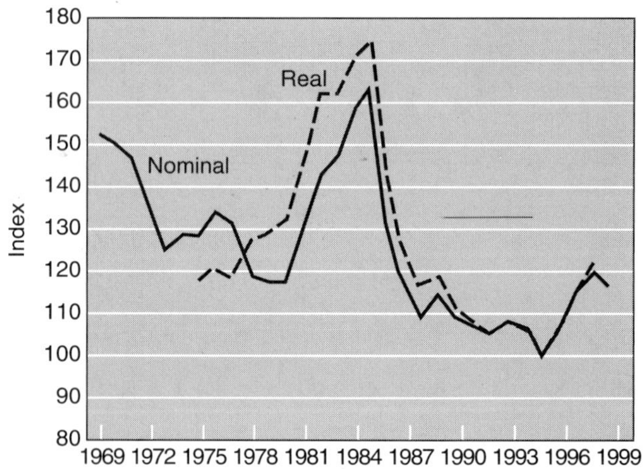

Figure A.7 Nominal and real effective exchange rate index for dollar, 1969–1999.* The nominal is a weighted average of selected bilateral rates. The real is the nominal rate adjusted for relative national price/cost changes.

*1995 = 100.

Source: IMF. *International Financial Statistics Yearbook.* Washington, DC: 2000.

GLOSSARY OF SELECTED TRADE-RELATED TERMS[1]

***Ad Valorem* Tariff** A tariff stated in percentage terms, calculated on the import value (e.g., a 30 percent tariff on imported steel plates).

Antidumping Duty The duty (tariff) assessed to offset dumping. In the United States, the amount of the duty depends on the dumping margin, as determined by the Commerce Department.

Antitrust Policy See competition policy.

Appellate Body A WTO body that entertains appeals of WTO panel decisions on trade cases.

Assimilative Capacity Concept from environmental economics that some environmental media have a (limited) ability to absorb wastes and render them harmless.

Autarky An economy that is closed to international trade.

Beggar-Thy-Neighbor Policy A trade or exchange rate policy that attempts to shift economic costs onto foreign countries. Especially prevalent during the Great Depression but also used today.

Border Tax Adjustment Allows countries to rebate indirect taxes on exports and apply taxes on imports equal to domestic indirect taxes on similar products. Indirect taxes include sales and value-added taxes.

Bound Tariff A tariff whose upper limit is contractually set in the GATT. Most U.S. tariffs are bound. The applied tariff is often less than the bound rate.

Brander and Spencer Trade Model Explained in Chapter 3.

Carbon Emission Trading Schemes Proposals for creating a market and thus a market price for carbon emissions permits, either within a country or internationally.

Cartel Agreement by firms in an industry to control a market by fixing prices, limiting output, or dividing the market among members. Generally illegal in the United States.

Collective Good See Public Good.

Commodity Agreement A cartel-like arrangement among producing (and possibly consuming) countries to stabilize or increase the price. Examples have included coffee, rubber, and tin.

Common Market A customs union that has freed up internal movement of goods, services, and the factors of production (e.g., labor and capital).

[1]Many trade terms are explained in the text and footnotes; this glossary is a supplement. Acronyms appearing in the glossary are defined in the list beginning on page xxiv.

Common Property Resources Resources such as fisheries or land owned in common, not as private property. If open access to these resources is permitted, there is a tendency toward overuse and abusive use—the so-called tragedy of the commons.

Compensation As used in the trade literature, trade concessions offered by country A to country B when it takes an action that diminishes contractual benefits enjoyed by country B.

Competition Policy Regulations to encourage competition and limit anti-competitive practices such as price-fixing and excessive concentration of firms in an industry.

Computable General Equilibrium (CGE) Model A numerical/mathematical characterization of an economic system taking into account interactions among markets. Used for policy analysis.

Concession In GATT parlance, an offer to reduce a trade barrier.

Convertible Currency Currency that can be freely bought or sold at market rates for trade transactions (trade convertibility) or for trade and capital transactions (full convertibility). Implies the absence of foreign exchange controls.

Countervailing Duty The tariff to offset a foreign government subsidy to exports. Ostensible purpose is to negate "unfair" trade.

Customs Union A free trade agreement that has also established a common external tariff against non-members.

Deadweight (Efficiency) Cost (Loss) In trade terms, the welfare loss due to inefficiencies associated with trade interventions (i.e., tariffs, quotas, subsidies).

Direct and Indirect Labor-Output Coefficients Measure the amount of labor used directly and in upstream input supplying industries to produce, say, one million dollars in export or import competing sectors. Their calculations require an input-output table. See also factor coefficient.

Dispute Settlement Panel If a complaint by one member against another is brought to the WTO and is not settled by consultations, a WTO-nominated panel of independent experts is constituted to determine the validity of the complaint.

Dumping Price discrimination, in which the good or service is sold at a lower price in the foreign market than in the home market or is exported at less than "fair" value. See Chapter 2 for details.

Duties Another name for tariffs.

Duty Remission Scheme A border adjustment in which duties paid on imported inputs to production are remitted to the producer when the product is exported. Helps maintain export competitiveness.

Eco-Labeling Certification and labeling schemes indicating that certain products have reduced or no adverse environmental impacts in their production, use, and disposal. Certification is done by private or joint private-public entities.

Economies of Scale (Scale Economies) A long-run situation in which increasing output results in decreasing average costs. Long run implies that all inputs to production are variable. Economies of scale can be the result of production functions that exhibit increasing returns to scale (an X percent increase in all inputs leads to a greater than X percent in output). But economies of scale can also be the result of spreading certain startup costs over a large volume of output.

Effective Rate of Protection (ERP) Measures the protection afforded to a process (i.e., value added), not a product. By considering nominal tariffs on inputs as well as output, the ERP can be positive or negative.

Elasticity The percentage response of one variable to a given percentage change in another. Trade examples include the elasticity of supply or demand for exports or imports in response to price change.

Escape Clause (Safeguard) Provision in U.S. and GATT law permitting a temporary trade restriction if a domestic industry is suffering serious injury from increased import competition.

Ex-Ante versus ***Ex-Post*** The former refers to the estimation of the effects of policy change before it happens; the latter considers the actual effects after they happen.

Exchange Rate Pass-Through The extent to which an exchange rate change results in an equivalent import price change (measured in domestic currency) or an export price change (measured in the foreign currency). Varies between zero and 100 percent.

Export Targeting The allegation that one country deliberately concentrates its exports of a particular good on a specific foreign market.

Externalities (external economies/ disconomies, external benefits/costs) The effects of the action of one economic agent (firm, consumer, government) on the welfare of another economic agent, where the effect does not pass through markets. Can be positive or negative. Uncorrected externalities lead to market failure (inefficiency in the price-market system).

Factor Coefficient As used here, the value of an input per unit value of output. For example, the expenditure on labor per million dollars worth of output of autos. Direct and indirect labor coefficients would include the use of labor in auto production but also the indirect use of labor in inputs to auto production (i.e., steel, rubber). Calculating this requires an input-output table.

Factor Price Equalization (FPE) Theorem Explained in Chapter 5.

Fair Labor Standards The attempt to insert certain minimum labor protection obligations in trade agreements such as the WTO and NAFTA. See Chapter 10.

Fast Track Congress delegates authority to the President to negotiate trade agreements and in return promises to vote such agreements up or down, without amendment. Now known as Trade Promotion Authority (TPA).

Foreign Direct Investment (FDI) Investment by a firm across borders with intention to have at least partial control over the enterprise. FDI is generally defined to be at least 11–14 percent of equity and ranges up to 100 percent.

Free Trade Agreement (Area) (FTA) An arrangement among countries in which trade barriers against partners are substantially or totally eliminated but each member maintains its own tariffs against nonmembers.

General Equilibrium Model (Approach) Used for the study of the interaction among markets simultaneously, including production and consumption. Contrasts with partial equilibrium analysis, the study of a single market without considering repercussions with other markets.

Gravity Model A statistical model attempting to explain the volume of bilateral trade flows, using distance (a proxy for transportation costs) and other explanatory variables such as size, per capita income, etc.

Heckscher-Ohlin Trade Model Explains the pattern (composition) of trade on the basis of differences among countries in relative factor endowments and differences among products in relative factor intensities. For example, countries abundant in unskilled labor (e.g., Vietnam) will tend to produce and export labor-intensive products (e.g., shoes or toys).

Imperfect Competition All market structures other than perfect competition. Includes monopoly, oligopoly, monopolistic competition, and, on the input side, monopsony, etc.

Import Penetration Ratio The ratio of imports to either domestic consumption or domestic production. Can be calculated for a specific product or to include all imports.

Import Substitution (IS) The now discredited development strategy of industrializing by restricting or eliminating imports of manufactures. Extensively pursued in developing countries, especially in Latin America, in the middle post–World War II period.

Import Surge A rapid increase in imports of a particular product. Can cause adjustment costs for the domestic industry and its workers.

Infant Industry Argument The proposition that a new industry may need temporary trade protection as it starts production but that it ultimately will become competitive without protection. Implies some failure in the private capital markets.

International Trade Commission (ITC) An independent quasi-judicial U.S. government agency that determines if there is injury to a domestic industry in dumping and countervailing duty cases; investigates injury and recommends remedy in escape clause cases; and conducts trade research.

Intra-industry Trade A situation in which a country both imports and exports goods within a single industrial classification. May be an artifact of the classification system or may represent specialization in very narrow product varieties. Often explained with monopolistic competition, scale economies, product differentiation type models.

***Keiretsu* System** Term for the unique interlocking corporate relations structure (e.g., producers and suppliers) in Japan.

Large Country A country whose imports or exports of specific products are sufficiently large in international trade so that they influence international prices. For example, despite its small GDP, Vietnam is a "large" country with regard to trade in rice.

Margin of Preference The difference between a preferential tariff rate and the MFN rate.

Marketing Board Government or government-sanctioned institution to promote production and sale of a specific commodity. In some instances governments require domestic producers to sell to the board, which, in turn, becomes the country's export monopoly.

Mercantilism An old economic doctrine emphasizing the accumulation of gold or currencies as the source of national wealth. Consequently, a trade surplus is seen as inherently desirable. Now discredited by (most) economists, but the popular view that exports are good and imports are not good hangs on.

Monopolistic Competition A market structure characterized by a large number of sellers of broadly similar but differentiated products and easy entry and exit of firms.

Monopsony Control over demand for a good, service, or production input. By restricting demand, the monopsonist depresses the price of the good or service.

Nash Solution (Nash Equilibrium) A game theory term to describe a situation in which each player has chosen its best strategy, given the strategy chosen by other players.

New International Economic Order An unsuccessful attempt in the 1970s to radically alter the role of developing countries in the international economic system. Elements included commodity agreements, improved export market access, and altering the terms for MNC investments.

Nominal Exchange Rate The exchange rate as determined in currency markets, not adjusted for differences among countries in inflation rates. See also Real Exchange Rate.

Nominal Tariff The published tariff rate on an imported product (*ad valorem* or specific).

Nontariff Trade Barriers (NTBs) A catchall term to include all barriers to trade other than tariffs. Includes quantitative restrictions, discriminatory government procurement, certain customs valuation practices, and many more.

Nontradable Goods and Services Goods and services that are not imported or exported, primarily because of high transportation costs.

Nullification or Impairment A GATT term to describe an action by one country that reduces contractual trade benefits enjoyed by another.

Oligopoly A market structure characterized by a small number of firms that act strategically (i.e., consider each others actions with respect to pricing, product lines, marketing, etc.).

Outsourcing The general term for a firm allocating a part of the production process to an outside firm. For example, a U.S. insurance company may outsource data entry to a specialized firm in India.

Polluter Pays Principle (PPP) Adopted by the OECD in 1972. States that governments should not subsidize pollution-abatement expenditures undertaken in the private sector. The PPP has now acquired equity overtones—the polluter should compensate victims of pollution. The acronym PPP also refers to purchasing power parity, a different concept. Purchasing power parity is the attempt to convert domestic currency expenditures in various countries into a common currency so that a unit of that currency could purchase the same bundle of goods in all countries.

Precautionary Principle The concept supporting regulation of technologies and products that might be harmful to health or environment, without a clear demonstration that harm would necessarily result.

Predation (predatory actions) Attempt by a firm to drive rivals out of business and establish greater market power by lowering its prices or by other practices.

Preferential Trade Agreement (PTA) All agreements such as FTA, CUs, and CMs that violate nondiscrimination (MFN) in trade. PTAs are authorized by GATT Article XXIV but are subject to certain restrictions.

Prisoners' Dilemma A game theory term describing a situation in which the players, acting rationally, do not cooperate, although cooperation would be in the interest of all players. A regulatory "race to the bottom" is often described as a prisoners' dilemma situation.

Public Good A good or service that exhibits nonrivalry in consumption (one person's use does not preclude use by others) and nonexcludability (technical difficulty in excluding users once the good or service is produced). Gives rise to a market failure.

Quota Rent The difference between production cost and the selling price that is inflated by a qualitative restriction such as a quota or VER. The capture of quota rent by the importing or exporting country depends in part on market structure.

Real Exchange Rate The nominal exchange rate adjusted for prices (or price changes) in the home country and its trade partners. A better measure of changes in international competitive position than the nominal exchange rate.

Ricardian Trade Model Trade model attributed to the 19th century economist David Ricardo. Explains that trade takes place on the basis of relative, not absolute production costs. Relative cost differences attributable to differences in relative labor productivity, as among products and countries. Classic example is Portugal's exporting of wine and England's exporting of cloth in the 19th century.

Rules of Origins Regulations specifying what fraction of the value of a product must be produced within an FTA or CU to qualify for duty-free movement within the area.

Safeguard See Escape Clause.

Sanitary and Phytosanitary Agreement (SPS) A WTO agreement concerning regulation of imports for food safety and animal and plant health reasons.

Selectivity With regard to trade, allows countries to restrict imports from some but not all countries in an escape clause action.

Small Country A country whose trade is sufficiently small that it does not influence international prices.

Smoot-Hawley Tariff Historically high U.S. tariff enacted in 1930. Widely seen as triggering tariff retaliation and contributing to severity of the Great Depression.

Social Issues (Social Clause) The attempt to introduce social concerns, mainly environmental protection and "fair" labor standards, into trade agreements.

Specific Tariff A tariff stated as a monetary amount per unit imported (e.g., a tariff of $1.20 per gross of imported clothespins). The restrictive effect varies inversely with the price of the import.

Spillover Benefits See Externalities.

Stopler-Samuelson Theorem (S-S) Explained in Chapter 5.

Strategic Trade Policy Explained in Chapter 3.

Tariff Commission Predecessor to ITC.

Tariff Dispersion The extent to which a tariff structure is uniform or non-uniform across products. Economic theory shows that widely dispersed tariff rates are more distortive than relatively uniform rates, even if the average of both structures is the same.

Tariffication Conversion of NTBs (mainly quotas) to tariffs. Dirty tariffication is the practice of setting more restrictive tariffs than the initial quota.

Tariff-Rate Quota A system in which a certain quantity of imports of a product are assessed a low or zero tariff, but over-quota imports are assessed a higher duty.

Technical Barriers to Trade (TBT) The collection of regulations pertaining to imported products that may restrict trade. They include labeling requirements, safety standards, packaging requirements, product health, safety and environmental standards, and many more. Governed by the WTO's TBT agreement.

Terms of Trade In its simplest form, the ratio of a country's export to import prices.

Theory of Domestic Distortions Asserts that if a distortion arises in the domestic economy (e.g., monopoly, externality in production), the best policy response is a domestic measure. Trade measures to address domestic distortions are second-best and may worsen welfare.

Trade Creation The displacement of inefficient domestic production by more efficient partner country production in a PTA. See Chapter 6 for elaboration.

Trade-Related Investment Measures (TRIMs) Trade requirements placed on foreign investors, mainly minimum export requirements and minimum domestic sourcing of inputs. Now controlled by the WTO's TRIMs agreement.

Trade Diversion Displacement of efficient imports from third countries by less efficient imports from a partner country in a PTA. See Chapter 6 for elaboration.

Trade-Weighted Currency Index Measures changes in a currency's value with use of trade values as weights for bilateral exchange rates. Also known as the effective exchange rate index.

Trigger Price As used by President Carter's administration, a minimum price for imported steel, prices below which would automatically start a dumping action.

Unfair Trade In a strict sense, restricted to instances of dumping and government subsidies. Loosely used to describe a wide variety of trade-related practices by one country that another country objects to.

Variable Levy A device through which the level of a tariff automatically adjusts to the difference between world market prices and some target domestic price. Used in the EC's agricultural policy for protection.

Waiver Formal authorization from the WTO to deviate from a legally binding obligation.

NAME INDEX

SUBJECT INDEX